"*Genius at Scale* offers profound insights into the approaches and skills crucial for driving innovation within organizations, revealing how collaboration, experimentation, and continuous learning can catalyze transformation. These concepts resonate with my own workplace experience in fostering a culture that inspires purpose, empowers leadership, and encourages a growth mindset."

—TAN SU SHAN, CEO, DBS Group

"*Genius at Scale* is the exact right book for right now! The stories and research provide readers with a bold road map for navigating complexity while also issuing an urgent call to reimagine how cocreation, deep connection, and productive challenge unlock real innovation and impact."

—BRENÉ BROWN, *New York Times* bestselling author, *Strong Ground*

"In an era of material AI-driven disruption, people-centered innovation isn't optional—it's essential. *Genius at Scale* offers a compelling road map for leaders navigating real-world innovation challenges, reminding us that in a world of exponentially accelerating change, our greatest advantage is our ability to learn, adapt, and empower others to do the same."

—OMAR ABBOSH, CEO, Pearson

"In *Genius at Scale*, Linda A. Hill, Emily Tedards, and Jason Wild reveal both the art and the science of betting big. By taking readers inside the day-to-day work of large-scale change at leading companies and organizations, this book will help leaders in every walk of life think and work bigger."

—RAJIV J. SHAH, President, the Rockefeller Foundation; author, *Big Bets: How Large-Scale Change Really Happens*

"*Genius at Scale* is a practical guide for leaders who want to innovate at scale—not just within their organizations but across entire ecosystems. By spotlighting courageous and generous individuals from around the world, it shows how the roles of architect, bridger, and catalyst can unlock collective genius and transform complexity into opportunity."

—LUCA DE MEO, CEO, Kering

"*Genius at Scale* is a must-read for any leader keen to unleash innovation at scale. Through vivid case studies, Linda A. Hill, Emily Tedards, and Jason Wild bring to life their brilliant idea of leaders as architects, bridgers, and catalysts, offering powerful insights that will deeply resonate with both established executives and emerging leaders."

—**HUBERT JOLY**, Senior Lecturer, Harvard Business School; former CEO, Best Buy; and bestselling author, *The Heart of Business*

"The ABCs of innovation! A must-read for leaders at all levels looking to drive meaningful change in business and society."

—**PARMINDER KOHLI**, Chairman, Shell UK

"*Genius at Scale* gives leaders a clear framework to drive innovation and impact through culture, clarity, and cocreation. Not just vision—execution."

—**JACOB BENDFELDT**, Global Head of Strategy, Transformation, and AI Partnerships, Microsoft Research

"In an era when AI scales faster than organizations, *Genius at Scale* reminds us that the real leverage is human—connecting people, purpose, and incentives. It shows how to design relationships that convert purpose into performance and make innovation repeatable, not accidental."

—**ATSUSHI TAIRA**, cofounder and Chairman, The Edgeof; General Partner, Alpha Intelligence Fund

"*Genius at Scale* gives leaders license to be ambitious about driving an organization through powerful forms of collaboration. Managing an organization of highly talented people is a big leadership challenge. The authors' ABCs—architect, bridger, and catalyst—provide a framework for maximizing that talent in service of ambitious goals."

—**MICHAEL BRANDMEYER**, Global Head and CIO, External Investing Group, Goldman Sachs Asset Management

"*Genius at Scale* is a remarkable exploration of the often overlooked leadership qualities needed to bring about landscape-altering innovation. Linda Hill, Emily Tedards, and Jason Wild illustrate how the most powerful engines of growth come from building a generative ecosystem for consumers, communities, suppliers, and competitors alike. The book is inspiring, not only for the C-suite but for all, as it reveals how leadership and innovation can come from unexpected places, regardless of rank, function, or title."

—**AUDREY CHOI**, Chair, Generation Foundation; former CMO and Chief Sustainability Officer, Morgan Stanley

"*Genius at Scale* is an inspiring and practical guide to leading innovation in today's complex world. Through vivid stories and the ABCs of leadership—architects, bridgers, and catalysts—the authors show how great leaders build cultures of cocreation, forge powerful partnerships, and ignite movements that transform industries and societies. A must-read for anyone serious about driving meaningful change."

—**AVI HASSON**, CEO, Startup Nation Central; former Chief Scientist, Ministry of Economy, Israel

"The best book on innovation I've read in at least ten years. We know driving change requires a complex combination of cultural shift, digital acumen, structural change, and bridge building within and across organizations. But Hill, Tedards, and Wild build on years of research to give us detailed accounts of what this actually looks like on the ground. I loved the stories. I'll be recommending this book to everyone I know who grapples with these kinds of challenges."

—**REBECCA HENDERSON**, John & Natty McArthur University Professor, Harvard Business School

"*Genius at Scale*'s framework of leaders as architects, bridgers, and catalysts captures the essence of exceptional innovators worldwide. The principles in this amazing book are universal, as they transcend geographic and market boundaries to deliver results across diverse contexts. This is a vital read for any leader in today's dynamic and complex world."

—**JING HONG**, Founding Partner, Gaocheng Capital

"This book brilliantly takes the concept of 'collective genius' to a whole new level. It's filled with truly valuable and insightful observations of leaders driving innovation at scale around the globe."

—**REIKO KASHIWABARA**, Senior Vice President and General Manager, Global HR Department, Mitsubishi

"Grounded in a decade of research on exceptional leaders, *Genius at Scale* equips today's executives with the mindset and skills to navigate an evolving, complex business world. Through a clear framework, it shows how cocreation, collaboration, and experimentation drive innovation with speed and scale—a powerful guide to sustainable success."

—GLAUBER MOTA, CEO, Revolut Brazil

"*Genius at Scale* delivers uniquely inspiring, keen observations on how real innovation happens—by leaders who architect cultures, bridge boundaries, and spark movements. This book stands out for its current, fresh, practical wisdom and vivid stories that show how collective genius (over lone genius) truly transforms organizations and society at large."

—MICHAEL WARSAW, Chief Design Officer, Haworth

GENIUS
AT
SCALE

GENIUS AT SCALE

HOW GREAT LEADERS DRIVE INNOVATION

LINDA A. HILL, EMILY TEDARDS, JASON WILD

Harvard Business Review Press • Boston, Massachusetts

Copyright 2026 Linda A. Hill, Emily Tedards, and Jason Wild

Printed in the United States of America

10 9 8 7 6 5 4 3 2 1

The web addresses referenced in this book were live and correct at the time of the book's publication but may be subject to change.

Library of Congress Cataloging-in-Publication data is forthcoming.

ISBN: 978-1-64782-750-2
eISBN: 978-1-64782-751-9

The paper used in this publication meets the requirements of the American National Standard for Permanence of Paper for Publications and Documents in Libraries and Archives Z39.48-1992.

To leaders who unleash genius in our organizations and communities.

With gratitude,
Linda, Emily, and Jason

Contents

PART THREE

THE CATALYST

Building Movements

GENIUS
AT
SCALE

Introduction

How do great leaders drive innovation at scale? By sharing the driver's seat. Leading innovation has always been an uphill climb, especially in successful corporations where it is hard enough to consistently execute the core business. While innovation was long considered an add-on, it is now an imperative. Organizations that fail to innovate will fall behind as competitors find more efficient and effective means of delivering value to customers and stakeholders. Communities and nations that fail to innovate will be unable to address the social, political, and environmental challenges that threaten their very existence.

When the new CEO of an established financial services firm was charged with future proofing his company against digital-first competitors, he invited an entrepreneur—who had recently joined through an acquisition—to stay on and help lead the effort. Though hesitant, the entrepreneur accepted. And the outcome, as we'll describe later in this book, was extraordinary. Together, he and the CEO led the organization's transformation into a tech company in the payments space. They infused innovation into the firm's culture, forged unconventional partnerships, and built a generative global ecosystem comprising corporations, startups, governments, and civil society. In a single decade, the company saw a tenfold increase in market capitalization, while helping billions of people gain access to the formal economy.

If you were the entrepreneur, would you take the CEO's assignment? The first time one of us (Linda) asked a classroom of executives at Harvard Business School, only three of eighty-five participants raised their hands—even *after* knowing the outcome.

Many talented leaders are reluctant to take on roles leading innovation. We understand all too well why they might be hesitant: it is hard and risky work, with no all-purpose road map through its increasingly complex terrain. Global crises have amplified our interdependence, and innovating in silos is no longer viable. Emerging technologies—the stuff of science fiction not long ago—have made "business as usual" obsolete. Speed is the mandate; good ideas are abundant, yet execution is hard and expensive and often feels too late.

All of this begs some sobering questions: How can leaders inspire in themselves and others the sense of imagination and possibility required for continuous innovation? How can they embolden others to take the risks required to *act*, rather than plan, their way to the future?

We wrote this book to show emerging and established leaders that there are tenable ways forward. In the pages ahead, we will meet exemplary individuals from across the globe who built teams, organizations, and broader ecosystems that routinely generated innovative ideas, and also *scaled* them—that is, implemented them in practice so they fulfilled their intended purpose. For some leaders, scaling meant launching new products and services. For others, it meant expanding into new markets or amplifying social impact. The contexts are as diverse as they get: startups, legacy companies, nonprofits, governments, family businesses, and social enterprises.

These stories show definitively that innovation rarely results from the caricatured "aha" moment of a solo genius. Rather, we'll see through the eyes of our leaders that both ideation and implementation are ultimately processes of *cocreation*—collaboration, experimentation, and learning among people with differing perspectives. We'll see that *collaboration* entails weaving together both diversity of thought and constructive conflict to create a marketplace of ideas. We'll see that *experimentation* involves actively testing and refining hypotheses while embracing the inevitable false starts, failures, and pivots that come with trying something new. And we'll see that *learning* happens when individuals and collectives reflect on the knowledge and insights gained from experiments and adapt their courses of action.

Leading Innovation, Then and Now

The book in your hands builds on groundwork laid in *Collective Genius: The Art and Practice of Leading Innovation*, written by Linda and coauthors Greg Brandeau, Emily Truelove, and Kent Lineback in 2014.[1] At a time when research focused either on innovation or on leadership, the book looked at how they intersected. It showcased how leaders from Pixar to Volkswagen built teams that innovated not once or twice but time and again. Although these leaders were visionaries, they recognized that their job was not to get others to follow them into the future. Their job was to invite others to cocreate the future with them. They wanted everybody in their organizations to see themselves as innovators. As one leader put it, everyone has a "slice of genius" waiting to be unleashed and harnessed for the collective good. Consequently, they adopted a very simple, local definition of innovation, which is also at work in this book: *anything that is new and useful to their team or organization*. It could be a product, service, business model, or process; it could be incremental or breakthrough. With hindsight, it's clear that the book captured a paradigm shift in our understanding of great leadership.[2]

In the decade after *Collective Genius* was published, Linda continued her fieldwork and brought new partners to the table. By 2022, she and collaborators had conducted longitudinal studies on leaders in eighteen countries and twenty-one industries. They found that the leadership paradigm introduced in *Collective Genius* still held, but it did not go far enough.

By that point, Emily and Jason were part of the conversation. Emily had been working with Linda on the on-the-ground research that forms the backbone of this book. As a young researcher, she was interested in relationships between business, government, and civil society and continues researching these dynamics in contexts ranging from energy transitions to economic development. In the last years, Emily has built new intergenerational forums at Harvard, bringing graduate students and senior executives together to explore the most pressing questions of our time.

Jason, meanwhile, brought the key perspective only a practitioner could have on what it takes to overcome the myriad barriers to innovation and build truly customer-centric, technology-enabled organizations that innovate consistently and maintain relevance. Jason and Linda first met when she was studying IBM for *Collective Genius*. Having worked in various tech companies including "Big Blue," Salesforce, and Microsoft, Jason experienced firsthand, over and over, that innovation is more about people than technology. This insight has become Jason's guiding ethos as a strategic adviser, and since meeting Linda a decade ago at IBM, he has gradually shifted roles from subject of study to co-investigator.

To collect the stories in this book, we spent thousands of hours in the field, up close and personal, observing leaders and their teams at work for years.[3] We conducted hundreds of in-depth interviews (many over videoconferencing, thanks to the pandemic) and pored over company records. Some leaders we met early in their careers, some late. They are high-ranking executives, middle managers, individual contributors, and entrepreneurs. They have diverse cultural, professional, and educational backgrounds and work in industries ranging from consumer products, health care, and aviation to high tech, agribusiness, and education.

Across our studies, the three of us observed that some leaders had a masterful ability to drive innovation, despite an ever more demanding landscape. Our mission was to understand who these great leaders are, what they do, and how they think and behave.[4] From their stories, a framework began to crystallize.

The ABCs of Leading Innovation

Whether developing a vaccine in record time or extending financial services to billions of unbanked people, the exceptional leaders in this book managed to get multiple organizations to collaborate, experiment, and learn together. These leaders saw emerging technologies not as disruptive but as tools for unleashing and harnessing *collective genius at scale*—what we call genius at scale for short. Genius at scale is not simply about activating collective genius in-house, but forging partnerships and strategic movements, amplifying influence by spurring cocreation across sectors (companies, government, civil society) or the globe.

To drive genius at scale, these leaders relied on a repertoire of interrelated roles: *architect*, *bridger*, and *catalyst*—what we came to think of as the

FIGURE I-1

The ABCs of leading innovation

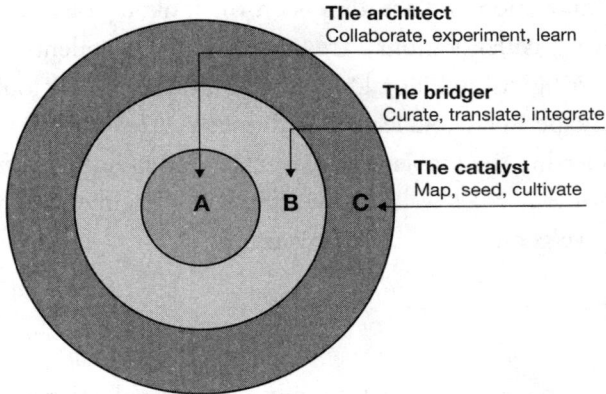

The architect
Collaborate, experiment, learn

The bridger
Curate, translate, integrate

The catalyst
Map, seed, cultivate

A B C

ABCs of leading innovation. These roles might be visualized as concentric circles. Architects largely work within their team or organization, building innovative communities by fostering the culture and capabilities that enable cocreation. Bridgers work at the boundaries of their enterprises, building partnerships with those outside their walls to access essential talent and tools for innovation. Catalysts go even further, launching movements that activate and spread innovation across broader ecosystems. (See figure I-1.)

Architects

The architect is the foundational role of the ABCs, building innovative communities prepared to cocreate not only inside but also outside organizational boundaries. Architects understand that they cannot mandate innovation; instead, they *invite* their colleagues to think and act differently by reshaping the social environment in which they do their work.

Architects invite everyone in their organization to participate in innovation and build the *culture* and *capabilities* required for them to do so. By instilling shared purpose, values, and rules of engagement, architects build a sense of community that encourages the *willingness* to innovate. By helping their colleagues amplify and navigate their diversity of thought, and overcome fears of risk and failure, architects embed the *ability* to collaborate, experiment, and learn.

Architects pay attention to the emotional, intellectual, and organizational barriers to innovation and are always on the lookout for resolutions. Are silos hindering collaboration? Are performance or talent-management systems deterring risk-taking? Do people have the digital tools and data they need to experiment and learn expeditiously? And perhaps most importantly, is leadership the problem—are leaders getting in the way? These are just a few of the hurdles we'll see our architects grapple with as they unleash collective genius in their organizations.

Bridgers

Leaders today recognize that they rely on external talent and tools to bring their organizations into the future. Bridgers have the unenviable job of facilitating cocreation between their internal colleagues and partners outside their organizational boundaries—a role that requires exercising influence without formal authority.

Bridgers build partnerships with different organizations—often with vastly different priorities, constraints, capabilities, and work styles—to innovate together. In doing so, they build relationships grounded in mutual trust, influence, and commitment. Bridgers carefully *curate* potential partners; they *translate* across those partners to build common understanding; and *integrate* their disparate intentions and actions so they can develop and scale new products, services, and processes.

Bridging is a difficult, hands-on, time-intensive form of leadership, and it is often underappreciated since much of it happens behind the scenes. Innovating feels all the more complex and risky when working with outsiders. A high degree of emotional intelligence, patience, and diplomacy is required for bridgers to navigate the vexing conflicts that arise.

Catalysts

If architects build innovative *communities* within organizations and bridgers build innovative *partnerships* at their boundaries, then catalysts galvanize *movements* to drive innovation far beyond their organization's boundaries.[5]

Catalysts *map* their ecosystems: the evolving landscape of stakeholders, their interdependencies, along with emergent opportunities and barriers to innovation. They *seed* tangible opportunities for others to engage in multiparty cocreation, fulfilling individual priorities while advancing collective aspirations. Last, catalysts *cultivate* those seeds, equipping stakeholders with the mindsets, relationships, and tools needed to sustain the movement's momentum over time.

The ecosystem metaphor in business practice and research tends to evoke a gatekeeping mindset: positioning one's organization as the central hub controlling information, resource flows, and the customer interface in a value chain.[6] The catalysts in our book adopt a different approach, emphasizing synergies, sustainability, and shared value.

. . .

The ABC roles are not only complementary, but as you will see, our leaders often span multiple roles or deliberately choose to don one mantle while delegating the others to trusted colleagues. That said, in this book, we focus each story on the primary role—architect, bridger, or catalyst—that a particular leader played to accomplish extraordinary things for their organization.

Among ourselves, we sometimes joke that Linda is the architect (intensely focused on getting the culture of a place right), Jason the bridger (eager to seek out and connect tools and talent), and Emily the catalyst (embracing how interconnected the world is and the ripple effects across it). But even in writing this book, each of us has jumped across roles from time to time, an experience that we felt sharpened our interpretations of the leaders we studied.

A Road Map to *Genius at Scale*

Chapter 1 provides a snapshot of the ABCs in action. We'll see the CEO of Mastercard work with parties both inside and outside the company to transform its culture and seize the digital future. From there, we divide the book into three parts—highlighting stories that exemplify each individual ABC in turn.

In part I, we meet *architects* from three iconic legacy organizations. At Pfizer (chapter 2), the architect reinvents an incumbent's clinical supply chain to better collaborate in an increasingly digital world. At Procter & Gamble (chapter 3), the architect introduces a new operating model of experimentation to address competitive threats with more speed. And at Cleveland Clinic Abu Dhabi (chapter 4), two architects build a workforce that is able to learn and adapt its model of health care to a new context— seven thousand miles away from US headquarters. These stories of established companies bring into sharp relief the headwinds against innovation, including entrenched mindsets, work routines, and discomfort with digital tools and data. We will see how each leader broke down barriers— including their own mental models and behaviors—and profoundly transformed their company's culture and capabilities.

In part II, we meet leaders at Delta Air Lines (chapter 5), the Dubai International Financial Centre (chapter 6), and again Mastercard (chapter 7)—all illustrations of the role of the *bridger*. These leaders navigate the messy intersections of corporations, startups, and regulators. We'll see how each bridger establishes robust relationships across organizational boundaries to access critical talent and capabilities for innovation.

In part III, we introduce you to *catalysts* from four entrepreneurial ventures—avatarin (chapter 8), African Food Changemakers (chapter 9), the Francescana Family (chapter 10), and Sampark Foundation (chapter 11). From the outset, our catalysts adopted a systemic view of the business and societal challenges they aimed to address and the key stakeholders they depended on. By launching innovation movements, these catalysts strove to unlock collective genius at the scale of industries, sectors, regions, and nations.

In the epilogue, we conclude our journey through the ABCs by introducing you to the first executive we ever met with the title "chief catalyst officer." Using her zigzag career through luxury, technology, and venture capital, we invite you to turn inward: How can you prepare yourself and others to lead innovation—with a realistic, yet optimistic, view of the demands ahead?

The completion of this book was extended by the pandemic. We made an agonizing decision (fellow book writers know how much you want a book to get done) to go back out into the field to observe how our leaders coped with the unprecedented global crisis. We are so glad we did. We witnessed human ingenuity at scale: people innovating in new ways to save our companies, communities, and of course, our lives. We suspect many are tired of hearing about Covid-19 but we have included some of these stories because they illuminate key insights about leading in an ever more dynamic, complex, and interconnected world.

. . .

Our world demands a new kind of leader—one who can bring together the work of myriad actors and navigate inevitable tensions: aspiration and pragmatism, individual and collective ambitions, support and confrontation, short- and long-term thinking, structure and agility.[7] Accepting such a challenge can be daunting. The ABCs are emotionally and intellectually demanding, but they are also more necessary than ever before.

Our work is informed by the extensive writings of scholars and practitioners on leadership and innovation (we have posted online a full bibliography of the over seven hundred books and articles we relied on, available at https://hbr.org/book-resources). But in this book, we focus on telling stories. We have sought to convey each leader's narrative from their perspective as much as possible, letting you hear their voices through direct quotations.[8] Our leaders, though exceptional, are far from perfect, and they would be the first to admit this. But these individuals are mastering a difficult art, and their examples are highly instructive; we encourage you to pay attention not just to what they do, but *how* they do it, and *why*.

We hope that watching these leaders at work will inspire and empower you. As you will see, they are not driving innovation alone. They have learned to lead beyond their formal authority, sharing the driver's seat with the communities, partnerships, and movements they've enabled. Given the existential challenges in front of us, we need many more leaders willing and able to become the kinds of architects, bridgers, and catalysts shown in this book. Whether you are an emerging or established leader, this book is meant to show you the art of the possible. We hope it will embolden you to cocreate the future you imagine for your organization, your community, or the world.

The ABCs of Leadership

Ajay Banga at Mastercard

*The single biggest differentiator in this company is the culture—
the willingness for leadership to take thoughtful risks, push the envelope,
be innovative and creative, feel the pressure of competitive paranoia,
and have a sense of urgency. Culture trumps everything.*

—Ajay Banga

When Ajay Banga became CEO of Mastercard in 2010, he knew the company's future was in jeopardy: the rise of digital technology was about to disrupt the global payments industry. Mastercard needed to innovate if it hoped to compete.[1] Yet when surveyed, most of the company's seven thousand employees didn't share that sense of urgency. They ranked innovation *twenty-sixth* out of twenty-seven factors "most important" to the company's success.

For Banga, the greatest threat to Mastercard's future lay within its own walls. He had inherited a company with a conservative and consensus-driven culture. As far as his new colleagues were concerned, the organization's years of success—including its $13 billion market capitalization post-IPO in 2006—only confirmed that its culture had served it well.[2] But Banga saw two options for Mastercard: evolve or die out. Evolve was the only solution, and sure enough, when Banga stepped down in late 2020, the company's market capitalization had grown to nearly $335 billion.[3]

After decades of being known as a credit card service, Mastercard had rebranded itself as a "global technology company in the payments industry."[4]

Over his decade-long tenure as CEO, Banga would implement what many felt were radical measures to overcome internal barriers, embrace emerging technologies, and embed new innovative mindsets and behaviors across Mastercard. Banga understood that innovation required cocreation—collaboration, experimentation, and learning—both within the company and with external partners. He knew he couldn't drive the needed transformation alone, so he enlisted cadres of leaders throughout the organization, and they got to work. Banga *architected* an environment inside of Mastercard—the foundation for cocreation—consisting of a sense of purpose, shared values, and rules of engagement. To introduce new digital talent and tools into the organization, he empowered *bridgers* to facilitate partnerships across organizational boundaries. Finally, Banga and his team went a step further: they acted as *catalysts*, using their corporate platform to ignite a global movement for financial inclusion—improving the livelihoods of more than a billion unbanked people across the globe along the way.

When Culture Gets in the Way

To appreciate Mastercard's transformation under Banga, we must begin with the state of affairs he inherited. With its iconic "Priceless" campaign, the company was often perceived to be a business-to-consumer brand.[5] However, Mastercard operated for decades as a membership association and even after converting into a private share corporation in 2002, it still served only a single customer—banks. "The company was very successful, but it was very narrow," said Michael Miebach, head of the Middle East and Africa operations at the time. "It was organ-reject syndrome for new ideas"—particularly when it came to new technologies and ways of working.[6] Because Mastercard's payments infrastructure was strictly regulated and helped power economies around the world, its leadership had come to prioritize security and reliability over all else.

Over time, top-down decision-making discouraged open discussion and produced a culture of conformity. Sachin Mehra, now CFO, joined Mastercard in 2010 as the group executive and treasurer. "When I came here," he recalled, "the culture was one where people would come into a meeting and ask, 'Boss, what do you want me to do?'" Another executive, Michael Fiore, echoed that sentiment: "No one wanted to make a decision unless it had gone up the chain and the CEO was okay with it."[7]

What Banga found at Mastercard was what we often observe at incumbent organizations. People hesitate to say what they truly think and instead defer to tradition and hierarchy. A healthy respect for experience and expertise devolves into a culture of compliance. Rather than risk confrontation, even talented and passionate people learn to "go along to get along."

Mastercard's board wasn't blind to the company culture, but only in the wake of the 2008 financial collapse did the board members realize it represented an existential threat. The company had survived the crisis, but it needed to either "batten down the hatches" to ensure survival or "fight its way out," according to chairman Richard Haythornthwaite. After interviewing various candidates, Haythornthwaite recalled, "I invited Ajay to the UK and within twenty minutes, it was really quite clear that he was exactly who we wanted. He brought the balance of being able to think through the risk of the company but, at the same time, could help the company step into the future and be aspirational."

Like many of his new colleagues, Banga was from the banking industry; however, he understood that his personal background and career trajectory were unconventional. "There was nobody that looked like me in the American top ten companies," Banga said later. "I think it was an enlightened board that didn't care about how I looked or where I came from." Born into a Saini Sikh family in India, Banga graduated from the prestigious Indian Institute of Management in Ahmedabad, Gujarat.[8] He started his career working in sales, marketing, and country management at Nestlé and then at PepsiCo. In 1996, he joined Citigroup and rose to become CEO of the bank's Asia-Pacific business. Banga developed a reputation for building successful multinational businesses able to take advantage of global scale, while also delivering customer experiences tailored to local circumstances.

When Banga became Mastercard's CEO in 2010, its market capitalization was $27 billion, up from $13 billion in its IPO.[9] Most incoming CEOs would have been pleased to inherit such a rising tide, but Banga, like Haythornthwaite, sensed danger. The company looked impressive on paper, but was it ready for ever more demanding expectations of stakeholders? This included everyone from customers to the markets to governments—in the face of increased competition from incumbents like Visa and American Express *and* digital-first players like Apple, Google, and Alipay. With little pressure within the company to fight for deals, it had begun to slip in head-to-head competitions. Banga was frustrated: this should have been a wake-up call—and yet, many of his colleagues were dozing. How could he, as CEO, fuel a sense of urgency to innovate?

Architecting the Environment

Banga recognized that leading innovation was not about getting people to follow his vision into the future, but to invite Mastercard's employees to join him in proactively creating the future of the company. His task was to build "a culture where people saw themselves as empowered agents of change," he said. To elicit the mindsets and capabilities required to work in new ways, he would have to craft an environment that was conducive to collaboration, experimentation, and learning. This meant purging the company's ingrained focus on stealing incremental points of market share from admittedly formidable competitors. Instead, he would raise the company's collective aspirations, reframing *why* they existed, *who* they served, and *what* they would do going forward.

Rather than jockeying with old rivals for the 15 percent of global payments that were electronic, Banga illuminated a massive untapped opportunity: the other 85 percent of the payments market consisting of cash and check transactions, many of which were conducted by "unbanked" individuals and small businesses in emerging markets who had no access to the formal financial system. Mastercard's true competition, as Banga saw it, was not Visa or American Express, but cash itself. His commitment to what he came to call a "World Beyond Cash" would shift the company's view "from short-term card share or account wins to a much larger and longer runway for growth," as he explained. It also aligned with Banga's personal motto of "doing well" by "doing good." As Haythornthwaite described, "Ajay had a wonderful speech that I would sell tickets to if I could, where he talked about the World Beyond Cash. He did it with such passion and pulled people along with him." Financial inclusion, Banga insisted, was both a business imperative and a societal responsibility—an ambition that could only be met if Mastercard embraced innovation.

Building on the company's present strengths, Banga introduced a simple three-pronged framework—"Grow, Diversify, Build"—to shape his colleagues' attention and guide decision-making toward the future he envisioned.[10] *Grow* meant continuing to compete—and with increasing success—against Visa and others in Mastercard's core payments business. "Authenticating and securing card-based transactions was still at the center of our day-to-day work," Banga said. "The more we grew it, the more we strengthened everything else we do." *Diversify* meant introducing new services and expanding Mastercard's customer base to include people and institutions that were not typical customers—from large corporations like Walmart and Lufthansa to governments and small businesses in emerging markets. Serving these new customers would become "the wellspring of our creativity and ability to expand and scale our capabilities," noted Banga. Finally, *build* meant creating entirely new businesses and revenue streams, which would require new capabilities.

Going forward, Banga asserted, half of the company's financial resources and management attention would go to growing the core product, a quarter would go to diversification, and a quarter would go to experimenting with new sources of growth. All budgeting exercises would include short (twelve to eighteen months), medium (eighteen months to three years), and long-term investments (four years and beyond). "Ajay was making a point that we needed to start being more innovative across the company," Mehra remarked. "He was showing 'I am willing to put my money where my mouth is. So you better come along for the ride as an employee of this company.'" Martina Hund-Mejean, CFO at the time, championed the strategy: "I said to people, 'We are crafting for the next hundred years, but there won't be a hundred years if we don't survive the short term.'" Thus began a new era at Mastercard.

Since the grow component was what the company knew best, Banga focused much of his effort on instilling the mindsets and behaviors to diversify and build. He recognized that the embrace of new technologies would be essential, as would diversifying its talent base internally—beyond the typical North American ex-banker or consultant profile that Mastercard tended to hire. As Banga explained, "If you surround yourself with people who you've worked with and studied with for a long time, you will all have the same blind spots." Instead, he sought talent with experience in government, nonprofits, consumer product companies, and technology companies, among other areas.

Banga knew that increasing the diversity of perspectives would feel uncomfortable in a company whose people were accustomed to decisions by consensus. The potential for conflict was obvious. To encourage collaboration across these differences, he decided to unify the company around a new code of values he dubbed the "Mastercard Way." A "relentless focus on our customers," in Banga's words, was the core of the Mastercard Way. Banga expected his people to have an intimate understanding of customers' diverse priorities, capabilities, and constraints. Doing so for an expanding set of customers required Mastercard to embrace those with different backgrounds and expertise. Above all, customer-centricity meant being hungry to win their business. Instilling this hunger, however, would be one of Banga's biggest challenges:

> I sat in a conference room after we had lost a major deal, and the only thing I heard was, "Oh, we didn't want to do that deal." I said, "There is no such thing as a deal you didn't want to win. There's only a deal you couldn't figure out how to win at a price that you thought was useful to you. I'm not here to listen to you give good reasons for why you didn't win."

Banga worked forcefully to kill off any complacency—what he saw as Mastercard's "worst enemy." Through his own daily communication and actions, he instilled a sense of urgency and accountability.[11] He firmly reminded employees that "procrastination was not [their] friend." A colleague noted, "Ajay was very tough. There was no excuse for not making the numbers. There was also no excuse for not advancing the financial inclusion agenda." This no-excuse mindset extended to interactions among employees. When Banga heard complaints about bottlenecks between managers and their people working in different geographies, he instituted a new policy: if an employee request sent to a manager went unanswered for seven days, it would automatically be considered approved. (The policy was rescinded once managers got the message and began responding more promptly.)

Perhaps the most difficult new value to embed at Mastercard was thoughtful risk-taking. The fears of risk were deep-seated—and rightly so, to some degree: their business was regulated for good reason. "Ajay was never cavalier on risk," noted Timothy Murphy, chief administrative officer at the time. Banga made it clear that regulatory compliance, reliability, and customer trust remained paramount. Yet, unlike many in his position, Banga equally understood the dangers of inaction. "A lot of his driving force came from his belief that failure to act is itself opening the company to risk," said Murphy.

Banga emphasized that while it wasn't possible to have "perfect knowledge" about every decision, it was possible "to take risks thoughtfully and exercise your judgment." He applauded and issued bonuses to anyone who took ownership of well-reasoned risks—even when the results fell short of expectations. At the same time, he gave bonuses to individuals who had courage enough to kill their own projects and free up resources for other experimentation.

Undergirding all these values was a broader concept that Banga called the "decency quotient," or "DQ" for short—a principle he hoped would shape every Mastercard interaction, internally and externally. "Decency serves as the foundation for the kinds of relationships and respect that drive innovation, urgency, and enterprise-wide thinking and behaviors," Banga explained. "DQ also informs how we regard our employees and every single element of their lives, both inside and outside the office." Once again, Banga walked the talk with this value. He mandated several changes to Mastercard's incentive systems, including competitive wages, equal pay for equal work, parental and bereavement leave, an expanded program of stock ownership, and industry-leading levels of retirement contributions. Banga also expected other leaders at Mastercard to be exemplars of the culture of decency, insisting

FIGURE 1-1

The Mastercard way: Decency quotient

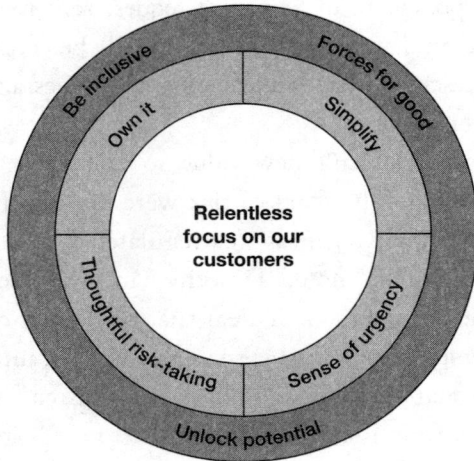

that they regard leadership as a "privilege"—not a preordained right. (See figure 1-1.)

Bridging Across Boundaries

As Banga worked to establish an environment for cocreation inside Mastercard, he also began introducing emerging technologies into the organization. As Banga put it, "The thought that we could figure out all the tech internally was a fallacy. We needed to find ways to allow the body to absorb from the outside, so it filtered into our bloodstream." The *bridger* he chose for the task, an Irishman named Garry Lyons, had recently joined Mastercard when the company acquired his startup, Orbiscom—a pioneer in virtual credit card numbers and blockchain technology in payments.[12]

According to Banga, he told Lyons to "make the culture care about innovation, wake us up to the innovation happening around us, be our eyes and ears to the outside world, and scare the crap out of us." At the same time, Banga recognized that in an environment unaccustomed to breakthrough innovation, he would need to create space for Lyons to think and act differently. Banga gave Lyons his own budget separate from corporate finance, building a "moat," as he put it, between him and the CFO. As Banga explained:

> My role was to protect Garry—to make sure nobody stood in his way. . . . We needed the company to be challenged—both from inside and from outside. I told [him], "I will give you a budget, your job is to disrupt me, and you never have to give me a spreadsheet to prove any projects. Your money is my money; . . . you're beholden only to me." I even told him, "I don't care if you go and drink Guinness all day long, but if you don't give me two new things to launch every year, I will fire everyone."

With significant autonomy and money to spend, Lyons elected to launch Mastercard Labs ("Labs")—a specialized innovation unit that eventually expanded into a global network of R&D labs. Under Lyons's leadership, Labs became Mastercard's "bridge between the legacy and the new," as Banga put it. Lyons and his team kept a pulse on technology trends by partnering with technology companies, startups, and venture capitalists. They hired specialized technology talent, who applied cutting-edge tools and methodologies to generate new payments solutions. At the same time, Lyons and his team actively primed those in the core business to embrace Labs' new offerings and innovate in their roles. They hosted awareness campaigns, upskilling sessions, hackathons, and other competitions to showcase emerging technology—and, most importantly, to get people involved in innovation.

By the end of 2013, Lyons had made significant progress on introducing new digital products and services. But Banga was especially pleased by a different metric: an in-house survey showed that employees had begun to rank innovation as the number one factor most important to Mastercard's future, up from number twenty-six *just three years before*. "Garry changed culture," Banga remarked, so "he got promoted."

By the time Lyons stepped down from his role as chief innovation officer in 2018, he had expanded Labs' scope to include a full-fledged corporate accelerator program and an innovation service for customers. Even Mastercard's core legacy systems had been upgraded to support cocreation. By embracing a more modular and flexible "API-first" approach, partners from across the financial landscape could seamlessly integrate with Mastercard's technology—enabling all sorts of new payments solutions, including the engine powering Apple and Google Pay.[13] Lyons's successor, Ken Moore, continued this trajectory of cocreation—forging closer bridges between Labs, external partners, and Mastercard's core business to fit the company's evolving needs. (Chapter 7 will delve deeper into the extensive bridging role that both Lyons and Moore played at Mastercard.)

Catalyzing a Movement

Through Lyons's and Moore's bridging efforts, Mastercard began to expand its influence across the broader financial ecosystem, positioning it to drive cocreation on a much greater scale than Banga could have imagined in 2010. When he first articulated his vision of a World Beyond Cash, Banga understood that delivering financial services to underserved communities would require digital technology and innovation. New banking, telecommunications, and regulatory infrastructure needed to be built from the ground up—and this was not something Mastercard, nor any single institution, could shoulder on its own. Thus, to advance their financial inclusion agenda, Banga and his colleagues at Mastercard would need to enable numerous local stakeholders—governments, banks, fintech startups, telecommunications providers, nonprofits, and civil society organizations—to cocreate in new ways.

This scale of innovation required Banga and his colleagues to cultivate movements across local ecosystems—that is, to step into the role of *catalyst*. For Banga, mobilizing key stakeholders started with earning their trust. He understood that he and Mastercard couldn't march into countries and tell them how they should build and run their economies. As Banga expressed, "It's not our birthright to do business in your country. We *earn* the right by proving that we can create value for your citizens. . . .

It's about attitude." Banga personally took responsibility for earning the confidence and commitment from national governments worldwide. "Societal trust was the foundation to play in all countries," he said. In his view, Mastercard needed to expand its entire circle of support and value creation to engender this trust, which meant shifting its role in society from "gatekeeper at the heart of commerce" to "collaborative facilitator of commerce and economic opportunity."

Banga and his colleagues launched numerous initiatives to spark collaborative problem-solving across African economies. In South Africa, Mastercard partnered with the government and private banks to transition disbursements of monthly government assistance programs from cash to bank-issued Mastercard debit cards. Within a year, South Africa's banked population increased by 22 million, or about 15 percent.[14] In the process, it also cut out 900,000 fraudulent grant recipients from the system, saving the government about $200 million.[15] In another partnership, Mastercard collaborated with the Nigerian government to issue 13 million national e-identification cards to citizens.[16] Following that success, the company established the Center for Inclusive Growth—a hub dedicated to partnering with local organizations to experiment with new distribution channels, micropayments, and digital-identity solutions in contexts with unreliable electricity or telecommunications infrastructure.[17]

At a 2015 meeting of the World Bank, Banga made an unscripted public pledge to build further momentum for financial inclusion: Mastercard would bring 500 million people into the formal financial system by 2020.[18] Over the following five years, Banga would help Mastercard launch even more impactful partnerships—each creating powerful opportunities for hundreds of millions of people and businesses.

Through his catalyst leadership, Banga not only deepened the company's reputation as a trusted adviser and partner to a growing array of nontraditional stakeholders, but also drove material business growth. Mastercard would eventually achieve its goal of reaching 500 million people two years early. In 2020, Banga, in turn, raised the previous commitment from 500 million to 1 billion people, while also setting new goals to help 25 million women entrepreneurs and 50 million micro and small businesses connect into the digital economy.[19]

Making the Case for the ABCs

When Banga stepped down as CEO in 2021, he passed the company on to his successor, Michael Miebach. Miebach had also played a significant role evolving Mastercard into a financially inclusive digital powerhouse that was unrecognizable when compared with the "credit card company" Banga had inherited in 2010. Mastercard's market cap had grown by ten times.[20] The story behind the numbers, however, is the transformation of culture—what Banga called "the single biggest differentiator in this company." In her appraisal of the Mastercard transformation, senior vice president Deborah Barta observed:

> For me, it was the top down. If innovation wasn't supported at the top, there was not a lot that middle managers could do to change culture. You had to be willing to invest. I respect Ajay to the ends of the earth for believing that we had the power to change. At the top, Ajay was promoting it. He spoke it. He believed it.

Banga understood that as the leader of the company, he was a stage-setter for innovation. As an architect, his job was to create an environment—to set the tone—for Mastercard's employees to be willing and able to join him on the exhilarating and taxing journey of forging their collective future. He recognized the importance of infusing new talent and tools from outside, and he chose to delegate the task to skilled bridgers, who established the partnerships necessary to drive digital transformation at Mastercard. As a catalyst, Banga mobilized numerous global stakeholders to become agents of financial inclusion. Along the way, he found himself leading not just a corporation but a global ecosystem into the future. Perhaps the greatest testament to Banga's leadership was his appointment in June 2023 as president of the World Bank—his largest platform yet for expanding the economic horizons for even the most marginalized.[21]

We've used Banga's story at Mastercard as a vivid illustration of all three roles we've observed among leaders who foster genius at scale—architect, bridger, and catalyst. The rest of this book will explore the three roles in depth, focusing on the constellation of mindsets and behaviors they entail. While the roles are deeply intertwined in practice, in each of the book's three parts, we focus on a single ABC. Many of the leaders you'll meet, like Banga, were in positions of significant formal authority in established organizations. But many others were middle managers or entrepreneurs starting out.

As you will discover in their stories, formal authority is often a limited source of power when leading genius at scale. Being an effective architect, bridger, or catalyst is not tied to formal roles and titles—they are practices that can and should be embraced by all leaders of innovation, no matter their level or function in organizations.

THE ARCHITECT

PART ONE

ARCHITECT

Building Community

Architects recognize that innovation is, above all, a voluntary act. Trying to mandate the mindset and behaviors required for cocreation is a futile effort. Instead, architects shape the social environment inside their teams and organizations to allow cocreation to emerge organically.

By building a sense of community around a shared purpose, values, and rules of engagement, architects refashion their organization's *culture*. A shared purpose keeps their teams aligned and energized through the arduous journey toward the future. Shared values and rules of engagement guide how they interact and problem-solve to meet the evolving needs of customers and key stakeholders.

Along with culture, architects develop key *capabilities* for innovation. They help their people embrace diversity of thought and the conflicts that come with creating a true marketplace of ideas. They encourage them to *act*, rather than *plan*, their way to novel solutions—learning and adapting along the way to inevitable missteps and even failures. Finally, they empower their organizations with analog and digital tools to make cocreation a more inclusive, disciplined, and repeatable process.

Architects rely on different levers to invite innovation within their organizations. They are deeply attentive to how structures, operating models, and configurations of tools and talent influence the willingness and ability to cocreate. They make deliberate changes to eliminate barriers and introduce enablers. But, perhaps most importantly, they also constantly calibrate and recalibrate their own leadership practice: they figure out when to lead from the bottom up and when to lead from the top down, when to support and when to confront, when to be patient and when to demand urgency, and when to emphasize learning and development versus performance.

In the next three chapters, we'll witness architects at three storied organizations—each over a century old and a leader in its industry. We chose to profile architects in these contexts because of the challenges posed by their rich legacies. Their colleagues took tremendous pride in past achievements and were reluctant to unlearn mindsets and behaviors that had served them well for so long. The not-invented-here syndrome was alive and well, so their teams were slow to adopt outside perspectives and new technologies. And finally, all three were in regulated industries where quality and safety standards understandably rendered them risk averse.

Although the task of driving innovation often seemed like "mission impossible," as one of our architects described, these leaders managed to build innovative communities within their organizations that could *collaborate*, *experiment*, and *learn* in new ways. While these three functions are intertwined in practice, each of the following chapters will center on how an architect fostered one in their organization.

CHAPTER 2

Collaboration at the Speed of Science

Michael Ku at Pfizer Global Clinical Supply

Together we continuously innovate, determined to adapt to unanticipated challenges and deliver hope to patients.

—**Michael Ku**

On November 9, 2020, Michael Ku, the vice president and head of Pfizer's Global Clinical Supply (GCS), was up early after a fitful night.[1] He logged onto a video call with leaders from across Pfizer's research and development unit. Pfizer and its German partner BioNTech had cocreated an mRNA vaccine for Covid-19. For months, Ku and his team had been working at breakneck speed to complete one of the fastest clinical trials in history, and the first phase-three results were in. Ku was about to learn whether their efforts to "make the impossible, possible," as he put it, had paid off.

Developing a vaccine of any kind typically takes up to ten years. But in March 2020, Pfizer CEO Albert Bourla had committed to spending as much as $2 billion up front on an expedited clinical trial R&D program, declaring Pfizer would "go all in" to develop a vaccine and save lives.[2] The program, Lightspeed, aimed to dramatically compress the usual timeline without compromising quality and the trial's integrity—requiring Ku's team to be more agile and innovative than ever.

A small but critical unit at Pfizer, GCS manages the packaging, labeling, operations, and logistics for hundreds of clinical trials worldwide. Even under normal circumstances, this is an extremely complex job. For the Covid-19 vaccine, Ku and his colleagues worked hand in glove with actors across Pfizer, BioNTech, government, and numerous suppliers to solve problems as they emerged. As John Ludwig, senior VP of Pfizer Medicinal Sciences, recalled:

> It was clear we were not going to have enough vials to run the study with our standard reserve doses. It was a problem I couldn't solve. . . . That had to come from Michael and his team. . . . I said to Michael, "This is a Wild West scenario. . . . How are we going to pull this off outside the norm while maintaining quality standards?"

Now on the video call, Ku held his breath as the phase-three results were read. Many were already hailing their work as "the clinical trial of the century," but Ku was cautious. An mRNA vaccine had never been approved before, yet they had already started making millions of doses. If the trials were a success, Pfizer could begin vaccine distribution immediately, potentially saving millions of lives.[3]

Ku wondered what would happen if they did not cross the finish line. But then, he heard the words he'd been listening for: among the over forty thousand adult participants, the vaccine was found to have an efficacy rate of more than 90 percent.[4] Pfizer and BioNTech could seek emergency-use authorization immediately.

Ku quickly gathered his GCS colleagues on another video call to share the news. Their team, he reminded them, had produced a veritable "avalanche of innovation" to deliver those clinical studies in record time; now they could pause to enjoy this moment of success. Through tears and laughter, the team shared stories of the countless roadblocks they'd navigated—"the wrath of Mother Nature," hurricanes and wildfires, border closures, and lockdowns—as they transported precious vials under extraordinary temperature conditions.[5] Not a single shipment was lost.

What's more, Ku's team had somehow continued orchestrating logistics for almost four hundred additional trials across the globe.

How did they pull it off? This chapter recounts the ten-year backstory of how Ku and his leadership team prepared GCS to triumph over unthinkable constraints. Ku, a middle manager, built and shaped a culture of innovation—a consummate architect. His mandate had been to lead the digital transformation of the supply chain. But in the end, it was not technology that explained their success; it was their sense of community that got them through the stresses of "living vial to vial," as Ku put it. It was their spirit of *collaboration* that enabled GCS to be willing and able to experiment and learn together with their partners, pulling off one of the fastest clinical trials in history and saving millions of lives.

An Outsider Coming In

Ku was born in the Philippines and grew up in Canada. He became passionate about health care when he landed a job as a technician in a local pharmacy, where he "loved putting on the white coat to help patients."[6] After receiving his bachelor of science in toxicology and a minor in computer science, he moved to the United States to pursue an additional bachelor's degree in pharmacy and a doctor of pharmacy. He interned in pharmacy operations supporting patients at a Boston hospital before moving into the biopharmaceutical industry. As Ku put it, his career took him from "touching the lives of patients, one at a time . . . to now touching the lives of entire populations and countries."[7]

In 2011, Ku was working for Genzyme Corporation, a biotech company, when he received an unsolicited call about a position at Pfizer. Ku and his Genzyme colleagues had just spent thirteen years building out the company's global clinical supply organization, where he discovered his penchant for solving complex operational problems and managing layers of internal and external relationships to address them. To prepare himself to scale his growing organization, Ku had even completed an MBA while working full-time.

Pfizer was looking for someone who could lead a digital transformation of its clinical supply chain. Ku's friends warned him not to leave the fast-paced world of biotech and join big pharma. But he was excited by Pfizer's patient-centric mission and the prospect of a leadership role in an organization supplying more than one million packages of investigational medicines for clinical trials at eight thousand sites in seventy-plus countries each year. "It was the largest opportunity in the industry," Ku said, "a pinnacle position."

Despite his due diligence before accepting the job, Ku says he didn't appreciate just how complex his task would be. Although he immediately understood why Pfizer had one of the highest-performing clinical supply chains in the industry, Ku also saw that it was overstretched, and its technology "close to end-of-life." Pfizer had undergone three large-scale mergers and acquisitions, and the clinical supply chain had implemented an aggressive outsourcing strategy, reduced its head count, and begun moving from fourteen operations facilities to a single internal packaging and labeling site.

Meeting his team for the first time, Ku knew that his identity as an outsider "set off alarms" in a company that normally promoted from within. He also understood that he was looking at the survivors of a long series of changes and layoffs; innovation was the last thing on their minds. People had their heads down, working in silos to meet the demands in front of them. Collaboration for them, Ku observed, meant "getting along and going with the flow," whereas Ku knew from experience that diverse perspectives and pushback was critical for innovation.[8]

Starting with the "Why"

During his third week on the job, Ku took the stage at the clinical supply chain's ad hoc town hall meeting. The room at Pfizer's site in Groton, Connecticut, was at full capacity, with global members attending virtually. Ku saw this as his "defining moment." If Pfizer was going to have a premier physical and digital clinical supply chain, Ku knew where he had to start to gain the team's trust. "The big piece for me was to get everybody together to focus on the *why*," he said. "You have to have your purpose and the *why* before you do your *what* and *how*."[9]

"First and foremost," Ku told his new colleagues, "I am all about the patient."[10] He recounted his experiences caring for patients on the front line, how he understood what it meant to hold a sick patient's hand. He'd seen up close how a clinical trial's success depended on the site's health-care providers storing, preparing, and administering the drugs correctly. Following strict protocols and gathering precise data was imperative—yet the systems that companies used to support health-care providers were neither user-friendly nor agile.

Ku explained his ambition to build a "patients-first, physical and digital, end-to-end" supply chain at Pfizer. That meant taking responsibility for the *entire* clinical patient experience. The supply chain didn't end when the drug shipment left Pfizer or even when it arrived at the hospital conducting the clinical study. Keith Jackson, then a group lead of Clinical Supply Strategy and Management (CSSM), later reflected on Pfizer's process before Ku arrived: "When we shipped product to a hospital or clinical site," he said, "we were done. That was the end of our supply chain."

But Ku was introducing an entirely new philosophy: the process ended only when "the clinical trial patient took the right product, at the right dose, at the right time, at the right temperature, and in the right location"—a mantra he would repeat in the years ahead. Health-care providers at clinical sites were their *partners* in delivering quality clinical trials. And for them to do their jobs effectively, Ku insisted, supplying information was just as important as delivering products. Moreover, the seamless convergence of information and products would require a significant boost to GCS's technology and data capabilities.

As Ku spoke to his teammates, he felt rising skepticism in the room. Many of his new colleagues had been at Pfizer for decades. Although they'd been hearing about digital transformation for years, they'd also gotten the job done using traditional analog systems. In a regulated environment like theirs, they did not feel change was worth the risk.

Ku was all too aware of the difficult journey ahead. To get his new colleagues to embrace digital technology, data, and new ways of working, he knew he had to first build a culture of innovation. Ku was not patient by nature. Nevertheless, he knew that culture change takes time and was careful not to disrupt things too quickly. Most important, he would keep the entire leadership team (LT) he had inherited, as well as the extended leadership team (eLT).

Ku spent the rest of 2011 on a global listening tour, meeting every one of his colleagues and key internal and external partners. He recognized that there was no substitute for face-to-face interaction when it came to building connections and earning trust. His goal? To encourage a new mindset about the meaning of their work. He used every conversation to remind people that the purpose of the clinical supply chain went beyond delivering packages; it was about "bringing hope to patients," what he shorthanded as putting "patients first." For Ku, this was not a tagline but an ethos. It meant working in an integrated way to deliver an impactful, holistic experience for patients. He encouraged everyone he met, including vendors, to define what patients first meant to them personally, exploring together the role each could play in realizing their purpose. As one colleague observed, "Michael modeled the behavior that he wanted from the team. He listened to everyone, no matter the level of the organization." He reminded his colleagues that their investigative medicines could well be the "last hope" for many patients; therefore, speed and efficacy were imperative. By the end of Ku's tour, he'd identified a glaring barrier to collaboration on his team: siloed thinking.[11]

Collaboration for Innovation: Embracing Diversity of Thought

Decades of research tell us that innovation is most often a group effort—an interplay of ideas that emerges only through interactions of people with different viewpoints, experience, or expertise. Albert Einstein, a genius by any standard, referred to innovation as "combinational chemistry . . . about taking ideas, half-baked notions, competencies, concepts, and assets that already sit out there and recombining them. . . . What's new in many instances is the new mix." Einstein reminded us that most innovations come about through a process of simply looking at "old problems from a new angle."[12] Ku's next task as an architect was to encourage his colleagues to do just that.

As Ku dug into the root causes of siloed thinking and behavior across GCS, he learned that many of his colleagues had stayed within one function for their entire Pfizer careers, some for decades. For Ku, the challenge ahead would be guiding people out of their comfort zones to embrace other illuminating perspectives and possibilities—to help them "get comfortable being uncomfortable." He chose three areas of focus.

Bringing the Outside-In Perspective

Architects can help their organizations embrace new perspectives by intentionally exposing them to people with different expertise and experience. To help his LT "break frame," Ku decided to add new people to the team, including high-potential employees from within GCS and from Pfizer's upstream and downstream partners. Not only that, Ku also invited leaders from other business functions, such as development operations, finance, and procurement, to attend the team's monthly meetings, depending on the agenda.

Having expanded the LT from six to sixteen people, Ku wasn't surprised when his colleagues worried the size was becoming unwieldly. Others questioned why they should share decision-making rights with subordinate "high potentials" as well as people outside clinical supply. As he listened to his colleagues' concerns, Ku took this as an opportunity to be transparent about the "why" behind his decisions. The LT depended on perspectives both inside and outside GCS if they hoped to implement the best decisions on behalf of patients. "We needed their voices in the room," he explained.

"It took a long time to build trust," noted Jeanne Quattromani, a GCS business administrator. Ku mandated that the LT begin meeting monthly and face-to-face—which had never been their regular practice. Slowly but surely, transparency and inclusive decision-making by the LT began to set the tone for change throughout GCS.

Bringing the Patient Perspective

Ku insisted that another key perspective was missing across their supply chain: the patient. "All patients aren't created equal," he said. In 2012, Ku introduced his first major structural change—an entirely new team, Clinical Research Pharmacy (CRP). Ku hired clinical research pharmacists— talent that had never been part of Pfizer's supply chain—and charged them with generating and sharing information about the experiences of patients and health-care professionals at clinical sites. But Ku underestimated the strong internal antibodies at GCS. Rather than embracing CRP's insights, his colleagues deliberately excluded the team from pertinent conversations. "There was a fear that they were being replaced with pharmacists," recalled CRP leader Stephen Kay, "which obviously wasn't the case."

Ku recognized that architecting something new and getting people to embrace it were two different things. To create opportunities for the clinical supply chain members to arrive at their own conclusions, Ku encouraged them to join him at clinical site visits launched by CRP. For many, these visits were the first time they witnessed the daily challenges healthcare professionals faced when preparing and administering drugs. They saw for themselves the problems that could emerge as professionals deciphered complex instructions to prepare an investigative medicine.

Ku recalled that when his colleagues "saw the product that they packaged sitting on the shelf in the hospital, they started to understand how their role in the clinical supply chain was critical in delivering the product *and* information to the clinical sites." The value of CRP members as advocates of health-care workers and patients in the field became self-evident. Ku felt encouraged when the LT decided to institute "Patients First Awards" for which people could nominate colleagues across functions and levels, based on their patient-centric efforts. One of the first nominations went to a packaging and labeling team.[13] It had created stickers to remind them of whom their finished package would ultimately touch, for example, a pediatric cardiology patient or geriatric oncology patient.

Bringing the Global Perspective

In the spirit of inviting new mindsets and behaviors—rather than forcing them—architects tend to ask deliberate and thoughtful questions instead of making declarative statements.[14] In one of his first eLT meetings, Ku asked a question that previous leaders had never explicitly posed: "Where are our patients?" As the team began to discuss the many countries they served, they made the decision to officially rename the clinical supply chain "*Global* Clinical Supply"—to communicate (and remind themselves) that they served patients worldwide.

Yet, a year into his role, Ku still did not feel GCS was truly embracing a global perspective. GCS was supplying trials to clinical sites in seventy countries, but its teams were located only in the United States, the United Kingdom, and Japan. No one from GCS had ever visited many of their far-flung clinical sites where trials took place, yet they regularly made crucial decisions about those sites without appreciating the local health-care contexts and regulatory landscapes.

Just as CRP had begun to help Ku's colleagues embrace the nuances of the patient experience, Ku decided to establish new GCS teams in Asia and Latin America to help the organization grasp the challenges and opportunities of running clinical trials in those regions. Once again, the established leaders on Ku's LT resisted. Was this the best use of their resources? Would it not complicate their work unnecessarily? But Ku insisted the investment would best serve their patients: "We needed people on the ground that knew the local practices, spoke the local language, and could make partnerships that would create the best insights to mitigate risks." He created a set of online forums to give GCS colleagues based in different geographies opportunities to discover the commonalities and differences in their local circumstances.[15]

To further broaden mindsets, Ku began rotating his direct reports and high potentials across functions, offering them stretch assignments. He delegated the expansion of GCS's global organization to Laurent Dhervilly, then a high-potential leader with technological expertise who shared Ku's vision but had little experience managing virtual or global teams. Ku knew that new digital tools would be crucial for GCS to become an integrated global organization.

Collaboration Is Not Consensus

While diversity of thought is essential for collaboration, it also increases the potential for conflict. Architects understand that fostering a true marketplace of ideas requires that divergent viewpoints are voiced, tested, and debated. Innovative solutions emerge when a group searches for ways to take the best of the proposed options—even ones that at first seem in opposition—to find what we call integrative or "both/and" (as opposed to "either/or") solutions.[16]

By 2013, Ku felt encouraged to see that, by diversifying the talent in the room, GCS had begun to see the value of different points of view.

However, as much as Ku encouraged candor in meetings, he rarely saw the kind of open, robust discourse he knew was key to cocreation. He observed that GCS (and Pfizer more broadly) had a "deeply polite and respectful culture." While this collegial environment had clear benefits, it also meant that meetings were fundamentally about coming to consensus, rather than identifying the best ideas. Instead of raising a dissenting voice, people kept quiet, not wanting to be seen as "the problem."

To help his colleagues speak up and engage in productive discourse, Ku introduced a simple "complexity scorecard" consisting of red, yellow, and green circles, like those found on stoplights. High-complexity projects were red, since they carried the most risk, and low-complexity projects green. This created a neutral, shared language for spurring debate about projects that—given the culture of politeness—would never have been challenged. The scorecard was used in regular operational reviews to discuss risks more openly—for example, what made the packaging and logistics more complex for one investigative medicine versus another? Still, in the first meetings using the scorecard, Ku found that few were willing to categorize any clinical study as red. He had to constantly remind his team that "red isn't 'bad'—red means 'pay attention'" because the study contained highly complex elements.

In addition to the complexity scorecard, Ku became a champion for a Pfizer initiative called "OWN IT," which promoted a sense of company-wide accountability. Ku encouraged his colleagues to use "Straight Talk" coins that Pfizer provided, which meant that if someone wanted to introduce a sensitive topic or offer critique during a meeting, they could place a coin on the table. This action told everyone in the room that the person intended to speak candidly, in a patient-focused way—not to assign blame.

Adapting Leadership Style: The Key Lever of an Architect

Ku's story so far illustrates the many levers architects have at their disposal: instilling a sense of purpose and shaping the talent profile, team structure, and processes. But perhaps the most important lever available to leaders is their personal style as an instrument of cultural transformation. The best architects are deeply self-aware of the experiences they create for others through their actions and words. They periodically ask themselves, "How do people experience me, and how do people experience themselves when they are with me?" For Ku, this behavior was learned over time.[17]

Ku's embrace of the corporate OWN IT initiative caught the attention of Pfizer's senior leadership. They rewarded him with the opportunity to work with a leadership coach and receive 360-degree feedback about his management ability. Ku learned that, despite his best intentions to empower people, his colleagues experienced him as being "directive." His coach helped him realize for the first time that *when* and *how* he spoke up in meetings affected people's sense of psychological safety and the quality of discussion. Ku admitted that in meetings, "Everybody quieted down after I said my opinion. Nobody else said anything."[18]

Ku's coach suggested that as the most senior person, he should speak last to avoid inadvertently shutting down discussions. This didn't come naturally to Ku. "Michael didn't hold back," said Delayn Haynes, then head of GCS's CSSM unit. But over time, Ku found ways to encourage debate. Haynes described one such change: "Sometimes he'd stand up and take four steps back from the table and let us go and have a discussion. We were quite a diverse team and if somebody had something to say, they'd say it, but he let us have those discussions."

Coaching also made Ku more conscious of his rhetoric.[19] For example, his GCS colleagues were sensitive to his frequent use of the words "change" and "transformation"—which they perceived as dismissive of Pfizer's traditions and culture. Ku soon adopted the term "evolution" instead. "Evolution respects past achievements and builds on them to get better," a colleague pointed out to him.

Ultimately, Ku came to understand that the cultural transformation he hoped to drive required his own personal transformation as well. While most leaders might choose to keep their 360-degree feedback to themselves, Ku initiated a dialogue with his leadership team about their inputs. "Here are the things I heard," Ku told them. "I want to make sure I understand everything. Here is what I expect to do, and I need your help to make sure we've got a strong team." Ku was modeling the kind of vulnerability and openness he wanted his team to practice. Thereafter, members of the LT noticed they began to bond and work with each other more constructively. Everyone was becoming more comfortable speaking up, as one team member observed, "even with those more senior to them. . . . It started to change the organization for the better."

Improving Collaboration with Digital Technology and Data

By 2016, Ku felt that GCS had learned how to "walk together." He and his colleagues were beginning to feel like a community with a sense of shared purpose and values. They'd developed rules of engagement for how to solve problems together, including a common lexicon for managing conflict and risk. Now it was time to learn to run together.

Information was still traveling to clinical sites in "big binders full of forms," Ku said, which were cumbersome and inefficient for communicating with partners. Pfizer intended to scale its clinical trial portfolio in the years ahead. To keep up, Ku knew GCS had to evolve its legacy systems of record into more agile, end-to-end "systems of engagement and insight."

Ku and his leadership team mapped out an ambitious digital strategy. It included, for example, leveraging big data, machine learning, and simulations to create the seamless end-to-end flow of physical products and information. But they knew it would take time and energy for people to learn to work with these tools. GCS's digital evolution could only be as effective as the people who implemented it, both in-house and at partner sites.[20]

As they began making initial technology investments, Ku and his team found a way to communicate the value proposition of each new tool—*why* and *how* it would help GCS deliver on its purpose. Through vivid storytelling and interactive demonstrations, they illustrated how simplifying the preparation and administration of investigative medicines could accelerate data generation and get life-saving drugs to patients faster. Ku encouraged his colleagues to develop their own use cases of how new digital capabilities could improve the patient experience.

Still, some GCS members struggled with the new technologies. Others wondered why they must use digital systems when their analog ones were perfectly functional. When colleagues asked hard questions about how to weigh data against their experience in decision-making, Ku changed his rhetoric—from saying decisions should be "data-driven" to the more accurate statement of "data-informed."[21] He began to personify "data" as just another collaborator. "It's like data is the guy sitting in the chair next to us," he told them, "and we get to ask him questions." By introducing visualization tools and dashboards that improved user-friendliness, GCS staff began to see how data created more alignment in their day-to-day activities to achieve their goal of "running together."

Expanding the Sense of Community

In 2016, after years of advocating for the patient in meetings, Ku was proud to see that other leaders were now adopting this role. As LT member Richard Hwang recalled, "patients first" became a guiding norm during debates: "In the end, even if Michael did not mention it, another member would mention, 'If we do this, is it going to be best for the patient?' So, I do think that the culture piece really was the foundation to help us to be able to make tough decisions together."

GCS's strong sense of purpose opened new opportunities for collaboration with colleagues inside and outside of Pfizer. The CRP team, for example, proactively began working with Pfizer's consumer division, using a simulated consumer home in Richmond, Virginia, to test packaging of clinical trial products with focus groups. Ku was impressed by the insights this internal partnership generated. In an on-site test where a parent needed to dose a child, he observed, "When we took the families into the 'Pfizer Consumer Home,' the children, of course, ran around distracting mom and dad—just like at home. . . . If the parents couldn't administer the medicine in this setting, then we weren't clear enough with our instructions."

The eLT designed a team-building exercise where GCS members created a twenty-foot mural depicting images symbolizing "bringing hope to patients." One image, painted by a pediatric oncology patient, spelled out the word "HOPE." An eLT member suggested creating lapel pins of this image for everyone in GCS. And when visiting GCS offices around the world, Ku was touched to see people proudly wearing their HOPE pins.

Such symbolic gestures kept the shared "why"—bringing hope to patients—front and center. The HOPE mural was later displayed at Pfizer's world headquarters in New York City.

Democratizing Innovation

Even as GCS and its partners became more collaborative, Ku still found people slow to embrace technology and its promised innovative ways of working. The problem, from what he could tell, was that his colleagues conflated "innovation" with "invention." At Pfizer, the scientists were the innovators; supply chain members were executors. As a result, teams focused their attention on what they *should* be doing, not what they *could* be doing. Ku, a hockey fan, knew this mindset had to change. To paraphrase one of his hockey heroes, Wayne Gretzky, "We need to go where the puck is going to be—not where it [is] or has been." To do that, Ku needed to find ways to democratize innovation: to encourage everyone to see themselves as innovative problem-solvers, on the lookout to create something new even in their daily routines.

He started by sharing in a town hall meeting an inclusive, expansive definition of innovation: "anything that was both new and useful."[22] Innovations didn't need to involve technology; they could be a new way to manage inventory or cut inefficiencies. For example, the complexity scorecard was an innovation because it was both new *and* useful, fundamentally changing the quality of conversations during operational reviews.

Ku adopted another Pfizer-wide mantra—"Dare to Try"—and used it in meetings when his team hesitated to do something unfamiliar. Missteps and intelligent failures were relabeled as "learnings." GCS's Patients First Awards were expanded to include a special "Learn Fast" award (adapting the "fail fast" language of startups to Pfizer's highly regulated business, with its focus on quality and safety).

This celebration of learnings enabled Ku's group to feel safer exploring opportunities to improve their operations. For example, the Latin America team decided to test certain process assumptions they held, found that many were unfounded, and made changes that collapsed operational timelines in one country from fifty-five days to twenty. "I had always thought that innovation was only related to digital," reflected Viviane Arantes, the head of GCS Latin America. "I didn't think there was any easy way I could innovate in Latin America. But I completely changed my way of thinking. With everything I did, I constantly thought, 'What can I do differently?'"

Soon this mindset translated to how GCS teams applied digital technology to their work. Ted Bradley, then head of Clinical Supply Logistics, explained how his team overhauled a legacy system that tracked regulations for seventy individual countries:

> We digitized and uploaded our distribution plans and country specifications into a single platform with a country architecture, and when people were preparing distribution plans, we made it very easy to input the requirements and have a more comprehensive view of the country intelligence picture.

Meanwhile, Ku worked with GCS's digital teams to develop a data marketplace that would help teams coordinate their innovation initiatives with more "discipline" by centralizing data from across GCS. As the "single source of truth," it made the group's entire portfolio of digital assets visible and served as their center of excellence for data governance, data cleaning, and data integration.

Building Decision-Making Muscles

It took nearly seven years, but Ku could see that GCS was increasingly comfortable generating and implementing new ideas. For example, drawing inspiration from Amazon, teams created mobile phone apps. One team created the Kit Verify App to support clinical sites, and another created the Shipment Notification App, a first-ever for a clinical supply chain.

Amid these encouraging innovations, however, Ku saw that his colleagues were too often reluctant to kill projects that had stalled, creating what some referred to as "walking zombies." Anticipating more budget constraints, Ku and his colleagues affirmed that GCS could ill afford to dedicate resources to efforts not creating value for patients. Ku partnered with an outside organization to assess why his group found it so hard to kill projects in a timely fashion. When Ku and the eLT reviewed the survey data, they learned that GCS members struggled with effective decision-making. More specifically, their long-held discomfort with "creative conflict" continued as a key barrier. Instead of resolving conflicts as they emerged, teams tended to escalate tough decisions to the senior team.

Now that the problem had become visible, Ku saw an opportunity for his LT to model the behavior they expected from GCS team members. "I challenged the leadership team to go on their own and think through the data, our processes, and structures," Ku said. "I trusted them to develop a plan to address the decision-making issues themselves." At first, however, the LT struggled to agree on a solution; they kept trying to persuade Ku to weigh in. Each time, Ku resisted and told them to go back to the drawing board.

In May 2019, after months of debate, the LT returned to Ku with a proposal. They suggested new decision-making bodies called "tetrads": cross-functional teams of people from Pfizer's different line functions. This was a significant departure from GCS's existing structure, where a single leader was accountable for a function's decisions. Kay described the tetrads as the "patient-focus boards." Haynes added that "the intention was to align ownership across GCS and create a point of contact in each of the functional lines. We wanted to empower the next layer down in the organization. It was not just about giving them permission to make decisions, but to enable them to learn to analyze risk and think more strategically."

Implementing the tetrads was a developmental experience for all of GCS—one that Ku recognized was only possible because of the trust they'd nurtured together. For those appointed to the tetrads, exposure to other functions' ways of operating provided key stretch opportunities. It took time for the tetrads to find their footing, but they soon became an important driver of innovation. Kay noted how "one tetrad came up with ideas around distribution for our gene therapy programs that our leadership team would never have thought of. That to me . . . was worth all the perseverance it took to build these groups."

Almost ten years in, Ku could see that GCS was becoming the patients-first, physical and digital, end-to-end supply chain he'd envisioned back in 2011. Ku's team had managed to build out GCS's global footprint while leveraging digital tools to maintain their close sense of community.

At the end of 2019, these gains were tested when Ku decided the CRP team should expand to Manila, Philippines—charging GCS member Fae Wooding to lead the effort. Mentored by Ku, Wooding worked thoughtfully to extend GCS's patients-first culture. Through remote onboarding sessions and cultural exchange initiatives, she built a global CRP team that helped GCS leverage time differences to operate twenty-four hours a day, five days a week.

These new efficiencies came just as Pfizer announced a new strategy: the company began divesting its consumer and off-patent products to focus exclusively on innovative, patient-tailored medicines and vaccines. Ku could see that GCS would need to operate within a "new clinical trial paradigm": to deliver with "velocity—speed with purpose." As 2019 came to an end, Ku's prediction soon became reality—with a vengeance.

Meeting the Covid Challenge: Collaboration at Light Speed

In March 2020, Pfizer launched its Lightspeed R&D program to develop the Pfizer–BioNTech Covid-19 vaccine. "We started making millions of doses at risk," Ku said, "knowing that if the data didn't demonstrate adequate safety and efficacy, we would throw everything away."

With many at GCS ordered to work from home, the group adopted a remote, just-in-time operating model and decision-making cadence to remove what Ku called "white spaces" from every step in the supply chain. Decisions were made and immediately implemented. "There was no buffer," said Hwang. "Everyone was on alert and proactively preparing all the time to pivot instead of sticking to a defined plan." With Covid-19 vaccines, a shipment could arrive at a site at 6 a.m. and the patient could be dosed at 8 a.m. While speed was critical, it was never at the expense of scientific rigor.

To maintain the integrity of the trials, potential vaccines had to be tested in high-Covid-infected areas. Having developed one of the most advanced data marketplaces in the company, GCS rapidly consolidated data of infection rates and potential risks at clinical sites—everything that would limit supply movement, from extreme weather to lockdowns and border closures. Every effort was made to move vials proactively. "We couldn't have extra doses sitting on the shelf at one site when we could en-roll and treat participants at another," Ku explained. "The sooner we got participants in, the sooner we got data for submission to regulatory authorities."

On November 9, 2020, Ku and his colleagues received the news they'd waited for: the phase-three clinical trials were a success, and Pfizer and BioNTech could seek emergency-use authorization for their vaccine immediately. On December 2, 2020—266 days after the World Health Organization had declared a pandemic—the Covid-19 vaccine received its first global authorization for emergency use in the United Kingdom, followed shortly afterward in the United States.

Ultimately, Ku's team had demonstrated a new vision of what a supply chain could be—one driven by continual collaborative innovation. Covid-19 and all its variants would remain a formidable challenge for Ku and his GCS colleagues. They worked tirelessly on clinical trials for pediatric vaccines, "booster" vaccines, and even for an antiviral drug to reduce the more serious consequences of Covid-19—all done with the same fervor that went into the initial vaccine.[23]

Despite being "up to his eyeballs" in complexity as GCS's leader, Ku never ceased looking ahead to where the puck was going.[24] His next challenge as an architect was how to convert the radically new way of working that they'd learned during the crisis into business as usual at GCS.

Lessons Learned: Architecting for Collaboration

The story of Michael Ku and his GCS team illustrates just how arduous it can be for leaders to architect an environment where people are willing and able to innovate. Although Ku was hired to lead a digital transformation, he quickly realized that digital tools and data would not magically make a legacy supply chain more agile and innovative. His challenge was going back to basics: instilling in his team the willingness and ability to collaborate.

Unlike Mastercard's CEO Ajay Banga, Ku was architecting as a middle manager with limited control over things like budget and compensation. What he *could* shape was his team's sense of community—their mindsets and behaviors. "Patients first" was Ku's passion. But rather than forcing his "why" on others, he invited his team to come up with their own stories about what patients first meant to them. Ku listened to his colleagues and made thoughtful changes to the organizational structure, talent, and digital tools available to overcome siloed mindsets, fears of speaking up, and ineffective decision-making. Most significantly, Ku was willing to change his own leadership style to ensure a transformation of the culture.

Full of prodigious energy and naturally action-oriented, Ku nevertheless had the vision to be patient. He took the time to appreciate what had made his new team successful already and did the hard work of adapting himself to fit with what the team was ready for—from learning to speak last in meetings to deliberately adopting new rhetoric.

Collaboration is foundational for innovation, and Ku's story demonstrates what that means: the capacity of people to embrace their differences and work through them together. It took time and trial and error, but Ku found ways to help his GCS colleagues use robust debate to voice wide-ranging ideas and hone them into new combinations. Our research and experience have shown that many organizations fail to develop this muscle. In fact, we find more often that too little conflict—not too much—is what impedes innovation. Why? We all know what it feels like to have our ideas belittled or rejected; it is not easy to stay in the fight. We all know how hard it is to critique a beloved colleague's pet project, even when everyone in the room believes the project should be killed. Finally, we have all seen what can happen to those who challenge the status quo too often; they are labeled contrarians or disruptors, and over time their opinions are ignored.

That's why it is essential that architects, like Ku, devote time and attention to instilling a sense of community—the glue to hold groups together as they traverse the rocky social terrain of cocreation. Ku and his team's efforts to architect for collaboration unlocked GCS's capacity to experiment and learn, not only within the team but also with key stakeholders inside and outside Pfizer. How fortunate that Ku's GCS colleagues came to see themselves as innovators—willing and able to put patients first—just in time for a global pandemic, when we all became the patient.

CHAPTER 3

Experimenting into the Future

Kathy Fish at Procter & Gamble

It's time to innovate how we innovate.

—Kathy Fish

Procter & Gamble (P&G) is a global consumer products superpower.[1] Billions of people worldwide use P&G products on a weekly, if not daily, basis. Founded in 1837, P&G dominates US retailers, with the Tide brand alone accounting for nearly 20 percent of total US laundry detergent sales in 2022.[2] In the personal care aisle, brands like Crest and Gillette take up a disproportionate amount of shelf space. In home cleaning, it's Cascade, Bounty, and Swiffer. In baby care, it's Pampers and Luvs.

For Kathy Fish, a chemical engineering major at Michigan State, landing a position at P&G was a dream job. Her interview with P&G, she said, was a "defining moment" that changed the course of her life.[3] In 1979, Fish moved to Cincinnati, Ohio, where she would raise her family and build a storied career in the R&D division of one of America's most iconic companies.

Over four decades, Fish witnessed P&G's steady and prodigious growth, which many attributed to the company's ability to turn continuous innovation into a science—or, at least, a predictable machine.[4] P&G's "stage-gate" methodology became the industry standard—separating R&D, manufacturing, marketing, and sales into discrete linear stages. It required big investments and long timelines, sometimes up to ten years to get the seed of an idea "cooked" in the lab and onto retail shelves. As Marc Pritchard, P&G's chief brand officer, explained, the method worked well—at least when "we had the luxury of time."

When the 2008 financial crisis hit, the company's category growth sunk to an all-time low amid turbulent commodity prices and foreign exchange rates. As Fish put it, "The flywheel stopped turning and people started doubling down on activity and cost savings." Rather than churning out breakthrough products that had once transformed entire categories, P&G was delivering mostly incremental innovations—a new product color, a flavor variation. Business units (BUs) were producing "more initiatives but not innovation that improved consumers' lives by solving real problems or creating new possibilities," Fish explained.

By the early 2010s, as Fish reached the senior ranks in R&D, P&G was facing a new competitive landscape. The rise of the internet, social media, and other digital technologies enabled scores of startups to begin shattering many long-held assumptions at P&G. In the razor business, for example, Dollar Shave Club was beating P&G's Gillette, but not with better razors or by dominating traditional retail outlets. Instead, the startup provided personalized facial care regimens (pre-scrub, razors, aftershave), marketed mostly through YouTube ads. It also eliminated the hassle of in-store purchases with a subscription model, shipping directly to consumers.

Historically, P&G's competitive advantage had relied on technical superiority, economies of scale, mass marketing, and strategic retail distribution. But the product economy was shifting to an experience economy, and digitization was raising expectations for end-to-end personalization. Dollar Shave Club, Harry's, Glossier, and countless other direct-to-consumer newcomers were competing by new rules and business models, leveraging consumer data to innovate with agility. P&G's size, age, and complexity—benefits in its historic past—were becoming liabilities.

As the company stood unfavorably against its new class of competitors, investors blamed P&G's innovation engine, and in 2014, almost half of its executive team was replaced.[5] During that shake-up, Fish became chief technology officer—soon renamed as chief research, development, and innovation officer. She would now oversee the seven-thousand-strong R&D function and the company's innovation portfolio across all the category-driven BUs.

Corporate R&D would continue making long-term investments in "transformative platform technologies" that could have broad impact across the BUs. And while P&G was making significant investments in its digital transformation, Fish knew fundamental change was needed to catapult the company into the twenty-first century. "P&G's innovation machine was broken," she said. The BUs needed to evolve their high-capital, time-intensive, stage-gate approach to innovation—or get left behind.

The Invitation to Innovate

As one of the most senior leaders in a 100,000-person organization, Fish could have approached P&G's transformation as a directive from the top. But decades of experience had taught her that, to succeed, any change initiative at P&G had to be more bottom up and "organic," as she put it.[6] P&G's sixty-five brands served more than five billion consumers.[7] The heads of the category-based BUs owned most decisions about products and talent. They were accountable for clear, largely shorter-term financial metrics and, understandably, leaned toward tried-and-true methods for generating profit. Fish's empowering leadership style and political savvy were well suited for the task. As one of her colleagues described, "She is a strategic master. She is introverted, some would say soft-spoken. She chooses her words very carefully. She has real conversations with people. She's very focused on where we need to go. She pushes hard but is fair."

Fish's first task, she decided, was to articulate a clear value proposition for change. The BU leaders would need a compelling reason—a *why*—anchored on P&G's corporate purpose to "improve the lives of the world's consumers." A researcher at heart, Fish got to work investigating the history behind P&G's billion-dollar products. What she and her team found was surprisingly consistent. The products at the core of these mega-brands weren't built purely on a single great technical concept; they represented a confluence of factors—functional performance, packaging, brand messaging, and retail execution. These were products that offered high value for consumers and retailers and dramatically elevated the individual category's performance overall.

Over decades, brand products like Crest toothpaste, Tide laundry soap, and Cascade dishwasher detergent had raised expectations such that consumers couldn't imagine using alternatives. Mary Lynn Ferguson-McHugh, CEO of Family Care and P&G Ventures, noted that P&G had a history of "disrupting the way jobs could be done. People still mopped, but used Swiffer, as opposed to an icky old rag mop. . . . When we got it right, we did it really, really well."

Fish announced that these game-changing products shared the single special quality of "irresistible superiority"—a concept that embraced P&G's technical expertise but was more expansive, embracing the consumer experience from start to finish. Their value proposition, as Fish put it, was "holistically crafted to make an emotional connection . . . in the advertising, in how it speaks to [consumers], and in the details of the package and the product as [they] use it." Fish sought to make this P&G's new aspiration for innovation: it was no longer enough to be "functionally superior," she insisted. P&G had to *earn* the right to be "bought again and again."

At a company that tended to hire overachievers, Fish wasn't surprised that people quickly adopted the goal of "irresistible superiority"—a phrase that became an "immutable law of P&G's business," said Pritchard. The real challenge would be to architect new multifunctional ways of working to deliver irresistibly superior consumer experiences. P&G now had to "innovate how we innovate," said Fish.

Lean Innovation: A New Way to Experiment

Fish and Pritchard agreed that every single P&G employee—not just those in R&D—had a role to play in accelerating the quality and speed of innovation. Even those on the commercial side of the business would have to learn to develop and test ideas collaboratively. Fish and her C-suite colleagues stepped into their role as architects and aligned on the task before them: to instill within P&G the culture and capabilities required to *experiment* and bring groundbreaking consumer propositions to market—cost-effectively and with speed.[8]

Fish decided to investigate the methods used by startups and digital companies. "All of a sudden a light bulb went off," she said. "What we were trying to do was so consistent with lean innovation"—a disciplined way of developing and bringing to market new products, services, and business models, quickly and inexpensively.[9] It relied on multifunctional teams to run small-scale experiments in the marketplace to ensure that innovation remained grounded in real consumers' needs.

When Fish presented the idea to her C-suite colleagues, they were intrigued. Rather than making large investments up front for product development (P&G's stage-gate process), lean innovation leveraged micro-investments tied to ninety-day milestones. This ensured time and resources weren't wasted on initiatives that would ultimately fail. Lean innovation, they hoped, not only would help P&G de-risk its investments but would help the company develop new mindsets and behaviors for experimentation.

This was essential. New and useful ideas rarely spring forth in final form, ready to be implemented. Innovation is usually the result of a lengthy, messy, recursive process of deliberate trial and error. Even framing the right problem to solve can require numerous iterations. Dead ends and missteps are to be expected. And the iterative testing and pivoting do not end once great ideas or concepts are generated—they continue through the scaling process.[10]

Leaders in any organization are expected to deliver results. It's understandable that they would prefer to set goals, make plans, execute them, and monitor progress until goals are achieved. But as much as leaders would like to *plan* their way to innovation, their job as architects is to help their teams and organizations *act* their way instead. It's like shifting from leading an orchestra to a jazz ensemble: while their sheet music provides some guardrails, the musicians have to improvise, listen, and adapt to each other as they perform.[11] The shift can be uncomfortable for all. Fear of failure looms large. Efficiency and economies of scale may suffer. There is a constant tension between delivering a solution and exploring as many ideas and variations as possible, for as long as possible. It is no wonder Thomas Edison defined genius as "1 percent inspiration; 99 percent perspiration."[12]

Fish and her colleagues recognized that introducing lean innovation would be a wholesale departure from P&G's traditional operating model and would not be easy. The challenge wasn't so much technological, as Fish explained to us when we first met her; it was cultural.[13] Lean innovation would require P&Gers to develop the courage to "fail fast"—to put works in progress in front of consumers, collect feedback, and pivot—which would prove challenging in their context. As one HR leader reflected, "When you hire 'type A' people who are at the top of their class . . . , they don't fail. When you've always been right, failing isn't really something [you're] used to or understand."

To socialize leaders into the method, in July 2016, CEO David Taylor convened the executive team and BU presidents for "innovation tourism" in Silicon Valley. Fish invited lean startup and innovation thought leaders Eric Ries and Steve Blank to introduce their methodology to P&G's leaders, and the team got a chance to observe startups in action.[14] During the presentations, Fish was encouraged to find that work in the newly formed P&G Ventures and in P&G's Fabric Care were consistent with lean methods. Leaders in these organizations had begun to see the promise of merging the speed and agility of lean innovation with P&G's vast trove of market data and powerful marketing and distribution channels.

In the months after the Silicon Valley tour, Fish was heartened to see lean innovation "spread like wildfire" through P&G. Because the methodology is based on including perspectives from different functions, it encouraged an "entrepreneurial culture" across the company. Lean innovation "provided a much more open and welcoming umbrella," reflected Karen Hershenson, strategic operating leader. "Everybody could see [themselves] to be more entrepreneurial, more so than the term 'innovation,' which could be misunderstood as technical. It has helped free people. Ultimately, we want everybody to see that to be innovative is their job."

Although the BU leaders were eager to get started, not everyone was clear on how exactly to implement lean innovation in their organizations. At the end of 2016, Fish decided it was time to formalize the new methodology at the corporate level. She partnered with Bionic, a consulting firm of successful entrepreneurs that had developed a process and organizational structure to operationalize lean innovation within large corporations.[15] Together they launched GrowthWorks—an initiative to embed the process across P&G. Fish and Pritchard decided to co-lead the effort. "The future of brand building is experiences," said Pritchard, "and that requires teamwork—which Kathy and I try to model wherever possible." Demonstrating the collaboration they wanted to see from others, Pritchard said, was an innovation in itself. "We weren't a connected organization before. The commercial and technical weren't together, so Kathy and I made a commitment to change."

Fish and her C-suite colleagues, including the CEO, agreed that if they wanted BU leaders to adopt GrowthWorks, change should be "business unit-led, and corporately supported," as Fish put it. Their question, then, was how to *invite* the BU presidents to cocreate a new way of working at P&G. True to this aim, Fish and her colleagues approached the implementation of GrowthWorks as an experiment in itself—they would start small, collect feedback, and pivot together with the BUs.

GrowthWorks: Implementing a New Operating Model

After GrowthWorks was announced, highly respected leaders from across P&G began approaching Fish and Pritchard, asking to join in the effort. Over the next months, a full-fledged GrowthWorks team was incorporated under Fish's corporate R&D group, comprising eighteen multifunctional experts who were passionate about transforming the company. Chris Boeckerman, who became GrowthWorks's director of innovation capability, noted, "When I got this job, Kathy gave me a handwritten note to tell me how important this job was for P&G." An invaluable resource to Fish and Pritchard, this team installed within each BU a growth operating system—a mini-entrepreneurial ecosystem comprising four types of roles:

1. *Two or three founders* formed a dedicated, multifunctional team. One founder, either from the design or brand function, provided insights into the consumer and business model; a second, usually

from R&D, provided technical and product design expertise. Using fast-cycle, inexpensive experimentation, these entrepreneurs identified and tested new product and service ideas to address consumer problems or opportunity spaces (for example, the rising scarcity of resources resulting from urbanization and climate change).

2. *An executive sponsor*, or an influential BU leader, at least at the VP level, worked with peers across functions to break down barriers and provide essential permissions and resources to the founder teams. At key milestones, the sponsor helped teams decide whether to pass, persevere, or pivot on their projects.

3. *A growth board* served as the venture capitalists in the internal ecosystem. They managed the innovation portfolio within the BU, assessed the founder teams' learnings at key increments, and invested metered funding based on a project's demonstrated potential. The growth board was cross-functional, typically comprising people from the BU leadership team.

4. *The operating system*, a small, multifunctional team within the BUs, provided the founders specialized support in operations, supply chain, logistics, finance, rewards, and other areas.

To oversee all GrowthWorks projects across the BUs, Fish and her C-suite colleagues served as the enterprise growth board, ensuring that the companywide portfolio was "sufficiently robust" and that learnings were shared across BUs. Fish noted that "part of the reason that we needed a portfolio was [because] some projects should die. That was an important learning for us as well. Projects with low odds of success would stay too long using valuable resources if we weren't intentional about killing them."

Meanwhile, the corporate GrowthWorks team served as a centralized concierge service to the BUs, conducting training and solving operational problems to ease the implementation of the growth operating system. As Fish's eyes and ears in the BUs, this team would become the hub of institutional learning and share emerging best practices from GrowthWorks across the otherwise siloed BUs.

Piloting GrowthWorks and Reframing Risk

Fish and the leadership team decided not to roll out the growth operating system across all the BUs at one time. Instead, they would "let each BU decide how they were going to run it and create some core central capability to help," said Fish. In January 2017, the corporate GrowthWorks team partnered with three BUs—Fabric Care, P&G Ventures, and Hair Care—to conduct pilots to experiment with the new structure and see how it needed to be adapted in each context.

The pilots were intended to "run water through the pipes" and identify "the cultural and organizational elements of P&G that made it harder to do this work," said Erika Long, the corporate human resources leader for GrowthWorks. The three pilot BUs were asked to define a grand challenge aligned with the "irresistible superiority" vision in an area that could either disrupt their business or become an opportunity based on where their industry was headed. Fabric Care decided on a portfolio of experiments to explore "clothes ready on demand." Hair Care focused on "scalp health for hair health." And P&G Ventures worked on "foot health at every life stage."

As the founder teams proceeded to test ideas with consumers, they met regularly with their VP executive sponsor and quarterly with the BU and Enterprise Growth boards. "We evaluated how fast the experiments moved through the portfolio," Fish said. One challenge that the pilots revealed was P&G's "solutions-focused mindset." As John Brase, vice president of Family Care, explained, "Historically, we always started with, 'What do we want to accomplish?' versus 'What's the real, unmet consumer tension?'" To evolve the mindset into one centered around the consumer, Fish and the GrowthWorks team adopted the slogan, "Fall in love with the problem, not the solution." This became "the framework for our innovation efforts," explained Mark Glogowski, associate director of the innovation capability team.

As the pilots unfolded, Fish and her colleagues began to realize just how much the fear of failure loomed in the minds of P&Gers—especially those in brand management who believed, as one said, "disruptive innovation is where marketers go to die." Lean innovation required experimentation, inevitable missteps, and the death of some projects—a tough sell in a culture where failure was viewed as akin to career suicide. Part of the problem was P&G's own internal talent metrics and career systems. Bionic's Anne Berkowitch noted, "P&G was used to tracking against concrete metrics where you could check the box—'Did you achieve this, yes or no?'—across the whole organization, not only in processes like procurement but also in talent performance. It made decision-making in this new way of working very uncomfortable."

To help founders feel safer working on high-risk projects, Fish implored the corporate GrowthWorks team to consider new ways of valuing and rewarding work. "We hire entrepreneurial thinkers," noted Long, "and then in our processes and systems, we tend to hold them back." This needed to change. Soon, Long and the HR manager for Fabric Care began using lean innovation principles to generate options for new career development pathways.[16] One idea they tested was "E-track"—an entrepreneurial career track for GrowthWorks founders. The compensation structure in E-track was tied to a sales target, a burn rate, and a new metric called "entrepreneurial stewardship," defined by the number of learnings projects generated and how far they moved through the funnel. "My goal," said Long, "was for people to see that failure was accepted and learning was rewarded."

Experimentation Requires Leaders to Work on Themselves

As they began rolling out the growth operating system for GrowthWorks in the rest of P&G's BUs, Fish and her team found that leaders' mindsets and behaviors were creating barriers to cocreation. Although they had advised BU presidents to appoint their best talent to GrowthWorks's founder teams—to symbolize that the work was important—some simply weren't willing to do so. "The first and hardest decision that anybody had to make was to put a dedicated team on these projects," recalled Julie Setser, vice president of corporate functions in R&D, innovation capability, and P&G Ventures. Fish and Pritchard devised an incentive: they offered to pay for Bionic to assist the BU heads with implementing GrowthWorks. "If somebody wanted to work with us and get the help of [Bionic], . . . then they had to declare a dedicated team," Setser explained. "This tactic initially seemed to work—but then we got to a deeper issue."

In each BU, the corporate GrowthWorks team conducted targeted "activation sessions" with founders. Although these sessions were enormously popular, early on they were often followed by a period of disillusionment. When the founders shared their work with their BU growth boards, they often received, at best, a tepid response. "That's when we realized we had to train the leaders *and* teams together to drive an actual behavior change in the organization," Boeckerman recalled. If teams felt discouraged by their interactions with leaders, they wouldn't be willing to do the challenging work of further ideation and experimentation.

Fish and her team observed that the BU leaders on the growth boards, although well intentioned, didn't quite grasp how to best engage with the nascent ideas and consumer feedback that was presented to them. In their meetings with founders, the BU leaders were making too many statements and not asking enough questions. And when evaluating projects at different milestones, these leaders focused on short-term investment and returns, rather than on the valuable learnings that had emerged from the founders' experiments. In short, the BU heads were struggling with creating an environment conducive for founder teams to take risks. Brase reflected on why they were challenged by their architect role. "[Family Care] is a $5 billion business. . . . We have a very developed business model and a certain way that we bring innovation to the market." Growth-Works represented a very different approach to pursuing growth than they were accustomed to.

Fish and the leadership team hired coaches to help the BU leaders adapt their leadership style. In the growth board meetings, the coaches asked leaders to reflect on how many statements they made versus how many questions they asked about the founder teams' ideas and experiments. They reminded leaders that their job wasn't to provide answers, but rather to ensure their colleagues were designing rigorous and relevant tests and engaging in honest reflections about the consumer-preference data they generated. If a new idea wasn't resonating with consumers, it was up to the BU leaders to encourage and help the team figure out what experiment to run next—or whether it was time to kill the idea and pivot to another. As Long added:

> We say leaders should ask four questions: "What did you learn? How do you know? What do you need to learn next? How can I help?" Culturally, those questions are so important. . . . "What did you learn?" takes away the element of pass/fail. "How can I help?" enables the teams, because [it shows that] they're expected to come in with what they need the leader to do.

Fish firmly believed that in each BU, all members of the growth operating system—not just the growth board members—had a role to play in encouraging risk-taking and learning. Thus, she also hired the coaches to onboard and train the founders, their executive sponsors, and the operating system teams on GrowthWorks principles and practices. With the help of the coaches, leaders and operators across the BUs learned how to create an environment conducive to experimentation through new ways of communicating and interacting. As Boeckerman observed, "This was critical because we all learned how to do this in a common language." Over time, Fish and her colleagues were encouraged to see more employees test assumptions and question company orthodoxies. More and more, they were creating spaces where people felt psychologically safe enough to push against the status quo.[17]

The Garage: Bringing New Talent and Tools into the Organization

As the BU leaders and founder teams became more comfortable experimenting together, Fish was pleased to see disruptive ideas begin to sprout. In ninety days, one founder team identified an opportunity space—that consumers hate running out of toilet paper and paper towels—and developed three disruptive solutions. One was the "Forever Roll," an oversized roll of toilet paper. Why was there so much excitement internally about this low-tech idea? Because in the entire history of P&G's paper business, no one had ever stopped to question the assumption that toilet paper rolls needed to fit in standard holders. After speaking directly with busy suburban moms about their pain points, this team came up with a plan to sell consumer starter kits including three Forever Rolls and a special stand-alone holder.

As more and more prototypes such as the Forever Roll progressed toward validation stages—where products and business models were refined through midscale tests with real consumers—the founders essentially had to establish a whole business. Suddenly, Fish and her team saw many GrowthWorks initiatives run into the same challenges: they didn't have the capabilities to manage legal compliance, process credit card transactions, publish a website, buy media, or manufacture a product at small scale, among others. "When you're part of the big performance machine," Pritchard noted, "you take all that stuff for granted." In his efforts to enable the Forever Roll team, Brase recalled, "I needed someone to build a grade-A e-commerce platform. We didn't have that skill here in Family Care. How could I find that? I didn't know how to hire a performance marketer!"

Following the broader GrowthWorks "pull" philosophy, Fish and Pritchard decided to jointly invest in a new set of centralized enabling capabilities for the BUs. Housed within the GrowthWorks team, they created "The Garage"—a bench of talent with expertise in design, research, product supply, IT, commercial, and media buying. The Garage would also include digital expertise new to P&G, such as user experience and user interface design.

By eliminating hiring frictions for the BU leaders, teams could source needed expertise from The Garage quickly as problems arose. While Fish and Pritchard's investment was meant to accelerate GrowthWorks projects, they did not want leaders to become dependent on The Garage. "Try it and then buy it" was the framing: once a BU experimented with the new talent, leaders were invited to hire them full-time. Thanks to The Garage, Brase contracted a performance marketer specializing in pay-for-performance advertising, as opposed to P&G's usual mass marketing. The "try it" period worked out so well that Brase decided to bring on the marketer full-time to continue Family Care's experiments with the Forever Roll. He described how The Garage "helped us find and develop skills and capabilities that we didn't have in our business. It has been an amazing enabler. If that wasn't there, we'd be in trouble."

While The Garage proved to be invaluable, Fish and Pritchard intended for it to be temporary. As Pritchard remarked, "We have a mission to put the GrowthWorks Garage out of business. . . . You can borrow it to get started, but we want you to build this in your BU. Build your own Garage—that's the next phase."

Overcoming Barriers to Incubation

By early 2018, Fish was encouraged that the investments in lean innovation were paying off. Several projects had succeeded in getting a proposed solution validated, and some, including the Forever Roll, were moving into incubation—the phase designed to maximize value and minimize the risk of increasing investments (see figure 3-1).

Lean innovation was starting to take root across P&G, but Fish could see that incubation would require a whole new set of capabilities—including a more agile product supply chain and operational infrastructure.[18] As Long noted, "We could make five products in a lab or five hundred thousand in the plant, but we couldn't figure out how to make five thousand. It was the midrange levels of supply that made incubate a challenge." The Forever Roll team, for example, had made its first prototypes by hand. Yet when they reached incubation, they found themselves limited by the capabilities of the BU. Family Care's manufacturing systems, like P&G's other BUs, centered on highly capitalized equipment;

FIGURE 3-1

Lean innovation methodology

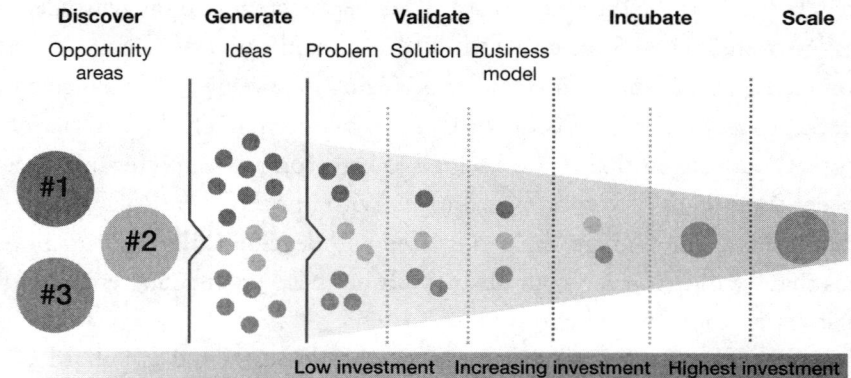

they were optimized for selling several hundred thousand cases of products per day. As Brase explained:

> Our next stage of learning was to transform our supply chain from huge, high-capital, low-cost, very-slow-cycle speed to fast-speed, low-capital, high-variable cost during the learning cycle. The question was, How do we create an agile supply chain to support this [direct-to-consumer] business to enable fast-cycle learning?

While the BU presidents had been willing to fund small-scale experiments, Fish observed that many were hesitant to make the stairstep investments required to support incubation. The GrowthWorks projects now faced a catch-22: they needed significant capital to run the large-scale experiments required to demonstrate ROI, but the BUs' finance groups were unwilling to release capital for nascent businesses that couldn't demonstrate rigorous financial metrics. If she and her team did not find ways through the incubation impasse, GrowthWorks was in danger of becoming a mere "hobby." The challenge, as Fish put it, was, "How [do we] make sure we are making the investments that we need in the mid to long term when there is so much short-term pressure?"

Fish and her corporate GrowthWorks team sought to enable on two fronts. For one, they began developing founder teams' ability to form and articulate value-creation hypotheses, to help them communicate more effectively with P&G's financial decision-makers. In addition, they created a designated "ring-fenced incubation fund"—a centralized funding resource that could support the BUs through this critical innovation phase. But most importantly, although Fish was reluctant to mandate change top down, she insisted it was time to hold the BU presidents personally accountable for innovation by putting mid- to long-term innovation metrics on their scorecards.

A New Portfolio of Projects

Despite the challenges of incubation, within three years of launching GrowthWorks, Fish felt that lean innovation was beginning to transform culture and capabilities across P&G. The corporate GrowthWorks team had activated more than eight hundred leaders and teams. Scores of founders were making progress on their projects, and The Garage was in high demand throughout the company. At the end of 2019, Fish and her colleagues reviewed the entire GrowthWorks project portfolio, and the results were stunning. "The first time we actually put it all together," Boeckerman reflected, "we saw there were over a hundred projects. It was amazing. . . . It helped to make it real."

GrowthWorks was not only generating bolder solutions to consumer problems; it was helping P&G learn to innovate with a fraction of the money and time—lessons that were spreading to the core business. "We're learning how to flex new muscles," said Brase. He continued:

> Anything like this in traditional P&G would've taken multiple years and multiple millions of dollars. Now . . . we are more comfortable learning on the fly with smaller bets. And if we get it wrong, it's a few hundred consumers. We sell to a hundred million consumers. The speed at which we're learning . . . and the cost that we're expending to get to that learning is night and day different.

Fish and Pritchard were also encouraged to see that multifunctional collaboration on the founder teams, growth boards, and operating systems was helping to bring their commercial and technical functions closer. A more integrated way of innovating was taking root, observed Pritchard: "What we think about is every aspect of the consumer experience and trying to make it better—the product, package, communication, the in-store, online, in-use, the after-use, and how it all comes together."

In January 2019, P&G headlined the Consumer Electronics Show (CES), one of the largest and most influential technology conferences in the world, for the first time. At the time, it was rare for CES to feature a non-tech company so prominently. But as a legacy company that had inched its way into the future—moving from making toothpaste and toilet paper to innovations like smart toothbrushes—P&G had earned the spotlight. During the P&G Consumer Experience Show, the company unveiled a selection of products from its skin and personal care, grooming, and home care businesses.

By 2022, the new products that P&G developed and scaled had begun to transform the way millions of consumers care for themselves and their homes. The company was starting to carve out a space for more nimble innovation, and already the new mindset was percolating across the business. A case in point was EC30, an array of P&G products for laundry, home, and personal care—all efficient cleaners that were environmentally friendly and convenient, with dramatically reduced size, weight, cost, and carbon footprint. The letters in EC30 stand for Enlightened Clean, and its products used an innovative technology to eliminate plastic waste by replacing bottles of liquid with tear-open packets to which the user adds water.

Although corporate R&D had worked for years on the foundational technology for more sustainable products, GrowthWorks was instrumental in cultivating the new mindset and capabilities needed to launch EC30 across the BUs. With a look and feel different from most P&G products, EC30 became its first brand sold directly to consumers via subscription model, an important foray into the new world of online retailers.

Leadership Lessons from Architecting P&G's Transformation

For incumbent companies like P&G, the only reliable path for driving market leadership and growth is innovation. But these same companies often fail at developing breakthroughs because of the kinds of barriers Fish and her colleagues faced. It is never easy to get even talented and ambitious individuals to embrace an uncertain future. Fish and other architect leaders overcome such challenges by creating environments in their organizations that encourage needed changes in mindset and behavior. She found the *why* and created a sense of urgency by building on the origins of P&G's success: irresistible superiority.

Fish also understood that to innovate at scale and with speed, leadership had to democratize innovation at P&G; it had to become the responsibility of everyone across the company, not just those in R&D. It was up to Fish and her colleagues to architect an environment in which BU leaders and founders would be willing and able to embrace cocreation—to take the professional risks associated with working in a very different way.

Innovation is a complex problem-solving process of trying, learning, adjusting, and trying again. While GrowthWorks provided a framework and principles for rapid, iterative experimentation within P&G, Fish and her colleagues had much to learn about how to collaborate across functions, design rigorous and relevant experiments, employ new data-analytic tools, make micro-investments, and pivot based on feedback. In addition, to encourage experimentation, the BU leaders had to unlearn well-honed habits and instead lead with more inquiry and less advocacy.

For Fish, driving this new form of experimentation wasn't about being decisive and making choices for others. It was rather about asking generative questions and creating the space for teams to try new ways of working and experience their strengths and shortcomings for themselves. Fish lived these values in her own approach to GrowthWorks. As much as she believed in the promise of lean innovation, she had the foresight and humility to introduce it as an experiment—to model cocreation from the top. She and her corporate colleagues did not thrust the new operating model upon the BUs but *invited* them to share ownership over its implementation and adapt it to their context. Along the way, Fish and her team were attentive to the structures, incentive systems, and leadership behaviors inside P&G that made failure and risk-taking uncomfortable. They smoothed the way for cocreation by actively alleviating frictions as they arose—filling talent gaps, providing coaching, and making new tools and resources available to unleash a spirit of entrepreneurship across the company.

Over four years, Fish and her team were able to begin disrupting P&G from within, redefining innovation as a consumer-led, multifunctional team effort—a complete turnaround from the company's longtime technology-led R&D efforts. One of Fish's colleagues reinforced that it was "the power of [Fish's] collaborative spirit" that created space for P&G's culture to change. "[Fish] won't be raising her hand and saying, 'I'm the one,' but she really is," said another.

By the time Fish retired from her role at the end of 2020, lean innovation had spread across P&G. By 2021, internal ratings showed that 75 percent of P&G's portfolio met their "irresistibly superior" standard—up from 30 percent when Fish and her colleagues began their transformational work.[19] Still, P&G's journey of "innovating on innovation" continued. As iterative experimentation became more embedded in P&G's day-to-day operations, the name GrowthWorks was retired. But the company continued adapting its performance management and reward systems to better support the innovative mindsets and behaviors needed for the twenty-first century.

In today's world, it is hard to imagine how incumbents across industries can prosper without leaders like Fish who are personally devoted to driving innovation at their companies. As Fish reflected, "The best thing we can do as leaders is to unleash our organizations to make a difference."[20]

CHAPTER 4

Learning How to Learn

Drs. Tom Mihaljevic and Rakesh Suri
at Cleveland Clinic Abu Dhabi

At Cleveland Clinic, unity is important in everything we do, and that is what separates our culture. Collective success brings individual success.

—Dr. Tomislav (Tom) Mihaljevic

True leadership thrives on humility and a relentless commitment to learning. Innovation and progress emerge when leaders remain open to new ideas, embrace diverse perspectives, and continuously challenge their own assumptions.[1]

—Dr. Rakesh Suri

From the moment Dr. Tomislav (Tom) Mihaljevic first heard of Cleveland Clinic's plans to open a health-care facility in Abu Dhabi, United Arab Emirates (UAE), he was eager to learn more.[2] A surgeon in the thoracic and cardiovascular surgery department, Mihaljevic understood the challenge too well: "This was considered mission impossible. Every international venture by a large health-care organization from the US had failed."

The location of Cleveland Clinic's foreign venture wasn't random. The not-for-profit hospital system founded in 1921 was ranked among the world's best, attracting patients from across the globe. Sheikh Zayed bin

Sultan Al Nahyan, the founding father of the UAE, had traveled regularly to Cleveland, Ohio, for care. Upon Sheikh Zayed's death, his son, Sheikh Mohamed bin Zayed Al Nahyan, now crown prince of Abu Dhabi, was determined to honor his father's wish of bringing high-quality health care to the UAE: safe, superior patient experiences backed by robust thought leadership in medicine.

In 2006, Mubadala Investment Company (the venture capital arm of Abu Dhabi's sovereign wealth fund) partnered with Cleveland Clinic to plant the seeds for Sheikh Mohamed's vision. The partnership had a false start. Cleveland Clinic brought a rotating management team to an existing three-hospital medical complex in Abu Dhabi staffed with local health practitioners.[3] Despite good intentions and effort, both partners were disappointed by the outcomes of this light-touch approach.

When Mihaljevic joined the initiative in 2011, Mubadala and Cleveland Clinic had decided on a new plan: to build a hospital in Abu Dhabi together from scratch. As chief of staff of the new project, Mihaljevic knew that both Cleveland Clinic and Mubadala would fundamentally have to *learn* by doing. Both partners, he noted, "had to commit to success, and with a healthy understanding that it was not going to be easy. This was a long-term commitment."

In the last two chapters, we've seen what it takes to architect organizations that can collaborate and experiment. In this chapter, we zero in on what's required for leaders to foster *learning* at the individual and collective levels. To transplant Cleveland Clinic's model of health care to the Middle East, Mihaljevic needed to build a team that was willing and able to let go of established assumptions and develop the contextual intelligence required to deliver health care to an entirely new patient population. His mandate, as he put it, was to hire "five thousand people from eighty-seven different countries, . . . form them into teams, and create Cleveland Clinic–quality care out of the gate."

In 2015, after nearly a decade of planning and construction, Mihaljevic was appointed CEO of Cleveland Clinic Abu Dhabi. He eventually recruited Dr. Rakesh Suri from Mayo Clinic as his chief of staff (who would later take over as CEO). Together, these trusted friends and friendly rivals (both were pioneers in robotic cardiac surgery) architected a world-class health-care institution in just a few short years—effectively scaling Cleveland Clinic's culture and capabilities seven thousand miles across the world from its main campus. The hospital's learning capacity would be put to the ultimate test as the first Cleveland Clinic location to confront the Covid-19 virus.

Scaling Across Geography: Architecting a World-Class Hospital in Abu Dhabi

Since the earliest days of his career, Mihaljevic had been deeply committed to expanding health-care access. He attended medical school in his hometown of Zagreb, Croatia, and trained in general and cardiovascular surgery at Harvard Medical School hospitals. He accepted a position at Cleveland Clinic because he was drawn to its "patients first" philosophy, and its collaborative, multispecialty team approach to health care.

When he transferred to Abu Dhabi, Mihaljevic found himself leading a team of fifty and overseeing twenty thousand construction workers who were building what would become their iconic 4.2-million-square-foot "hospital of the future." Mubadala and Cleveland Clinic stakeholders had agreed that every detail of the state-of-the-art facility should be designed to deliver a superior patient experience. As Gaurav Dixit, executive director of IT strategy and program management, later noted, "We didn't want patients to feel that they were coming to a hospital and getting treated. We wanted to provide them with the convenience as if it were their home, a hotel, or an airline to reduce their anxiousness." The hospital would be entirely paperless, and every light bulb and door would have its own IP address. Not a single wire would be visible in any patient room; each would be equipped with an "Interactive Patient Care System"—a single tablet where patients would watch movies, order food, and monitor their medical needs.

Mihaljevic recruited Suri to join him in "building the hospital up." The two surgeons knew each other well. Both had challenged the status quo, pushed the frontier of cardiac surgery, and launched robotic surgery programs at their respective institutions. Although it took three years for Mihaljevic to convince Suri to join him, in the end, Suri couldn't resist: "Everything in my life had been a step in being able to deliver on this dream, this vision of expanding access to world-class health care globally," he said. Cleveland's six-hour flight radius covered a little over three hundred million people; Abu Dhabi's covered three billion. As Mihaljevic put it, he and Suri would have an opportunity to help "better humanity on an entirely different scale." For his part, Suri was gratified to work with Mihaljevic; he felt they were "aligned on the fundamental values of innovation, a commitment to excellence, and empathy."

In addition to bringing top-notch global medical talent to the region, Mihaljevic and Suri understood that Cleveland Clinic Abu Dhabi's long-term objective was to educate the next generation of Emirati health-care practitioners and seed a sustainable local health-care industry. To that end, they couldn't just copy and paste US best practices from Ohio to Abu Dhabi. Rather, success would require learning with and from their Abu Dhabi stakeholders—including Mubadala, the government, and their patients—and cocreating a new model of health care suited to their context.

Building a Team of Innovative Caregivers

Under the terms of their partnership, Cleveland Clinic was the managing partner responsible for talent, sourcing, and patient care, while Mubadala was responsible for physical assets, financial support, and oversight on behalf of the country. Financial stewardship—what they referred to as a value-based care model—was a shared responsibility between the two entities.[4]

Mihaljevic and Suri's objectives were clear when recruiting Cleveland Clinic Abu Dhabi's "caregivers" (the term used to describe *all* staff at any Cleveland Clinic hospital campus, regardless of position). They recruited talent from across the globe, hiring only the most qualified and experienced health-care practitioners. In addition to expertise, the leaders looked deliberately for people who were "deeply resilient, self-aware, and able to manage ambiguity," as Suri stated. Each candidate was put through several rounds of rigorous interviews in Abu Dhabi, and those who would serve in leadership positions were also interviewed in Ohio.

New hires were onboarded and trained as much as possible with the cohort with which they would be working. In their communications with new colleagues, Mihaljevic and Suri made some very intentional choices to stress the importance of earning locals' trust. They emphasized, for example, that "it was a privilege to serve patients in the region" and that it was imperative to deliver superior care. Mihaljevic and Suri empowered all clinical and nonclinical personnel to "listen to patients and pivot to meet their needs every day"—and they modeled the behavior they hoped to see by adapting their own practices to their new environment. To guarantee 24/7 excellence, all physicians, including the CEO, took on tasks that senior caregivers typically did not (like making house calls).

Despite Mihaljevic and Suri's best planning efforts, Cleveland Clinic Abu Dhabi ran into operational difficulties soon after opening. They quickly realized that many of the Ohio caregiving processes didn't translate to Abu Dhabi. When forecasting demand, supply, and capacity, their models failed to consider how religious observances, like the annual month of fasting Ramadan, would impact patient behavior.

Perhaps most importantly, they soon realized that providing health care in Abu Dhabi was a family affair. "We couldn't care for patients as individuals," one caregiver observed. "There was a stronger collective energy, and health care became social. Our clinicians were diagnosing and treating *the family*." Fortunately, the hospital interior had been designed with this in mind. For example, instead of the standard open-floor layout divided by curtains, the intensive care unit rooms included a bed for family members. But caregivers had to learn that communicating and establishing relationships with patients' families was paramount. As Dr. Murat Tuzcu, chief academic officer, explained, "Many of our caregivers were not necessarily trained in a tradition where a relationship was part of the transaction with the patient and community that they served."

By definition, experiential learning is a nonlinear, iterative process. We know from decades of research that it isn't easy—especially in an ever more volatile and complex global economy.[5] It can be inefficient and can lead to false conclusions when people don't take the time to reflect on and consolidate lessons learned; and adapting to deliver on evolving expectations of customers and other stakeholders can be especially hard.[6]

As social architects, Mihaljevic and Suri understood the task ahead: they would need to absorb the insights from their first months and adapt to local expectations if they were ever to earn their new community's trust. To do that, they would need to instill in their caregivers the mind-sets and skills for continuous learning.

Harnessing Their "Unique Flavor of Diversity"

In 2017, Mihaljevic returned to the mothership in Ohio as president and CEO of the Cleveland Clinic enterprise. Suri became the CEO of Cleveland Clinic Abu Dhabi, just as their growing pains began to sub-side and hospital operations were running smoothly. By then, Suri had forged a strong relationship with Waleed Al Mokarrab Al Muhairi, chairman of the hospital board and deputy group CEO of Mubadala. "I was blessed to work with him," Suri declared. "He often said, 'We couldn't do this without you, and you couldn't do this without us.'" Al Muhairi made his ambitions for the hospital clear: Suri's new mandate was to grow Cleveland Clinic Abu Dhabi into the most "innovative hos-pital in the world" while executing against a five-year plan for financial sustainability.

Considering their growing portfolio of initiatives, including an aggres-sive timetable to launch the hospital's new research and education pillars, Suri and Mubadala installed new leadership. The new executive team was a heterogeneous group of thought leaders and innovators, diverse in terms of culture (from the United States, the UAE, Argentina, Turkey, and Canada, among others) and expertise (surgeons, operations directors, and digital experts). Cleveland Clinic Ohio and Mubadala had granted the team a great degree of autonomy "to lead locally" and "to move as innova-tively and as boldly as possible," said Suri.

With a caregiver population comprising more than eighty-seven na-tionalities, Suri saw diversity as the hospital's greatest asset when it came to innovation—that is, if they could embrace their differences and learn from each other. Even though Suri had helped to hire the four hundred physicians on staff and overseen their extensive onboarding process, when he conducted a series of listening tours, he heard disparate understand-ings of what it meant to put patients first. As one doctor explained, it was hard for caregivers to leave behind sentiments of "this is how we do it in Egypt" and "this is how we do it in Italy."

Suri learned that even something as standard as putting together a "crash cart"—the equipment and medications used to resuscitate a patient—led to heated debates. Sue Behrens, the chief nursing officer, recounted that when conflicts arose over contents of the crash cart, she encouraged her team to reframe disagreements as opportunities to learn from one another's best practices. After much back and forth, the team reassessed the North American crash-cart standard, incorporated what they learned from others who worked in different countries, and created something suited to their needs in Abu Dhabi.

When Suri heard how caregivers had cocreated a new crash-cart protocol, he felt profoundly encouraged. He began to imagine the kinds of innovation—both incremental and breakthrough—that could be unleashed if such a learning orientation were scaled across the hospital. To create a learning culture, Suri insisted that he and his leadership team model and reward behaviors like humility, curiosity, and candor.

The Executive Team Learns to Learn

Suri's early leadership team meetings revealed a stumbling block. "At the beginning," one team member explained, "there weren't a lot of lengthy, back-and-forth conversations in the executive team meetings. People weren't always expressing their opinions."[7] Suri saw that lack of candor as a sign that his own team did not feel safe enough to speak their minds. He reminded them that if they hoped to harness their complementary skill sets and perspectives, they had to practice "the right mindsets and behaviors"—including a willingness to be open and vulnerable.

Despite skepticism from many, Suri insisted that every team member, himself included, begin to meet biweekly for group coaching. Suri admitted that, as a surgeon, he was used to being the expert. He hoped coaches would help both him and his colleagues ask generative questions and challenge each other's assumptions. "Our coach even held me accountable in front of my team, which was amazing," he noted. "Those were the most revealing sessions." Over time, Suri learned to "acknowledge what he did not know" in meetings, and he adapted his personal style to encourage more pushback. Erika Maltese, manager of executive administration at the time, noted:

> It could be intimidating to go into a room of executives and say, "I don't understand this. I don't know." When the team was talking about something that wasn't [Suri's] area of expertise, he would be the first to sit back, admit he didn't know, and ask his direct reports to help him learn and understand. I felt much more comfortable asking questions when I saw him doing that.

With the help of coaching, the executive team learned to never allow what they called "silent thought bubbles" to exist. Instead, they began describing one another as trusted sparring partners and their weekly team meetings became their "sacred space," as Suri put it.

Cascading a Learning Mindset and Instilling Accountability

Suri understood that the learning muscles being developed on the leadership team had to scale across the hospital. After all, Cleveland Clinic Abu Dhabi's day-to-day execution happened throughout the hospital in "hundreds of milieus." "Every decision was the product of teamwork," said Suri, "not an executive leadership call from a centralized locus of control."

Suri insisted he and his fellow executives learn to temper their "doer" instincts—to not take the stage themselves but rather set the stage for others. Tuzcu noted how the best doctors did not necessarily make good leaders: "Leadership required a different set of skills, one of which was the ability to delegate authority and responsibility. For those who came from a traditional hierarchical structure, it took a big effort to learn to distribute and share leadership powers."

Suri helped his leadership team appreciate that their job was to create an environment where caregivers were empowered to innovate in their roles. Setting the stage, he explained, meant articulating a compelling, clear purpose and vision and establishing the values and behaviors by which people could fulfill them. As Suri put it, "align the organizational guardrails, and let the culture emerge."

The leadership team insisted, however, that with autonomy came accountability.[8] In partnership with Mubadala and Cleveland Clinic Ohio, Suri and his colleagues put in place key performance indicators (KPIs) pertaining to four priorities first established by Mihaljevic: patients, caregivers, organization, and community.[9] These KPIs served as the basis for each caregiver's personal performance scorecard. Many, particularly the nurses, weren't familiar with measuring outcomes through KPIs. "We had to teach them how to connect the dots," Behrens explained, "so they didn't feel [the KPIs were] just targets, but they understood the meaning behind [them]."

To accelerate knowledge sharing and accountability across the hospital, Cleveland Clinic Abu Dhabi adopted a practice from Cleveland Clinic Ohio: the tiered huddle system. Each day at 7:30 a.m., between twenty-five and forty managers came together to discuss what had happened in the past twenty-four hours and what would happen in the next. At first, some saw these as "shame and blame" sessions, as one person described, because people were expected to share not only good news, but also bad news. But, as one senior director recounted, attitudes shifted with experience: "As simple as the huddle was, it had such a big impact because there was a 'speak up' culture in the sense that if we saw something, we could catch it quickly. It was reported at the huddle and people were given action items to follow up by a certain date with the group." Within each department, cross-functional daily stand-up meetings took place as well.

Building and sustaining a learning orientation across Cleveland Clinic Abu Dhabi was not without its challenges. Because of visa requirements, the caregiver population was transient; most nurses, for instance, rotated on three- to four-year contracts. To sustain the right mindsets and behaviors, an organizational effectiveness (OE) team of fifteen certified emotional intelligence coaches was charged with listening for and addressing conflicts among caregivers in their day-to-day work. Through facilitated "norming sessions," the OE team helped teams develop their own rules of engagement and caregivers practice empathetic communication skills. These sessions were not easy; different cultural backgrounds meant different perceptions of how to behave toward one another.

With time, the OE group observed that teams began cocreating their own bonding initiatives. One coach, Bruce Perry, was pleasantly surprised to learn that a team of caregivers had launched a daily team-building group activity—a thirty-day plank challenge (a body-core strengthening exercise) during the year's busiest time. "They stepped out of the box," he noted, "not necessarily having the complete solution, but obviously [feeling] safe enough to take a risk for the betterment of the team. That, to me, was a wonderful example of creativity." Kate Brentley, an OE partner, noted that Cleveland Clinic Abu Dhabi was predominantly a "scientist organization of diagnosing and fixing," but to be effective, they had to shift their mindsets "from scientists to gardeners. We were sowing seeds, and when some [sprouted], we knew which ones to tend to more." That, she said, created a "ripple effect of successful experiments that enabled us to shift and nudge" the culture as the hospital grew.

Digital Tools and Data Support Learning and Innovation

Suri and the executive team made significant investments in digital technology and a self-service business intelligence (BI) capability to enable caregivers to experiment in their roles. A distributed network of data stewards and analysts centralized data from across the hospital's operations and made it available to everyone in the caregiver community. To increase the adoption of technology and data across the hospital, the IT and BI teams were remarkably proactive. Before releasing any new tool or feature, they conducted awareness campaigns, socializing caregivers in advance to the kinds of capabilities they'd be given and how they would help in their work. They conducted workshops, teaching caregivers to frame their data questions to glean productive insights and make data-informed decisions about patient care.

The BI team continuously monitored usage of their tools, which allowed them to gauge data maturity across the hospital. For example, in usage data for Tableau—a data visualization tool—the BI team could see that some caregivers were avid users, while others were not. The BI team was then able to conduct hospital walkabouts and lunchroom presentations, delivering targeted data-literacy campaigns to upskill less enthusiastic users. Similarly, the IT team relied on usage metrics to iterate and improve the user-friendliness of their applications.[10]

Over time, Suri was pleased to see caregivers across Cleveland Clinic Abu Dhabi embrace digital technology and data to innovate in their roles. Frontline nurses previously unaccustomed to using data were now running A/B experiments as part of their daily routine.[11] As a result, hundreds of ideas to improve the patient experience began to spring up across nursing—such as better ways to communicate with patients to mitigate the frustrations with wait times. "This was one of the most engaged groups of nurses that I had ever worked with," Behrens remarked.

This innovation mindset extended to the physicians. Working proactively with local regulators, the hospital had gained approval to experiment with cutting-edge, robotically enabled surgeries that couldn't be performed elsewhere in the world. Some, including Suri, were working closely with the IT team to develop ambient smart rooms, remote patient monitoring, digital physician interfaces, and telemedicine. "The physicians actually pushed *us*," noted Bryan Lord, chief information officer. "They wanted to move the needle—they wanted to innovate, and their excitement towards it drove us." As much as they pushed the technological frontier, Gaurav Dixit emphasized that their efforts remained grounded in the human experience:

> I still remember the interview we had with Dr. Suri when we were revamping our strategy. [Suri] said, "When I, as a physician, walk into a room, I don't want to see a keyboard and a screen. I want to interact with the patient." Our interfaces needed to become seamless so that the physician spent the maximum time actively talking to the patient.

By the end of 2019, Suri and his leadership team's efforts to architect an environment conducive to learning had unleashed a tide of innovation across the hospital. As a result, many of their operations were becoming more efficient; they were now ahead of schedule in their financial sustainability targets—a big win considering the ambitious timeline set by Mubadala. At the same time, however, the executive team noticed some duplication of effort: too many caregivers were still innovating in silos and weren't sharing learnings across the hospital. Working with their colleagues, the executive team created a new analog tool—a priority index—to channel caregiver experimentation toward the hospital's most critical challenges and opportunities.

Accelerated Learning: Leading Through a Fog

Just as Suri and his team were finalizing the upcoming year's budget and strategy, their ability to learn rapidly and collectively was suddenly put to the ultimate test. In January 2020, a mid-level manager from the infection control division spoke up during the hospital's 7:30 a.m. huddle. There were rumors, the manager said, that a flu-like virus originating in Wuhan, China, was spreading rapidly. It was unclear how serious the virus might be, but Suri's team decided to begin repositioning resources and preparing for a worst-case scenario. They immediately alerted their partners at Mubadala and Abu Dhabi's Department of Health as well as Cleveland Clinic Ohio. "I still remember people's faces on the video call," Suri recalled. "We were, in fact, the sentinels raising the flag across our international organization." As Mihaljevic remembered, "They triggered our response domestically. We started preparing everything from supplies to the organizational readiness, capacity, and training of our people. We began to have daily conferences with [Ohio] Governor Mike DeWine on how to prepare for the pandemic."

Before long, Covid-19 went from being a faraway issue to a "rapidly approaching freight train," said Suri. He and his team were accustomed to problem-solving with Cleveland Clinic colleagues in Ohio. The executive teams kept in contact through twice-weekly videoconferences because Mihaljevic, championing a "One Cleveland Clinic" philosophy, encouraged regular exchange of learnings across the global enterprise.[12] But with Covid-19, Suri and his team couldn't look to others for help because no one had the answers.

For the first time in his career, Suri felt like he was "staring into a fog." He decided that Cleveland Clinic Abu Dhabi needed to think of itself as the first responder for the UAE. "It was a life-or-death situation," one team member noted, "and every move we made would have implications for our caregivers, the country, and our colleagues in the United States." Al Muhairi remarked, "Nobody knew how bad it was going to get, and it was important for everybody to align on the fact that there was no playbook—we had to put the rules together as we went along."

Most important, Suri quickly realized that his surgeon instincts to take charge and steer the ship during crisis were not appropriate. "As a heart surgeon, when [you] see blood, the finger goes down and stops the bleeding," Suri explained. "It is ingrained in you that you have a responsibility to step in when everyone is scared. But that's the worst thing to do as a CEO . . . because it disempowers your team." Instead, he and his colleagues needed to create an environment where all caregivers could be "contemplative and creative rather than reactive problem-solvers."

Embracing a New Operating Model: The Working Hypothesis

Suri and his team saw every caregiver as a potential source of ideas for monitoring and managing the pandemic. They instructed everyone to start tapping their formal and informal networks for information about the disease. Since Cleveland Clinic Abu Dhabi's opening, Mihaljevic had always encouraged counterparts across the global organization to form their own coalitions and meeting cadence (i.e., there were monthly councils of the chiefs of staff and chief nursing officers). "That became the virtual superhighway of information and knowledge sharing," said Suri.

Suri insisted that everyone be as data-informed as possible. The hospital had been testing for variants of the disease since January and were aware of several. Their data scientists had developed an innovative approach to model the disease's trajectory that accounted for Abu Dhabi's demographics and cultural practices. Sifting through the local and global data, Suri's team could see that the virus behaved differently in different environments. One thing became clear: they needed to revisit their operating model because the worst was yet to come.

Going forward, Suri insisted that every decision should be treated as a "working hypothesis." They wouldn't know whether a decision was correct until collecting feedback on its impact. And as new information became available, everyone should be ready to pivot in lockstep.

A New Decision-Making Framework

As global guidelines for testing, clinical protocols, and protective equipment changed with each passing day, Suri's team soon saw that the hospital's existing decision-making structures couldn't handle the level of detail and speed required to operationalize all the necessary process changes. Using an emergency preparedness model from Cleveland Clinic Ohio, they created a Covid-19 task force, delegating decision-making closer to the front line.

While one might expect a hospital to put its most experienced leaders on such a team, Suri and colleagues selected a mix of twenty seasoned and early-career caregivers based on their subject-matter expertise, among other things. "We didn't want to be limited by historic or antiquated legacy ways of thinking," an executive team member said. "This was a new problem . . . which required a new set of solutions."

To learn and adapt "deliberately as a whole," as one caregiver put it, the hospital would need centralized, transparent communication. Everyone was instructed to route communications related to Covid-19 through the task force, which was given significant autonomy to vet ideas and implement process changes. For the few decisions requiring executive approval or sponsorship, the team had emergency powers to leapfrog traditional committees and go directly to the executive team. The task force met between the 7:30 a.m. huddle and the daily 9 a.m. executive team meeting; with this cadence, the hospital could share information and make and deploy decisions by 10 a.m.

Hyper-Empowerment

In late February 2020, Cleveland Clinic Abu Dhabi became the first academic medical center with US roots to treat Covid-19 patients. It introduced physical distancing measures across the hospital, expanded its emergency care footprint, and built out additional isolation capacity. But, Suri wondered, what if the hospital had to scale its efforts to serve hundreds or even thousands of patients?

Suri's leadership team had spent the last two years empowering caregivers to innovate; now, in his words, they had to "hyper-empower" them—to enhance their teamwork, agility, compassion, and resilience. "You can't know minute by minute what they're doing," Suri recalled. "Yet it's the minute-by-minute decisions that are critically important to save lives."

Suri and his team communicated this mindset, while reaffirming the hospital's four care priorities. They made a concerted effort to be fully transparent about the reasons behind any decision. Above all, Suri never hid how he felt: "I had to be honest and say, 'Yes, we're scared, the leaders are scared, the world is scared, but we're in this together.'"

Meanwhile, they worked side-by-side with Mubadala to take care of basics: managing the cash flow and ensuring an adequate stock of medicines, ventilators, protective equipment, and ICU beds. Mubadala also helped Suri and his caregivers coordinate care with others in the greater Abu Dhabi health-care ecosystem. "Leaders sometimes have a tendency to sit back and prepare within their four walls," Suri said, "but that narrative didn't work here. . . . There was no scenario where one hospital thrived, and another hospital suffered." Mihaljevic added:

> The way that Cleveland Clinic Abu Dhabi, the other hospitals, and the government worked in concert was . . . a reflection of the trust that had been built over years. . . . We had gone through a lot with our partners at Mubadala. . . . We had very deep, close, personal relationships. . . . We were fully aligned [that] what mattered was to have a system that worked for all people and that didn't put anyone at undue risk.

Managing the Emotional Strain of Continuous Learning

It was clear to Suri how cognitively and emotionally exhausting it was for caregivers to cope with Covid-19. With too much stress, it would be impossible for caregivers to be action learners able to absorb and adapt to their ever-changing circumstances. With the help of Mubadala, Suri and the executive team introduced new resources to support caregivers and their families' well-being: on-site sleeping areas and meditation rooms, nutritious food, online workouts, stress-reduction tools, and grief counseling. The executives modeled self-care, too. "Part of leading through crisis is about managing yourself," Suri said. "Muscling through, being exhausted, and wearing down your immune system were all potential failures in leadership in this pandemic."

Learning to Lead Remotely

By early March 2020, the hospital's new Covid-19 operating paradigm was in place. But while Suri was away on an emergency trip to the United States, the UAE instituted a fourteen-day quarantine requirement for anyone entering the country from the United States (by then considered a high-risk nation). "I was on the first plane to touch down after the rules were implemented," Suri said. He was immediately sent to a quarantined part of the airport and ordered to proceed directly home. In disbelief, Suri called Al Muhairi, who said, "Everybody will be watching you, and I advise that you lead in a way that others will want to follow." While Suri was eager to rejoin his colleagues, he knew he needed to set an example and abide by the regulations.

As Suri began his quarantine, he wondered, "How could I empower my team to be as effective as they could while providing the necessary air cover, resourcing, and empowerment—over a computer?" Most of all, he was concerned that his team was literally putting their lives at risk on the front lines while he was sitting safely at home. Suri sent messages to reassure not only his team and frontline caregivers but also all of the hospital's partners and stakeholders. "While he might have felt like he was less involved," one caregiver said, "we felt his leadership every day. . . . He was texting and calling people to ask what was happening, how people were feeling—checking in."

In the third week of March, all hospital meetings became 100 percent virtual as governments implemented lockdowns, work-from-home, and other social distancing measures. After years of working together with a group coach and learning ways to support one another most effectively, Suri and his team now found themselves undertaking yet another new learning: how to engage in rigorous team discussions in a virtual medium. For Suri, reading people's expressions and gauging tones of voice was challenging through a computer screen; he even sought coaching on how his facial expressions and body language came across virtually.

Every day, the leadership team engaged in strategic conversations and emotional check-ins. "People can change dramatically in crisis," one executive acknowledged. As everyone's fuses became shorter, the team worked hard to stay aligned. Whenever conversations became unproductive, one executive described, there was a process to help the group get back on track:

> Every time it got tense on the executive team, we took a break, reconfigured, opened up our willingness to be wrong and learn, and increased our level of humility, compassion, and forgiveness. We came back five minutes, half an hour, or a day later, whenever we were ready to listen to each other. This was the recipe for getting past any barrier. Our executive team meetings were truly a sacred space for us.

Running to the Fire

In early April 2020, Suri emerged from quarantine and relished the opportunity to walk among colleagues and thank them for all they were doing. "People had stepped up, responded, and collaborated in a bigger way than I had ever seen before in my leadership career," he said. Because of the transparency across the hospital, when caregivers learned of emergent challenges, they volunteered their help. For example, when it became clear that the ICU needed to manage inventory differently to prepare for an influx of patients, a young doctor began coordinating with ICU professionals across the country to share resources. "These remarkable people stepped up into a void and defined a new level of leadership," Suri remarked. "It was a new style of leader."

The hospital's caregivers thanked Suri and the executive team for their honesty and humility. Surgeons who were instructed to work from home volunteered for redeployment to the front line. "This was the highlight of their career," one caregiver noted. "They weren't running *from* the fire; they were running *to* the fire." As one executive recalled, "People were anchored to the purpose—patients first. Day in and day out, they knew that their efforts were for a noble goal. They were driven by it."

As the pandemic continued, Cleveland Clinic Abu Dhabi worked closely with local regulators and partners to bring telemedicine to life. In a matter of two weeks, the hospital pivoted its 1,500 daily consultations to telephone and video formats, freeing up space for an expanded critical care unit: the emergency department scaled from 200 to 1,000 visits per day and its inpatient capacity grew from 364 to 424 beds.[13] "This wasn't part of our strategy or business plan at all," one caregiver noted. "We rallied to respond to our patients' needs."

Ultimately, the hospital's response to Covid-19 was an exercise in collective learning, involving Abu Dhabi's Department of Health and the other six medical facilities in the Mubadala health-care network. Suri remarked, "We coordinated for the first time across the Emirates and across the nation with our so-called 'traditional competitors' to pool all of our resources so that we knew which patients needed to go to which hospital at which time and with which providers."

Later in the pandemic, colleagues from Cleveland Clinic Ohio volunteered to fly in to help their Abu Dhabi colleagues cope with local surges of the virus. Thanks to the sense of community across the Cleveland Clinic system, there was no sense of "not-invented-here syndrome" among caregivers. "The sense of togetherness; the sense of teamwork; the commitment to safety, excellence, patient experience—everything was exactly the same," Mihaljevic observed. This scale of cocreation was possible because of the leadership and culture that had been carefully nurtured since Cleveland Clinic Abu Dhabi's founding.

What It Takes to Architect Organizations That Can Learn Together

To scale world-class health care from Cleveland Clinic Ohio to Abu Dhabi, Mihaljevic and Suri had to hire and develop a special cadre of caregivers. They had to find top-tier professionals who could cocreate in a new context and work effectively with new partners and patients. They had to find people who were willing and able to learn and adapt.

In the best of times, that's what learning organizations do.[14] But what about in the worst? How many organizations can keep up the learning required to innovate and be agile when the changes are emotionally overwhelming, and evolving minute by minute? The research tells us that, unfortunately, many organizations don't pass the test. They fail to encourage the kind of deep listening and responsiveness that can help them face sudden, tumultuous change—like a pandemic.

True to Cleveland Clinic's long-standing ethos, from the beginning, Mihaljevic's and Suri's leadership was not about individual heroics; it was about unleashing all caregivers' slices of genius and harnessing them to deliver outstanding patient care. Moreover, to succeed, they could not simply copy the US culture in Abu Dhabi. Instead, they built a learning community. They were deliberate about their actions, from their microbehaviors and rhetoric to the resources they provided to caregivers. They adapted their leadership style, introduced coaching, rethought the operation of critical teams, and democratized access to technology and data. With persistence and consistence, Mihaljevic and Suri cultivated a sense of curiosity, humility, and candor where caregivers were able to question their own assumptions and express and debate diverse ideas.

The executive team stayed true to this ethos even amid the throes of the pandemic. Contrary to the popular belief that a crisis warrants top-down rule, Suri and his leadership team delegated decision-making, increased communication, were transparent about their fears and mistakes, and introduced new resources to support caregivers' ability to problem solve. Suri himself even learned to adapt his leadership style to a new virtual medium.

Thanks to their leadership, Cleveland Clinic Abu Dhabi caregivers became proactive learners, able to cocreate their way through the pandemic, even with organizations outside their boundaries. But as we saw with our other two architect stories at Pfizer and P&G, without a foundation of shared purpose and values—a sense of community—it is hard to imagine how this hyper-diverse organization, in incredibly high-stakes circumstances, would have been able to scale its collective genius.

THE
BRIDGER

PART TWO

Building Partnerships

T he speed and scope of technological change is amplifying an already accelerating reality: meeting today's opportunities and challenges requires leaders to do more than drive innovation within their own teams or organizations. Leaders must mobilize cocreation *across* organizational boundaries to secure the talent and tools needed to fulfill their ambitions—the work of the *bridger*.

When establishing external partnerships, leaders tend to prioritize governance, spelling out in meticulous detail legal safeguards like intellectual property rights, data-sharing provisions, and decision-making authority. Of course these matters must be addressed, but effective bridgers realize governance is just the beginning.[1]

As the locus of innovation shifts to organizational boundaries, leaders must foster cocreation among people with diverse expertise who no longer share the same team or organizational context. Bridgers understand that this increased diversity generates powerful new opportunities for innovation. But they also recognize it can create literal and metaphorical distance, increasing the risk of conflict, mistrust, and misalignment. Bridgers, thus, take on the hands-on and often emotionally demanding job of helping others embrace and work through their differences.

Bridgers focus their attention and energy on building *partnerships* across boundaries—robust relationships grounded in mutual trust, commitment, and influence.[2] In doing so, they perform three key functions: *curation*, identifying and engaging potential partners; *translation*, developing common language and understanding; and *integration*, aligning around shared intentions and coordinating work across partners. Like architects, bridgers use analog and digital tools to fulfill their role. We have already had a glimpse of this work in the stories of Michael Ku and Rakesh Suri. To survive the pandemic, Ku and his team cocreated "hand in glove," as he put it, with a range of partners inside and outside of Pfizer, while Suri and his fellow caregivers coordinated closely with government and their local competitors.

Our bridgers in part II are not the senior executives who formalize partnership agreements. They are the middle managers on the ground—tasked with execution—who navigate the day-to-day dilemmas of innovating with others who think and work differently. They operate in messy in-between spaces, establishing common ground, or social glue, among those with divergent priorities, capabilities, and constraints. By focusing on middle managers, we see the bridger's superpower in sharp relief: exercising influence beyond their formal authority.

Just as we used legacy institutions to illustrate the role of the architect, we use a common stage—innovation labs and accelerators—to introduce the bridger.[3] More and more corporations are establishing these separate units based on a body of research about "ambidextrous organizations."[4] The recommendation is structurally to separate out innovative work in dedicated centers of excellence to protect the everyday activities of the core business. Too often, however, leaders tell us that these innovation units don't deliver on their promises. They end up disconnected from the rest of the organization, chasing "shiny objects," as one of our leaders described it—ideas that never get implemented, commercialized, or scaled.[5] Why? We believe it's because they lack the right kind of leadership.[6] We find that where innovation labs and accelerators do deliver, there is a tenacious bridger behind their success.

CHAPTER 5

Why Bridgers Matter

Nicole M. Jones at Delta Air Lines

> *As aviation soars into its second century, we see technology as the tool to advance our mission of connecting people and creating opportunities. . . . At Delta, our focus is on applied innovation.*[1]

—Ed Bastian, CEO of Delta Air Lines

> *My team was like a Swiss Army Knife—multi-tooled, yet adaptable and versatile. When we all came together, it was magic.*

—Nicole M. Jones

As a tech enthusiast, Nicole Jones had attended the Consumer Electronics Show (CES) in Las Vegas before, but never did she imagine playing a role in the 2020 opening keynote.[2] Jones and her team were used to flying under the radar within Delta Air Lines (Delta), not taking center stage. She waited for her cue backstage as CEO Ed Bastian began:

> Why is an airline here delivering the opening keynote at CES? . . . We think the gift of flight is the ultimate innovation. It allows people to connect across vast distances. It opens up opportunities that simply aren't possible without a human connection. It brings the world closer at a time we need to be closer than ever before.[3]

Bastian went on to describe Delta's vision for the future of air travel. Beyond delivering superior in-flight journeys, Delta was investing billions in reimagining the airport experience. The vision of tomorrow promised seamless, digitally enabled door-to-door travel, from the moment passengers booked a flight to arrival at their final destination. Security wait times and boarding passes would be things of the past. Travelers would be guided through airports by parallel reality displays, allowing thousands of people to view personalized information on the same display simultaneously. The Fly Delta app, already loved by customers, would be a proactive "digital travel concierge," enabling every step in the journey.

This future was emerging because of the power of cocreation, said Bastian: "We're combining Delta's strength and scale with innovative startups to advance the future of travel."[4] With that, he invited Jones to join him on the CES stage.

In a career-defining moment, Jones introduced her team, The Hangar[SM] (The Hangar) to a packed auditorium. As Delta's first global innovation lab, The Hangar combined the airline's corporate capabilities with startups' latest technology to create real solutions for customers. Most ideas pursued in the lab, Jones said, came directly from Delta's own people: "Delta employees know our customers and our operation best. So we focus on applied innovation—which is about delivering real value to the customer experience."

Like most innovation labs, The Hangar was born of necessity. When Bastian first took over as CEO in 2016, Delta faced intense competition. Without continuous innovation and embracing new technologies, the airline wouldn't be able to keep up. Jones was chosen to build and lead a dedicated team, separate from the core business, to amplify Delta's culture of innovation. She and the executive team agreed that external partnerships would be key for catapulting travel experiences into the future. Jones and The Hangar, therefore, stepped into their role of *bridgers*— connecting nearly every Delta division with external partners, from research and educational institutions to startups and the venture ecosystem.

This is the story of how Jones built and led The Hangar to deliver its first award-winning project: a boarding pass based on biometric data. This might seem like a straightforward tech innovation. But as Jones and her team discovered, creating the biometric boarding pass required far more than connecting technical systems. It meant combining inputs from a host of disparate groups—teams within Delta's IT, operations, and marketing departments to stakeholders at CLEAR (a biometric technology startup), the Transportation Security Agency (TSA), and Customs and Border Protection (CBP).

Ultimately, Jones and her team shepherded the biometric boarding pass to the finish line by doing what bridgers do best: stitching together the social fabric required for cocreation across boundaries. The success of this project helped usher in a new culture of continuous innovation across Delta, a formidable challenge in an organization serving six hundred thousand customers every fifteen minutes and focused squarely on operational milestones.[5] Over time, The Hangar would become a launchpad for employee-generated ideas shaped by end-user needs and aligned with Delta's core business.

The Making of a Bridger

Jones grew up in Atlanta, Georgia—where Delta is headquartered—and earned a computer science degree and her MBA before taking on various roles implementing e-commerce technology in large businesses. From her first job at Price Waterhouse Coopers through positions at Macy's, IBM, and WarnerMedia, Jones said, "I focused on nurturing and implementing innovative ideas with employees [that] built the brand and drove long-term revenue growth."

In 2012, Delta recruited Jones to help build its new Delta Sky Media business, charged with boosting in-flight entertainment by selling content and advertising space. While Jones tended to approach her work like an engineer—"logically and tactically," she said—she quickly realized that building relationships would be key to getting things done at Delta. "There was a strong sense of purpose in Delta's culture," she noted, "and a family-like pride."

During her first four years at the airline, Jones rotated through positions in digital content strategy, marketing optimization, and retail strategy. She became familiar with each group's operating model, power dynamics, and decision-making processes, and learned how each function came with its own language and worldview. Although any initiative at Delta required senior sponsorship, she observed that middle managers' and senior leaders' priorities didn't always align, even within the same division. Appreciating such nuances enabled Jones not only to acquire an enterprise-wide view of Delta and the customer experience, but to connect with colleagues across a range of functions, gain senior leadership support for her ideas, and deliver outsized impact in her roles.

Opportunity Knocks

In November 2015, Jones read a headline on Delta's intranet: Gil West, chief operating officer, and Matt Muta, VP of innovation, had made a $5-million, multiyear investment in a 6,500-square-foot space in Atlanta's Tech Square. Tech Square was a hub for innovation centers, startups, venture capital, and academics at the Georgia Institute of Technology—with whom Delta already had a long-standing relationship. The executive team had previously sought to foster collaboration with local entrepreneurs and research groups but had found it difficult to forge and maintain those relationships. The plan was to build Delta's first "global innovation center" to facilitate these partnerships, and they were searching for a leader to spearhead the new team.

For Jones, the opportunity sounded exciting. She had been mentoring and investing in startups in Atlanta's budding entrepreneurial community for years and had many ideas for how startups could help Delta accelerate its innovation. Now, for the first time since joining the airline, Jones saw the chance to make those partnerships happen.

When Muta met Jones, he quickly saw she was the perfect candidate: "I was very keen on [Jones]. Her follow-through was just amazing. She had ideas of what she would like to see happen in this innovation center, and we started to communicate more and more." West and Muta were impressed by Jones's strategy, technology, and marketing background, but even more so by her people skills. "Her ability to bridge, to become an intersection between a large company and students and professors really came to bear," said West. "She was very powerful because people loved working with her. She was a problem-solver, a facilitator."

In September 2016, Jones took the helm of the innovation center (soon christened The Hangar). Her mandate was to help embed a culture of innovation across the company, and she had autonomy to explore what the center would do and how it would do it. She was given three months to develop a pitch for the executive team. Jones felt up to the task: "I am a builder. I like to start with a blank sheet and create something."

Designing an Innovation Lab for Cocreation

Jones immediately began a three-month benchmarking exercise, scanning the existing landscape of corporate innovation labs, accelerators, and venturing models. She was surprised by how much investment was going into these entities and how little value many created. She insisted The Hangar shouldn't fall into the same traps: "We knew we didn't want to be a team that people looked at and said, 'Oh, you chase shiny objects, completely disconnected from the rest of the business.'" Fortunately, West agreed: "We had to think about the problems we were trying to solve rather than just chasing technology."

Jones considered two potential paths for The Hangar. If she built a corporate accelerator, Delta could invest in and learn from leading-edge tech startups—but there was no guarantee their technologies would ultimately benefit Delta's business or move the needle on culture. By contrast, she could build an innovation lab, bringing together Delta colleagues and external partners to test and develop solutions directly aligned with the airline's needs.

Jones anticipated that involving those in the core business was the more difficult path in the short term. Many Delta employees had lived through the airline's bankruptcy in 2007, and employees at all levels prioritized operational metrics and risk avoidance; even small errors could inconvenience millions of passengers or worse. Still, Jones insisted cocreation was necessary to begin shifting mindsets toward innovation.

At the end of 2016, Jones and Muta made their pitch to Delta's executive team: The Hangar's mission would be to "incubate and invent solutions that empower employees and delight customers." The lab would center on four work streams: it would *orchestrate* (guide innovation strategy and partnerships), *explore* (rapidly develop and test), *build* (deliver innovative technology), and *design* (scale innovation companywide). While The Hangar would sit under IT, it would serve as an internal consultancy. Any Delta stakeholder could bring their ideas and challenges—operational, technological, or service-related—to The Hangar. Jones and her team would help validate various aspects of the problem and identify external talent who could help cocreate potential solutions. Importantly, Jones decided The Hangar would *only* facilitate the development of prototypes (minimal viable products—MVPs) to validate and thus de-risk further investment in the ideas. The core business would remain responsible for launching solutions since it had the capabilities to implement at scale. "We knew that the only way that our work would get integrated into the enterprise was if the entry point—the department or team where the idea landed—was behind it," Jones explained. To ensure this ownership up front, Jones insisted that The Hangar would only take on projects with formal sponsorship from a senior leader in the core business.

Building a Team of Bridgers

With Delta's leadership on board, Jones began hiring a team of designers, strategists, ethnographers, high technologists, and specialized engineers— "creative and eclectic" talent not usually found within the traditional airline context, noted West.[6] Jones knew her team would need to be able to relate to their diverse internal and external stakeholders to earn their trust. She deliberately sought people with unique cultural, professional, and personal backgrounds and interests, indications of flexible and creative mindsets. Other nonnegotiables included passion, self-motivation, and the ability "to leave pride of authorship and ownership of ideas at the door," said Jones. If all parties were going to commit to cocreation, her team needed to foster a sense of shared ownership. Their partners within Delta would take credit for the value generated—not The Hangar. "We had a vested interest in making sure that our partners worked together," she explained. "We wanted those in the businesses who collaborated with us to be the heroes."

In January 2017, Jones hired her first innovation strategist, Willy Barnett, a seasonal Delta gate agent who had just completed a PhD in marketing, consumer behavior, and technology. "I hired Willy because he had under-lying tech know-how, but he could also think big-picture, and he cared a lot about the human experience," said Jones. Her second hire was Carrie Moore, a former art teacher and design consultant, whom she tasked with building a design-thinking practice for the company. Like lean innova-tion at P&G, design thinking was a learn-by-doing problem-solving methodology: a nonlinear, iterative way to develop and test hypotheses while remaining grounded in the user experience.[7]

Jones also decided to leverage Georgia Tech's student interns as a con-tinuous source of fresh perspectives. Because she sought to build a highly autonomous team, she delegated the design of The Hangar's internship program to Barnett and Moore. Going forward, she involved every mem-ber of The Hangar—from designers to technologists—in vetting candi-dates for jobs or internships.

Building her team of bridgers required Jones to exercise her unique interpersonal abilities. Not only did she pull together diverse individuals, but she also facilitated the exchange of ideas across their conflicting ways of thinking and working. "Nicole was very diplomatic," Moore said. "She treated us all fairly, and that truly benefited our team's collaborative cul-ture. No matter one's experience or degrees, we all felt like equals. She listened to our recommendations, supported our visions, and empowered us to utilize our talents."

The Hangar's First Ninety-Day Sprint

In late January 2017, Jones was sitting in The Hangar's new, sparsely fur-nished office when she received an urgent email from West: Would Jones work with Delta's corporate security department—and an external com-pany, CLEAR—to develop a biometric boarding pass? Delta had made an equity investment in CLEAR, a US biometric technology company that used fingerprint data and iris (eye) scanning for identity verification.[8] The goal was to improve customers' airport experience by eliminating the wait times and pain points associated with presenting a paper boarding pass to go through security and board at the gate.

The turnaround time was tight. West asked The Hangar to deliver a prototype that could be tested in an airport in ninety days to determine the technology's viability for further investment. Jones and her team knew this assignment would be tough, but it was exactly the sort of project that, if successful, could earn The Hangar credibility within Delta. "We didn't have any capabilities within Delta to manage biometrics ourselves," Jones noted, "so we saw a win-win opportunity. The pilot would not only help make customers' lives frictionless in the airport, but it would also help Delta learn more about biometrics and scale their CLEAR investment faster." Jones also saw an opportunity for her team to test and develop an operating model for The Hangar going forward.

Jones immediately contacted Jason Hausner, managing director of passenger facilitation, and within days, the two held a kickoff meeting with The Hangar team—at the time, five full-time employees and four Georgia Tech interns. Together they framed the project and began to map the constellation of senior sponsors and internal and external stakeholders they would need to engage. CLEAR would supply the biometric identification hardware and software. Anything technology-related within Delta required building relationships with IT leaders and operators. The legal department would need to look at customer data and privacy implications. Corporate security and government affairs would work with TSA and CBP, the government gatekeepers that would provide approval for experiments in airports. And marketing would have the final sign-off before anything was put in front of customers.

Mutual Trust, Influence, and Commitment

Jones's experience had taught her that multistakeholder initiatives could easily stall if even one key individual didn't play their part. For that reason, she implored her team to "always build relationships before you need them." Jones stressed the importance of uncovering and empathizing with each partner's goals, capabilities, and limitations in their roles. Operators lower in Delta's corporate hierarchy, for example, would likely perceive the biometric boarding pass as nonessential work—and might see it as a personal risk to invest their time and energy in the project. Jones explained that her team had to be prepared to *bridge*. They would need to constantly remind stakeholders of *why* they were doing this work to earn and sustain their commitment throughout the project. Frequent communication and transparency about processes and problems would be key for earning and maintaining trust. Sharing influence—ensuring that everyone's input would be considered when making decisions—would be essential.[9]

Given the complexity and scope of actors involved in the biometric boarding pass exploration, Jones decided she would focus on bridging to key senior leaders, who could then support the initiative within their teams. She delegated the day-to-day project management to Barnett, who was just two weeks into his new job. In Jones's eyes, Barnett was the ideal bridger for the role. His years of working as a gate agent would earn him significant credibility with internal stakeholders, and his expertise in technology would allow him to communicate with CLEAR's technologists. Above all, Jones believed Barnett's user-experience expertise would help him keep stakeholders grounded in improving the lives of customers.

Building Mutual Trust

With Delta IT based in Atlanta and CLEAR based in Philadelphia, Barnett's priority was to create a communication channel between them to build trust and structure remote collaboration. While he immediately booked meetings with CLEAR's chief information officer, mobilizing Delta's IT team was more challenging. IT had experienced a costly five-hour outage the prior year—Delta's tech system in its Atlanta operations center went completely offline, inconveniencing millions of customers. The company's new CIO was now fortifying its IT infrastructure and establishing new priorities around systemic reliability. Understandably, everyone in IT was focused on reducing risks, not experimenting with innovation.

Without full participation from IT, Jones and Barnett knew the biometric boarding pass wouldn't materialize. Jones began leveraging her existing relationships within the company to advocate with Delta's senior leaders. Meanwhile, Barnett had learned from years as a gate agent that physically showing up at people's desks was sometimes the only way to accomplish things. He left The Hangar's offices in Tech Square and traveled to the airport to earn their trust in person. As he immersed himself within IT, Barnett began to make sense of the nuances of its decision-making processes. For example, while he first assumed he should be advocating with leaders higher in the command chain, Barnett soon realized that they were not necessarily the decision-makers. "There were some situations where a VP wouldn't do anything until a subject-matter expert *below* him said yes or no," Barnett recalled. "The expert rightly had more decision-making power."

Through their joint bridging efforts, Jones and Barnett were able to convince Delta's IT leaders to formally assign two people to the boarding pass exploration. But both understood that this didn't guarantee their trust in the initiative. They genuinely empathized and understood that their IT partners considered collaborations with The Hangar to be "special projects," separate from their already high-priority work. Thus, for Jones and her team, it was imperative to be considerate about their internal stakeholders' time constraints, deliberate about *when* they included them in meetings, and mindful that those meetings were efficient. One IT manager noted how The Hangar respected her team's priorities: "I trusted that Nicole, Willy, and the team would pull us in when it was the right time. . . . We had business demands to meet, and we didn't have time to waste."

Establishing Mutual Influence

Once the key contacts within Delta and CLEAR were identified, Barnett launched a series of meetings to determine what kind of biometric data should be used to identify a passenger—fingerprint or facial recognition—and who would own this data. Predictably, the conversations became lengthy debates. Every stakeholder had a different viewpoint, reflecting the priorities and concerns of their own group. At that time, facial recognition technology was faster, but less accurate. Fingerprint technology was slower, but more precise. A nonnegotiable requirement for both CLEAR and Delta's legal, security, and privacy departments was to maintain the security of passengers' biometric data.

Jones met with Barnett frequently during this time, coaching him to reconcile tensions by establishing mutual influence among partners. Instead of dwelling on technical details, Jones encouraged Barnett to recenter conversations on their shared intention: to "advocate for the voice of the customer, and make sure the innovation [starts] from the point of view of the human experience." Part of this involved helping stakeholders visualize and develop a collective understanding of the customer experience. An IT partner from the database architecture group reflected that they didn't often consider the end product: "How does the product look sitting on the counter in the airport? How does the customer feel?"

Through their efforts to instill a design-thinking mindset, Jones and her team allowed each of their internal and external stakeholders to appreciate their own and others' contributions in making the biometric boarding pass a reality. "We all became active partners in coming up with the end solution," one manager noted, "as opposed to just thinking of it as an IT integration. They guided us to collaborate through the solution and then work backward to figure out how to connect A and B."

Maintaining Mutual Commitment

After numerous conversations, the parties agreed to use fingerprints for their prototype and that CLEAR would continue to own the biometric data. But this spurred the next big debate: How would they design and execute the required back-end technical integration of Delta's and CLEAR's systems? The goal was to identify a passenger using a fingerprint in less time than it took to use a paper boarding pass. The team considered different ways to connect the two IT systems, and after weeks of further conversation landed on a solution: Delta and CLEAR would each build an application programming interface (API) to integrate their systems.[10]

CLEAR built its API in a week; Delta's IT team, however, missed key milestones. The ninety-day deadline was looming, but rather than push the sense of urgency, Barnett decided to slow down, have one-on-one meetings with his IT colleagues, and ask questions to understand the exact nature of their constraints. The problem he found wasn't one of technical know-how. Their lack of commitment stemmed from fear. They were deeply reluctant to open their internal systems to a foreign technology. Only then did Barnett fully appreciate how much Delta's IT system outage in the previous year had affected this team.

Jones helped address Barnett's roadblocks by communicating progress to senior leaders and maintaining a sense of ownership and enthusiasm among their stakeholders. "As the team encountered challenges," she said, "I tried to keep people excited, aligned on our North Star, and working toward a common purpose." West and Muta used their senior sponsorship powers to clear bottlenecks and instill a sense of urgency. After five weeks, Delta's IT team finished building and validating its API, at which point Barnett and Jones arranged for several other internal stakeholders (marketing and government affairs, among others) to help finalize the biometric boarding pass for testing at Ronald Reagan Washington National Airport.

Piloting the Prototype

Launch day was in sight, and just as Jones and Barnett were breathing a sigh of relief, they realized there was a big problem. Despite efforts to ensure all stakeholders were kept informed throughout the exploration, they had left out a key player. The airport gate agents would need to administer the pilot with customers, but they hadn't been trained to use CLEAR's fingerprint readers. Barnett acted quickly. He contacted the Agent Training Division and candidly acknowledged and corrected the misstep. Fortunately, the division agreed to help prepare thirty agents for the pilot.

On May 25, 2017, days before one of the busiest US travel weekends, the biometric boarding pass pilot launched in Washington, DC. Jones and The Hangar team observed intently as gate agents helped Delta customers use their fingerprints to enter the Delta Sky Club and board planes at one gate selected for testing. The Hangar and CLEAR teams were overjoyed that it technically worked. But as they expected, the qualitative feedback they received suggested the overall experience needed improvement. For one thing, gate agents and customers found the seven-second fingerprint reading process much too slow. "Fingerprints were accurate but not quicker," remarked Greg Forbes, part of Delta's airport customer experience division, "and customers did not like touching a surface touched by many others. I told the [Hangar] group, 'I think we're on the wrong path here. Biometrics, yes. Fingerprint, no.'"

Still, Jones was thrilled that her team was able to deliver a prototype and generate novel insights for Delta within ninety days. Given that facial recognition technology was improving rapidly, the airline's senior leaders were convinced to invest in further research and development. In the meantime, Delta would begin implementing fingerprint entry across airports to continue learning about biometrics and working through the back-end technological hiccups. For that, Jones and The Hangar now needed to identify a permanent home for the biometrics workstream in the core business. "We learned so much so quickly," Jones said. "The next question was, [Where's] the best place to scale?" The challenge would be identifying a team that would fund further innovation of the technology and drive its implementation in airports.

Handing Biometrics Over to the Core Business

From the beginning, Jones had believed that involving their partners within Delta at every step of the exploration—from problem validation to developing and piloting the prototype—would help prime them for the handoff.[11] While there was some initial reticence from internal colleagues, Jones and Barnett were able to position biometrics within the IT department's larger objectives. The Hangar eventually passed its biometrics project to Cheoukee Leung, manager of Delta technology—the IT counterpart to Delta Sky Clubs at the time—who'd been directly involved with the exploration. "Even though it was Willy's baby," Leung noted, "he could not keep holding it, and he understood that. A proper handoff, in my mind, was for the best, because it was better to have one team driving it rather than multiple teams."

The result was exactly what Jones had hoped for. Over four months, with Leung leading the initiative, a coalition of stakeholders from marketing, corporate security, and operations collectively took responsibility for the ongoing development and implementation of biometric technology solutions within Delta. By the end of 2017, Jones was amazed to see fingerprint entries rolled out to every one of the two-hundred-plus Delta Sky Clubs globally. Soon after, Jones was gratified to learn that Leung had been promoted to lead the airport customer experience IT portfolio, and had begun working with Hausner's corporate security team and CBP to develop facial recognition at Delta's international terminals. As Hausner reflected:

> We were applying what we had started with the biometric boarding pass exploration to other projects. Everything that we worked out initially [with The Hangar]—regarding meeting cadence, scheduling, how we attacked the problem, project management, innovation—we used as the template [for] other projects.

In 2018, Delta launched biometric facial recognition at Hartsfield-Jackson Atlanta International Airport—the busiest airport in passenger traffic worldwide almost every year since 1998—and became the first airline to have a fully biometric-enabled international terminal.[12]

Multiplying the Bridger Effect

In their biometric boarding pass exploration, Jones and The Hangar came to appreciate the enormous human effort required to execute what, at first, seemed like a straightforward technical integration. From day one, differences in goals, concerns, and working styles were on display. But as effective bridgers, Jones and Barnett were able to foster the mutual trust, influence, and commitment necessary for an innovative prototype to materialize.

After word spread about The Hangar's success, Delta employees from all over the company began approaching the innovation lab with ideas. However, Jones soon found that employees were "jumping to solutions."[13] As Muta explained, people had "preconceived notion[s] of what the solution should be, without really diving in to understand the problem." Jones began to worry that some were beginning to perceive The Hangar as an extra resource that could address items on their longstanding wish lists. But she insisted that The Hangar couldn't become a team to which people simply outsourced innovation. That's when Jones and her team took their learnings from the biometrics experiment and built an operating model—including new tools and methodologies—to systematize and accelerate their bridging work going forward. Beyond simply leading explorations, their objective was to help their partners within the core business develop their own capabilities as innovators.

The "Initiative Canvas": Framing the Problem

Moving forward, The Hangar team agreed they'd primarily source projects from within Delta's business units. They designed an extensive initiative canvas—an intake form crafted to help stakeholders succinctly articulate a problem and how resolving it would improve customer experience. This tool sparked dialogue that allowed The Hangar team to help their colleagues learn how to frame problems (rather than jumping to solutions) aligned with corporate objectives. Jones and her team would review the intake form with relevant internal and external stakeholders before beginning any new exploration—thus ensuring everyone agreed on the problem they were trying to solve and success metrics for any new MVP.

Earning Senior Sponsorship: The Importance of Storytelling

Jones's team also made sure to secure a business sponsor—typically a vice president—before beginning any exploration. This was crucial and often required first-rate storytelling skills. Biometrics simply wouldn't have been possible, for example, without West and Muta working at the top to secure resources and address bottlenecks. To gain such executive support, The Hangar team "had to learn to socialize ideas upward," Barnett explained, which was done through "strategic storytelling," added one designer. In pitching ideas to senior leaders, it became best practice to create one-page, fictional press releases or mini-stories with characters and narratives. "Writing a story was so much more efficient than doing a gigantic design concept," Moore noted. It helped an idea become more tangible and engaged business leaders more thoughtfully, while also creating guardrails for the imagination. "It was important to clarify what the concept was and what it was not," Moore added.

Evangelizing Design Thinking

Once a business sponsor was secured for an exploration, The Hangar team launched a four- to twelve-week cross-functional design-thinking exercise with the project's stakeholders. They delegated responsibility for each component of the MVP and defined the meeting cadences and rules of engagement for how different stakeholders would work together. They always began with deep ethnographic research into the employee or consumer experience, involving observations and interviews. To make the end-user experience more tangible, The Hangar team created *user stories* to understand customers' different personas and use cases as well as *empathy maps* to visualize the holistic customer experience—what the customer thinks, sees, feels, hears, says, and does.

While Jones intended these exercises to expand the imagination of colleagues across Delta's core business, many felt uncomfortable thinking this way at first. Even within The Hangar team, Jones observed that engineers sometimes wanted to jump to designing prototypes, and designers had to push back and advocate for the customer's voice. Other times, the designers had big visions for impact, but the engineers and strategists had to keep them grounded in technical feasibility and business strategy. All prototypes did not work out—and that was okay. "Failure is tuition" became The Hangar's mantra, and they developed standards and metrics to ensure learnings were captured as they iterated with their partners. That way, even if an experiment failed, they could apply the insights going forward.

Stakeholder Maps

The result of the design-thinking exercises was to land on a concept of a prototype worth developing and testing. To disentangle the inherently complex airline environment, The Hangar team designed systems maps (like customer-journey maps) that identified all the stakeholders required to execute the exploration. These maps visualized interdependencies and helped determine whether partners outside Delta would be needed. Stakeholder mapping also included possible unintended consequences, such as jobs that might be negatively affected by the innovation. "Looking

at both sides of the coin was a big learning," Barnett noted, "not just focusing on 'this is going to make the customer experience so much better'
but also empathizing with those whose work might change." Importantly,
to avoid inadvertently excluding anyone, stakeholder mapping was done
continuously throughout an exploration's life cycle.

Developing an Innovation Track Record

With its tools and methodologies in place, Jones and her team conducted
more than thirty explorations in The Hangar's first two years. Several
solutions were handed off to be scaled in the core business, including the
popular Delta consumer app, the wireless seatback entertainment system
that's now on every Delta aircraft (and which Delta sells to other airlines),
and handheld devices that enable gate agents to be mobile as they serve
passengers. In an organization of eighty thousand employees, it was easy
for these successes to be missed, so West encouraged Jones and her team
to publicize them internally and externally:

> We had to find our communication cadence—how do we com-
> municate this to the company, our customers, our investors,
> and our board so that they understand what we're doing and
> see the proof points? When the larger organization started to
> see the proof points and realize that The Hangar was making
> a difference, it built momentum. Then we were able to devote
> more capital and resources to it, and innovation became real
> business.

As trust and credibility grew, Jones and The Hangar were permitted to
push into more exploratory innovation, like parallel reality and other
emerging technologies that Delta had introduced at CES.[14] At the same
time, they were receiving more business requests than they could handle.
Jones and her team eventually began prioritizing requests based on projected cost, time, revenue, and potential impact on a net promoter score
(a standard internal metric). Although Jones made a commitment to help
all who asked, if The Hangar couldn't offer its full-fledged consulting and
project management services, her team facilitated connections to startups,

academic partners, and other vendors. Her team also began hosting technology reviews to expose internal stakeholders to the latest trends.

Over time, Jones began to hear encouraging signs that these relationship-building and upskilling efforts were beginning to impact Delta's culture. "They did a great job of setting up the infrastructure to help foster innovation at Delta," said Hausner. "I had not worked with startups at all prior to The Hangar. . . . When there is a project that The Hangar can't engage on, we're now able to actually manage ourselves, because they've helped us make connections and we can stay abreast of current technology."

At the heart of The Hangar's success was Jones's leadership—her ability to harness the collective genius of diverse teams and bridge their differences, while remaining grounded in the needs of the business. "Our COO was brilliant in creating The Hangar," Hausner remarked. "Having his executive sponsorship was huge, but it also needed the right leader to run it, and Nicole was amazing. She could take that mandate from the COO and put it into action."

Lessons on Why Bridgers Must Build Mutual Commitment, Trust, and Influence

Dedicated innovation units are often launched as if corporations will be able to work seamlessly with partners beyond their boundaries and integrate the new digital solutions they develop. Too often, however, they're designed with little regard for the social fabric required to operationalize partnerships in practice. Delta senior management didn't fall into that trap; they found in Nicole Jones a consummate bridger—an individual with enthusiasm, broad functional expertise, and a special talent for relationship building rooted in her own humility and emotional intelligence.

Every one of Jones's choices when building The Hangar was informed by her ambition to not simply deliver solutions but change culture—to unleash the "abundance of creative ideas" of her Delta colleagues, as she put it, and help embed the capabilities to realize them. Jones considered establishing a corporate accelerator, but she knew outsourcing innovation to startups wouldn't help the company realize its long-term objectives. Instead, she took on the more difficult path of cocreation: building an innovation lab in a way that made her internal colleagues an integral part of the process and triggered their own capacity to innovate.

Jones understood that facilitating cocreation across Delta's internal departments and external startups required building bridges to connect people with vastly different priorities, capabilities, and constraints both inside and outside the company. Crucially, her design choices started with a question: Why would anyone be willing to invest the time and effort—on top of their core responsibilities—to collaborate, experiment, and learn with The Hangar? From her prior experience, Jones intuited it was when partners share a sense of mutual commitment to a common goal, mutual trust in each other, and mutual influence over their joint work. She understood that partners like to know that each is well intended, there are no hidden agendas, and each will have a voice in deciding how they will work together.

Jones appreciated just how time- and energy-intensive cocreation could be. And she understood that to facilitate collaboration internally and externally, The Hangar first had to become a trusted entity. So, she hired a diverse team—including Barnett and Moore—who themselves had the mindsets and skill sets for bridging. Most important was her team's ability to share ownership: The Hangar's job was to set the stage for their partners to "look good," as Jones put it. She herself shared decision-making rights with her team, affording them influence in everything from hiring decisions to partnership management. She modeled how to mediate diplomatically between different perspectives (designers and engineers) and coached her team to do the same.

Jones coached Barnett to pay careful attention to building and maintaining quality relationships throughout. This started with empathizing with their partners. By immersing themselves with stakeholders at multiple levels, Jones and Barnett found that senior leaders and middle managers within a single team or department did not share the same immediate objectives and had to be engaged in different ways. Operators in IT, for example, didn't want to be involved in exploratory conversations. Leung remarked that The Hangar "would pull us in when it was the right time. . . . If the project had a lot of 'what ifs' or we didn't know what they were trying to do with the solution, we tended to step back." In addition, Jones and Barnett had to adjust to the fact that chains of command were messier in practice than they appeared in the formal organizational chart (e.g., experts in IT had more decision-making influence than the formal leaders).

Appreciating these nuances allowed Jones and her team to tailor their bridge-building accordingly. To earn and maintain commitment, they repeatedly reminded stakeholders of their shared intention—*why* they were doing this work and *how* it would help them achieve their individual ambitions. They communicated transparently and proactively to earn trust, keeping senior leaders informed throughout so that it wasn't a surprise when the time came to move an innovation from incubation to implementation. When problems or conflicts arose, they approached them with patience and curiosity. Barnett, for example, was able to take a step back at a critical moment to explore what was really happening within the Delta IT team when they missed their API milestone, and he and Jones then enlisted senior leaders to mitigate the anxiety associated with opening their systems.

Indeed, bridgers foster mutual trust, influence, and ongoing commitment by asking questions: Do we really know our partners' priorities, capabilities, and constraints? What kinds of emotional and material costs are we asking them to take on? Are we looking for both-and solutions whenever possible to address the desires or concerns of different parties? Are we generous in sharing recognition?

Above all, by sharing credit with internal stakeholders—and bringing them along in the journey—Jones and The Hangar were able to instill a sense of ownership for the ongoing success of any innovation they incubated. In doing so, she and her team not only became a trusted intermediary but also delivered a series of impactful solutions and helped colleagues across Delta develop their capacity to cocreate with external partners on their own.

CHAPTER 6

What Bridgers Do

Raja Al Mazrouei at the Dubai International Financial Centre

The secret to the renewal of life, the evolution of civilizations, and the development of humanity is simple: innovation.[1]

—His Highness Sheikh Mohammed bin Rashid Al Maktoum, vice president, prime minister of the United Arab Emirates, and ruler of Dubai

Our team spoke business with certain people, financial services and technology with some, and regulation with others. We needed to be able to capture all the different dimensions of the conversation . . . and make Fintech Hive beneficial for all parties.

—Raja Al Mazrouei

In late 2016, Raja Al Mazrouei, the head of marketing and corporate communications at the Dubai International Financial Centre (DIFC), was in her office reviewing the finishing touches on a major retail development project when her phone rang. It was a colleague on DIFC's strategy team.[2]

"Raja," he said earnestly, "I need to talk to you and your team about fintech. We are launching an accelerator. We need to brand it and give it a name. We will do all the background work, but you need to make it happen."

Al Mazrouei stopped in her tracks. "Fintech?" she asked. "What's fintech?" At the time, she had no way of knowing how momentous this call would prove to be.

Over the next five years, Al Mazrouei would turn the DIFC's vision into reality, building The Fintech Hive (The Hive)—one of the most successful startup accelerators in the Middle East. By 2022, The Hive had accelerated more than two hundred startups, which collectively raised more than $500 million in funding, created over a hundred jobs, and launched more than a hundred fintech products in the Middle East, Africa, and South Asia region. It was also ranked among the "World's Best Innovation Labs" by *Global Finance* in 2021.[3] Along the way, Al Mazrouei was recognized as one of the most influential thought leaders in fintech.

How did Al Mazrouei, who knew nothing about fintech at the start of this journey, pull this off? It was no small feat, especially given her position within a large government bureaucracy. Key to The Hive's success was Al Mazrouei's talents as a *bridger*. She built partnerships across incumbent financial institutions, high-tech startups, and regulators to enable them to cocreate the future of Dubai's financial industry.

Learning the Power of Relationship Building

Raised in what she described as "a traditional Emirati household" in Abu Dhabi, Al Mazrouei learned early on how to balance a strong respect for tradition while embracing the cutting edge. Her parents encouraged her from a young age to develop herself and contribute to her country. At university, Al Mazrouei was one of the first students to enroll in its newly developed information technology program. "When IT was first launched, it was the most difficult program," she said. "Nobody wanted to go into that, but I decided to try it. That was a transformation for me."

In 2005, after completing an MBA, Al Mazrouei moved to Dubai to pursue an IT career. She wanted to play a part in making Dubai one of the most innovative cities in the world. She landed a job at the DIFC, which had launched in 2004 when leaders of the seven UAE states realized the need to diversify their economies beyond oil and gas. (The UAE itself had been formed to safeguard and develop those rich regional resources, becoming an independent sovereign and federal state in December 1971.)

The DIFC was established by the UAE Constitution as one of several specialized "free zones" in the country. It operated according to British common law (as opposed to Islamic sharia law) and had its own regulatory body. After coming out of the 2008 financial crisis, the DIFC regained its earlier momentum, with its contribution to Dubai's GDP at 12.1 percent in 2013.[4] By 2016, it had become a thriving financial hub for both the country and region—housing more than fifteen hundred companies, including over four hundred financial services firms.[5]

At the DIFC, Al Mazrouei quickly earned a reputation for her sense of duty to her country. In conversations with colleagues, she'd often refer to Prime Minister Sheikh Mohammed bin Rashid Al Maktoum's ideals and vision for the UAE. Like him, she deeply believed in the role technology and innovation would play in the future of their economy. As Al Mazrouei saw it, she and her colleagues were working toward a bigger national purpose, one that would ultimately strengthen the country and the well-being of its people. Recalling his first meeting with Al Mazrouei, Abdulla Qassem—chief operating officer of Emirates NBD Group (one of Dubai's largest banks)—described her as "a servant leader who focused on people connections."

Al Mazrouei was promoted rapidly through the DIFC as her superiors took note of her diligence. She was a stickler for quality; nothing got out the door without her detailed review. In 2010, she was promoted to head of IT, charged with consolidating and optimizing back-end infrastructure. Three years later, she ascended to head of operations and then to a newly established position, senior vice president of marketing and corporate communications—her first customer-facing and creative role that, she admitted, was "outside of my comfort zone."

As a marketing leader, Al Mazrouei was tasked with a major assignment: building out Gate Avenue—the DIFC's 110 acres of real estate and retail space in Dubai's city center. The UAE had launched a national vision to make Dubai a global economic hub by 2021. Al Mazrouei's role was thus to transform the DIFC from a financial center into a "lifestyle destination"—a place where expatriates would want to work, live, and build their families.

Gate Avenue required Al Mazrouei to work with the broadest set of stakeholders she'd ever encountered: colleagues across the DIFC and other government agencies as well as local and global companies spanning retail, art, finance, and entertainment. It was in this role that Al Mazrouei realized just how much patience and diplomacy it took to meet clients' and partners' needs. "Making all the stakeholders happy was not easy," she recalled.

Just as Al Mazrouei was beginning to consider her next career step, her mentor—the DIFC governor, His Excellency Essa Kazim—encouraged her to do a semester-long executive education program. There, she reflected, "I realized my potential. . . . I had more confidence. When I came back, I said, 'You know what, there is nothing that I fear.' I decided to stay in marketing. But I felt freer." Upon returning to the UAE, Al Mazrouei even decided to experiment with new side endeavors related to entrepreneurship and investing, both within and outside the DIFC.

Envisioning the Future of Fintech

In 2016, just as Al Mazrouei was approaching the finish line for the massive, multiyear Gate Avenue project, the fintech accelerator request landed. DIFC's strategy team was working with a global consulting firm to determine how to build an accelerator program that would attract fintech startups to Dubai. Excited by the challenge, Al Mazrouei agreed to lead the branding and marketing strategy for its launch. She got to work learning all she could about the already burgeoning world of financial technology.

Through a series of information sessions, Al Mazrouei learned that the widespread adoption of smartphones had created opportunities to make digitally enabled financial services accessible to millions of people. Yet this evolution had largely bypassed the Middle East and North Africa region. Since 2010, only 1 percent of investments in the global fintech sector had found its way into her part of the world.[6] There was no doubt about the need for fintech: just a few years before, the region's unbanked population was a staggering 86 percent, one of the highest rates in the world.[7] She felt that the time was ripe for the sector, as more people were accessing the necessary technology in the region (smartphones accounted for 42 percent of broadband connections in 2016[8]).

Al Mazrouei could see that Dubai had many of the ingredients to support a robust fintech ecosystem: a healthy business environment with the right demographics, access to local and global markets, government and regulatory support, financial capital, and a growing economy.[9] But it was missing two key stakeholders: fintech startups and venture capitalists. Leaders of the DIFC hoped that creating an "innovation hub" would attract these groups, which other governments were already courting. At the core of this hub would be the government fintech accelerator, whose launch event Al Mazrouei was now managing.

As the DIFC's long-term strategy became clearer to Al Mazrouei, she realized that the purpose of the accelerator was not simply to attract fintech startups and venture capital; it was equally about helping established financial institutions within the DIFC to modernize. The accelerator was really a vehicle for cocreating the UAE's future financial industry. With this key insight, Al Mazrouei and her marketing team decided to convince leaders from *both* established financial institutions and startups to participate in the accelerator's launch event, alongside government representatives from the DIFC.

Turning Vision into Reality

On January 10, 2017, the launch of the Fintech Hive generated the most public relations coverage the DIFC had ever received. Energized, Al Mazrouei took over all communications and media for the accelerator. "Anything that came about fintech started getting sent to me," she remarked. "I just became fascinated by fintech." Two months later, Al Mazrouei learned that DIFC leadership was looking for someone with technology expertise and a strong marketing background to lead The Hive. She volunteered without hesitation, and by April 2017 she was the acting executive vice president of the accelerator.

Only after taking the job did she realize the immensity of the task. The Hive had already received two hundred applications for its first accelerator program, which at the time was nothing more than a website. She had no established team, process, program design, or even office space.

First things first, Al Mazrouei knew she had to build a team that could forge partnerships among their diverse stakeholders. She hired four people with wide-ranging technology and marketing backgrounds—three of whom were Arab and from the Gulf region, and all of whom happened to be women. Al Mazrouei surprised her DIFC colleagues by not requiring candidates to have previous fintech knowledge. Instead, she sought entrepreneurial minds who could move seamlessly across work functions while staying committed to The Hive's purpose: helping Dubai flourish through fintech.

Al Mazrouei made her expectations clear to her lean but growing team. Although she encouraged an informal and enjoyable work atmosphere, excellence would be key for The Hive to earn credibility within the DIFC and with external stakeholders. In all her leadership roles, Al Mazrouei explained, "I ate with the team; I had them on Instagram and Snapchat. But if they didn't deliver, I was very firm. . . . Things had to be perfect, and if they weren't perfect, I didn't approve them. If I didn't like something, I was vocal about it." Fatima AlHarmoodi, The Hive's marketing manager at the time, offered a complementary perspective from within the newly formed team:

> [Al Mazrouei] did not micromanage. She gave her team the freedom. She trusted us to organize our time, to get our work done. We took into consideration that she trusted us, and we made sure that everything was delivered. We knew what she would like, what she preferred, and how to work with her.

Al Mazrouei's team found a temporary office within the DIFC, which they began renovating into a modern coworking space. They got right down to work building The Hive's website and social media channels. Al Mazrouei insisted that, like the launch event, all communications materials must resonate with the more traditional priorities of the DIFC and legacy financial institutions *and* speak the language of future-forward global fintech entrepreneurs. The team's efforts to balance different stakeholders' points of view quickly began to pay off. "She understood what it meant to create a responsible brand," an executive at a financial institution observed. While The Hive's brand was more "playful" than the DIFC's, the same executive added, "It wasn't loud; it was very subtle. It always connected back to the nation. . . . It was the voice of the local."

As Al Mazrouei began promoting fintech through her DIFC networks, she was inspired by her colleagues' great suggestions for The Hive. As soon as construction of their coworking space was finalized, she launched a weekly forum—"Breakfast Buzz"—where any DIFC colleague could come brainstorm ideas at The Hive over tea and coffee. These meetings became enormously popular: people were eager to spend time in a colorful, relaxed environment, with open kitchens, beanbags, and phone booths.

Meanwhile, Al Mazrouei also activated her global networks for advice. In speaking with consultants, investors, and entrepreneurs, she learned that there were a few accelerator programs—such as Y Combinator and Techstars—that attracted startups by the droves. For The Hive to have this kind of pull, she realized, the world needed to know that Dubai was a place where startups could innovate.

After numerous conversations, Al Mazrouei envisioned the basic roles various stakeholder groups would play in The Hive's accelerator program and in creating a globally competitive, local fintech sector more broadly. Startups would bring promising new technologies, business models, and services to the region. Financial institutions ("sponsors") already established within the DIFC would provide mentorship and resources to help startups test and scale their businesses and learn from them in turn. And the DIFC's regulatory bodies would play an essential enabling role. They would create the legal framework necessary for innovation, educate startups about local regulations, and grant them a license to operate in the region.

Al Mazrouei and her team were also thoughtful about designing a strategy and revenue-generating business model that would "be beneficial to all parties," she said. While other accelerators charged startups a fee or demanded equity participation, they decided not to do so. The Hive's primary source of revenue would be its sponsors: they would pay a fee to participate in exchange for connections to a curated group of top-tier fintech startups.

With the program framework in place, it was time for The Hive team to begin the painstaking work of recruiting their first partners. Al Mazrouei understood that the critical first step would be identifying startups that sponsors would want to work with, and vice versa, as well as finding open-minded regulators; there would be little room for mistakes. But how could her team convince startups, sponsors, and regulators to participate in an accelerator program that didn't yet have credibility?

Curating the Key Stakeholders

From her years of doing business in the UAE, Al Mazrouei recognized that trust and buy-in had to be *earned* face-to-face.[10] Al Mazrouei and her team decided they should immerse themselves with each stakeholder group to understand their unique priorities, capabilities, and constraints. Interacting with each group, Al Mazrouei knew, required capturing a wide assortment of sensibilities: "You spoke business with certain people, financial services and technology with some, and regulation with others." Only with this contextual intelligence would Al Mazrouei and her team be able to enable their diverse stakeholders to innovate together.[11]

Regulators

The Hive team began by aligning with regulators, starting with people Al Mazrouei had met in her years at the DIFC. In these meetings, she and her team presented the types of financial technologies emerging across the globe. "We debated how we would regulate this technology," Al Mazrouei explained—"What was possible? What wasn't?" She listened intently to regulators' concerns about data use, compliance, and customer privacy. After several conversations, it became apparent that a whole new legal framework was needed to allow fintech startups to experiment in the region.

By empathizing with them and earning their trust, The Hive team eventually helped the regulators uncover an opportunity to innovate. Together, they created an innovation testing license that would grant startups preliminary permission to test and validate their products in the marketplace before earning a full license to operate in the region. This new "regulatory sandbox," as they called it, permitted startups to run small-scale experiments with a constrained set of real customers, while also protecting them: if any product or service failed within this environment, the transaction could automatically be reversed. Moreover, the sandbox enabled regulators to test provisional regulatory standards and learn from the actual experiences of customers interacting with startups, before settling on a full-fledged regulatory regime.

Sponsors

Leveraging her networks within the DIFC, Al Mazrouei began approaching financial institutions one by one for meetings with C-suite executives. While the DIFC brand helped open doors to meetings, she soon found that fintech wasn't at the top of their strategic agendas. To help make fintech more palpable to these corporations, Al Mazrouei decided to work with external experts to develop what would become an annual fintech report—a proprietary document capturing key global and regional fintech trends and investments in the industry. This report was crucial to help executives quantify and visualize the fintech opportunity, supported by concrete data.

In The Hive's first months, Al Mazrouei personally conducted more than twenty meetings with potential sponsors to review the fintech report. In every meeting, she made sure to listen to executives' priorities and concerns before she spoke. She tailored her communication to focus only on those fintech issues and trends most aligned with their particular interests. As buy-in was earned, executives invited The Hive to conduct priority workshops with their whole senior team, with the aim of identifying their top-three industry issues (even though they might not be about fintech). These constructive dialogues allowed Al Mazrouei and her team to step into the shoes of these executives before communicating how collaborating with startups could help them achieve their corporate objectives and address internal constraints. Moreover, Al Mazrouei assured each organization that any contractual agreement with The Hive would be customized to their corporate strategy and risk appetite.

Through these high-touch interactions, Al Mazrouei observed that many financial institutions shared similar priorities (e.g., accelerating digital transformation) and challenges (e.g., lack of digital expertise). She thought there was an opportunity for them to collaborate; there could be a real advantage if they started thinking of themselves as partners in modernizing the financial sector and driving impact for the nation. It was difficult to assemble the companies, but, relying on the DIFC's conven- ing power, Al Mazrouei eventually convinced executives from across the financial sector to meet. This is where her considerable skills as a transla- tor came to bear.[12]

Al Mazrouei knew that just sitting in the same room wouldn't neces- sarily lead to productive discourse. So, she and her team carefully choreo- graphed the meetings to ensure they were valuable to everyone. Using the annual trends reports as a platform for discussion, she always initiated the conversation by identifying the shared opportunities and challenges of the financial industry in the UAE, including its overall competitiveness in the global economy. (The first report became their baseline to assess collective performance as an industry each year.) Only once common ground was identified would Al Mazrouei invite the sponsors to share their individual goals, questions, and requirements. Sandeep Chouhan, then the acting CEO and COO of Abu Dhabi Islamic Bank and long- time colleague of Al Mazrouei, was especially impressed by her facilita- tive power among competing banks. "The first thing I found in her was really the guts to pioneer. . . . She got twenty-five banks sitting around the same table and openly sharing their strategy about wanting to mod- ernize the banking environment in the country."

Al Mazrouei and her colleagues secured four sponsors for the first ac- celerator program, all influential financial institutions in Dubai that shared the Sheikh's vision for the country: Emirates NBD, Dubai Islamic Bank, HSBC, and Visa. Once the sponsors were formally recruited, The Hive team worked to ensure that these relationships went beyond mere investment (their fee). They proactively built broad networks across all levels and functions of the organizations. "Managing the relationships was the most important thing we did," Al Mazrouei said. "We kept a very close relationship with all of them and knew the teams by name."

Startups

The Hive team used the insights they gained about sponsors' risk appe- tites and areas of interest to shape their ongoing strategy, including the types of startups and technologies they would pursue. Al Mazrouei de- cided they would recruit Series A fintech startups with a demonstrated viable product or proof of concept (PoC) in three areas: insurtech (fintech for insurance), regtech (focused on regulatory compliance), and Islamic fintech (which complied with sharia financial law).

Over the next several months, Al Mazrouei personally met with entrepreneurs across the globe, encouraging them to apply for the accelerator and sharing with them the promise of Dubai. To earn their trust along the way, she made another unusual design choice for The Hive. In addition to not paying a participation fee, the startups were welcome to join other accelerators as well (others typically demanded exclusivity). "We did that because our purpose was to accelerate the market," Al Mazrouei said, "so the startups [would feel] safe." AlHarmoodi said they didn't see other accelerators as competition: "Whatever helped the startups made us look good as well." Every touchpoint with startups—from The Hive's digital marketing campaigns to their online application forms—was monitored for engagement and iterated on frequently to improve performance.

Mutual Influence: Sharing Decision-Making Rights

Out of hundreds of startup applicants, The Hive team vetted a short list to interview for its initial cohort. Al Mazrouei then did what bridgers do best: she shared decision-making rights with The Hive's sponsors and regulators, giving them a say in the final selection process (to avoid conflicts of interest, the regulators did not vote). She understood that the process would be slower and more difficult in a group with such different points of view, especially given that most were not experts in technology.[13] But she was thinking long term. If The Hive's stakeholders were to build a robust fintech ecosystem together, they needed to have a sense of mutual influence and ownership from the beginning. It was better to institute a decision-making process that embraced all voices and "both-and" as opposed to "either-or" solutions.[14]

After two weeks of interviews and debate, eleven companies were chosen to join The Hive's inaugural accelerator program. One was Sarwa, which was creating a banking app to enable consumers to save money, invest, and trade stocks and exchange-traded funds all in one place. Jad Sayegh, cofounder of Sarwa, noted that he was attracted to The Hive because it prioritized getting startups regulated. "The innovation testing license would be our only chance to make something like that happen," he said. "This accelerator was built to get startups through that big hurdle. We didn't look at any other [accelerators]."

Another member of the cohort, norbloc, was developing a know-your-customer (KYC) solution powered by distributed ledger technology. KYC would enable financial institutions and governments to share sensitive customer data in a secure, seamless way and, thus, drastically improve customer service. Customers only needed to supply their information once, and based on their individual preferences, their data would be shared accordingly with other organizations in the norbloc network.

The startup selection process was indeed contentious at times and required all of Al Mazrouei's mediating talents, but by the end of the process, all agreed their first cohort represented a strong start.

Translating and Integrating Across Startups and Their Sponsors

The Hive's first startup cohort began the accelerator program with Bootcamp Week, which included meetings with financial institutions and outside professionals like law firms, compliance institutions, and large tech companies.[15] Al Mazrouei observed how intimidated startups were when they met with companies in corporate boardrooms. So, to level the power dynamics, she insisted these meetings take place in The Hive's coworking space. As Al Mazrouei said, the sponsors and regulators "need[ed] to sit in a different environment to understand what we were saying."

The regulators met with the startups biweekly throughout the program to help them learn about local and regional regulatory and compliance standards. "I think Raja put in a lot of effort to get [the regulators] involved and excited," said norbloc's CEO, Astyanax Kanakakis. Just as the startups were learning from the regulators, he observed that "the regulators were learning at the time as well." To his delight, Kanakakis added, they were "very pro-innovation" and the "atmosphere was absolutely fantastic and very collaborative."

The next phase of Bootcamp Week was a "speed dating" session, where each startup pitched its product concept to each sponsor. To prepare, startups rehearsed their pitches with The Hive team. Despite the on-boarding exercises she and her team designed, Al Mazrouei found that many of the entrepreneurs still struggled to communicate their value offerings in a way that was compelling to sponsors. Because of her intimate understanding of each financial institution's priorities, as well as the culture and business norms of the region, she coached each startup one-on-one to tailor their language and presentations to the specific needs of each financial institution. For example, she knew Emirates NBD had recently launched its first digital bank for millennial customers and was seeking to do the same for small and medium-sized enterprises (SMEs), so she encouraged norbloc to explain how its KYC offering could help Emirates NBD meet this goal.

Managing Discrepancies

After speed dating, The Hive team matched each startup with one or more sponsors with whom their priorities and capabilities best aligned. The sponsors were then expected to mentor the startups for a period of three months, collaborating with them to prepare their products and services for the market. Though enthusiasm was always high in early conversations, Al Mazrouei noticed that once the partnerships became operational, tensions between the startups and corporates began to amplify.

The norbloc team, for example, had been matched with multiple sponsors to develop pilot experiments of its KYC network. However, the startup found it difficult to pin down specific individuals at the sponsoring firms who could serve as a day-to-day touchpoint. "Everyone says, 'It's a great idea,'" Kanakakis shared. "But then they ask . . . , 'Where does the startup fit?' . . . We needed to find a champion within the bank—someone that would basically get this done." Al Mazrouei worked arduously to make connections where needed and nurture the "soft part" of the relationships between startups and large organizational sponsors. "She's very good at connecting people," said Kanakakis.

Even after identifying a champion, however, talent turnover was inevitable inside large institutions. Al Mazrouei observed just how frustrating this could be for the entrepreneurs. For norbloc, when a valuable partner moved to a new position, the team had to begin the relationship-building process again. One startup CEO recounted that in these instances, "Raja instilled a sense of urgency," and actively introduced teams to new leaders throughout the sponsor institution.

Despite The Hive's careful efforts to establish relationships, roadblocks continued to emerge throughout the mentorship period. Entrepreneurs, for whom time was money, became impatient with the corporations' operating models: a bank's "tech development and procurement cycles were just not as agile as that of a young company," said The Hive's senior program manager, Shereen Abdulla. Some startups entered the program with an "I'm better than a bank kind of attitude," as one Hive member put it. Other startups worried that the larger institution would engage them in conversations that went nowhere or try to copy their solutions.

Wherever possible, Al Mazrouei managed conflicts that inevitably flared up, first gently reminding startups and sponsors of their shared intention: "Because I have the tech background and . . . exposure to financial services, I was able to speak the language between the tech teams and the financial institutions and articulate the visions of their leadership." She reminded each stakeholder of *why* they were doing this work in the first place—emphasizing what each company originally wanted to achieve through the program. Then, Al Mazrouei encouraged the startups and the sponsors to empathize with each other's points of view, often finding herself playing the advocate for one party or the other. To help startups develop trust in their sponsors, for instance, she would explain why the financial partner felt certain (admittedly) time-consuming practices were necessary. At the same time, she encouraged financial sponsors to recognize how frustrating it could be for nimble startups to adapt to the slower pace of a large organization and urged them to move faster when they could.

While Al Mazrouei tended to intervene patiently in the mentorship relationships, if necessary, she shifted her style from enabling to directive. If she thought a sponsor could do more to help the relationship, she communicated that explicitly. She explained candidly just how demanding sponsors seemed to their startup partners, emphasizing the risks they posed to the entrepreneurs. In turn, when startups made unreasonable asks (e.g., costs of refining a PoC), she instructed them to imagine the sponsor's point of view and be more disciplined in how they managed costs.

On November 12, 2017, The Hive's first accelerator program concluded with a large in-person showcase filled with startups, sponsors, and regulators in the audience. Twelve startups presented their PoCs, including Sarwa, which had received an innovation testing license allowing it to test its consumer application with ten clients with a maximum of $50,000 of their assets. Sarwa had onboarded clients, developed a PoC, iterated, and had a market-ready fintech product in two months (a process that typically takes one or two years). It became the first of six startups in The Hive's first cohort to receive a full license for operation.

Al Mazrouei and her team were pleased with the outcomes of their inaugural group. They had run into many rough patches in the relationships between startups and financial institutions, but their bridging efforts enabled most startups in the cohort to find a home within a sponsor. As an Emirates NBD executive commented, these results proved the "power of collaboration and the great leadership of Al Mazrouei in ensuring engagement and tight coupling" of key stakeholders. Emirates NBD and norbloc, for example, decided to enter a formal business partnership. In these situations, AlHarmoodi described, "The sponsors took on responsibility for developing their relationship with the startups. For as long as each party liked, they could continue talking and working with each other." Within two years, norbloc and Emirates NBD joined forces to use the startup's KYC technology for SMEs with a trade license from the Dubai Economic Department. With this solution, SMEs could open a bank account with Emirates NBD in fifteen minutes—a far cry from the three to five months it had once taken. It was stories like these, Al Mazrouei noted, that "influenced the community. . . . It started to build the ecosystem."

Curate, Translate, and Integrate

As we've seen in the first half of this book, it is hard to cocreate within an organization and even harder across organizations. Nicole Jones and Raja

Al Mazrouei show us just how essential the role of the *bridger* is for driving innovation across boundaries—and it is not for the faint of heart.

Bridgers like Jones and Al Mazrouei have a deep awareness of the nitty-gritty, operational reality of ushering innovation from idea to the finish line, and the nuanced social interactions that happen along the way. They understand that innovating across boundaries requires partnerships. In practice, these relationships have less to do with formal contracts and more to do with evolving social processes that demand proactive, ongoing support from leaders.

As both Jones and Al Mazrouei have shown us, bridgers are the ones that ensure work stays on track, deadlines are met, and ideas ultimately turn into reality. They do this by building the mutual trust, influence, and commitment necessary for stakeholders, over whom they often have no formal authority, to cocreate. Al Mazrouei has shown us three interrelated ways bridgers *can* drive innovation across organizational boundaries—starting with *curating* the right partners.

Curation is about deliberately choosing *whom* to engage and why—not just which organizations but which individuals will invest their time, resources, and energy in the partnership on behalf of those organizations. For The Hive to deliver on its mandate, Al Mazrouei and her team had to select partners—cohorts of startups, sponsors, and regulators—who would be willing and able to work with each other. Al Mazrouei began by leveraging her personal networks within and outside the DIFC to survey the range of potential partners available. When approaching each stakeholder, she targeted executives in her initial outreach to firms but made sure to engage individuals at multiple management levels.

Curation requires trust, which is earned through deep listening, being curious and taking the time to empathize with how others operate and see the world. It requires a willingness to see the world through the eyes of various groups and individuals, and imagine how their priorities and challenges align and diverge. As we saw, executives and middle managers at Emirates NBD had different needs even though they shared the same organizational context.

Only with an intimate understanding of stakeholders' diverse needs can leaders begin to build bridges between them and others. Al Mazrouei and her team curated convenings of financial institutions based on shared opportunities and challenges; they brokered mentorship relationships based on complementary goals and capabilities. Curation is a continuous exercise. In Al Mazrouei's case, while organizational partners stayed consistent throughout the mentorship periods, people moved on, and new champions—equally committed to collaborating with startups—needed to be identified and included. Finally, as much as curation is about identifying potential partners, Al Mazrouei illustrated how it is equally about *compelling* others to participate. This is where translation becomes important.

For bridgers, *translation* is ultimately about building shared understanding. It means amplifying diversity and vocalizing differences, so that partners can learn to empathize with each other. As Al Mazrouei's case shows us, discrepancies can add friction as partners begin to work together; people can become frustrated by a slower pace or a different process, or when partners don't seem mutually committed. Bridgers diffuse such tensions through increased communication. They ensure that messages don't get lost in translation—that day-to-day operational delays don't get misinterpreted as bad intentions.

Al Mazrouei, for example, helped diffuse entrepreneurs' frustrations with corporate bureaucracy by encouraging inquiry into *why* these processes were in place—namely, to mitigate risk to customers. Still, sometimes messages didn't come through. As much as startups asked their sponsors for help, Al Mazrouei had to step in. She literally transported feedback to the relevant corporate stakeholder to ensure entrepreneurs' needs were heard and met. This required her to be more directive—to be the voice of the other partner, and level power dynamics to ensure mutual influence in the relationship.

Finally, the third way bridgers influence cocreation is through all the ways they help partners establish common ground—*integration*. Think of common ground as the physical bridge—the in-between space—that allows partners to bring their slices of genius together. Bridgers fill this space with a *shared intention*—a common priority that will help them reach their individual priorities. For Al Mazrouei, the annual fintech report became a device for motivating financial institutions to concern themselves with their collective performance *as an industry*.

Bridgers also foster integration by establishing shared ways of working, including *common language*, *tools*, and *processes*. Al Mazrouei and her team carved out numerous occasions for regulators, sponsors, and startups to develop common definitions around technology and regulatory standards that would allow them to work more effectively together. They carefully designed forums, such as the startup selection process, for sponsors and regulators to practice shared decision-making. Al Mazrouei managed inevitable conflicts and tensions with diplomacy and fairness—trying as much as possible to represent both sides, rather than frame their differences as trade-offs. Over time, startups, sponsors, and regulators developed their own shared practices; even forums like the Breakfast Buzz became a meeting place for all The Hive's stakeholders.

Through her bridging efforts, Al Mazrouei was able to build an accelerator program that began to have a transformative impact on Dubai's financial sector within just a few years. By 2019, The Hive was ranked as the world's tenth largest fintech hub and the third largest Islamic fintech hub. The 2019 iteration of The Hive's flagship accelerator program featured thirty-one finalist startups and more than a hundred mentorship pairings. The Hive had built a network of sixty ecosystem partners—law firms, investors, and others—who provided pro bono clinics and advisory support to the startups. They forged partnerships with accelerators across the globe, from Copenhagen to Tel Aviv, to cocreate new ways of adding value for their startups. Many corporations and governments even began approaching The Hive team to conduct bespoke consulting projects.

Demand for engagement with The Hive boomed; the number of startups and mentors continued to grow. But perhaps more importantly, their first sponsors continued to be deeply engaged with The Hive, and soon they developed their own capacity to cocreate with startups, independently of Al Mazrouei and her team. Spurred by this observation, and the demands of Covid-19, Al Mazrouei insisted that The Hive transition to a light-touch, virtual accelerator model, which they called "innovation sprints." With the sponsors managing the startup relationships themselves, The Hive team could focus its time on launching new accelerator programs—and scaling the number and stage of startups they served. One of these was Scale-Up, a new accelerator program powered by a digital platform model for post–Series A startups, venture capital firms, family offices, private equity firms, investment banks, and corporate and government funds. Another program particularly close to Al Mazrouei's heart was AccelerateHer, a mentorship program focused on growing the number of women in the region working in fintech.

In the fall of 2022, Al Mazrouei was offered another unexpected opportunity that would require her to bridge and scale innovation across an even larger and more diverse number of stakeholders. She left The Hive and in January 2023 became the CEO of Etihad Credit Insurance (ECI), the UAE's official export credit company—another position that would allow her to contribute to her country. Drawing on her background in technology and finance, she would architect a digital-first organization to help support UAE trade and the country's vision for economic diversification. She is now developing bridgers within her organization who can work across national and sector boundaries and build long-term partnerships with businesses, lenders, and investors. Fortunately, Al Mazrouei believes ECI's prospects are strong since "innovation is in the DNA of Dubai."

CHAPTER 7

Bridging the Legacy and the New

Garry Lyons and Ken Moore at Mastercard Labs

I am a big believer that incumbency with an open mind is unbeatable.

—Garry Lyons

We changed our name from Mastercard Labs to Mastercard Foundry, evocative of two things: creativity and delivery.

—Ken Moore

We introduced you to Garry Lyons in the first pages of this book. He was the tech entrepreneur who sold his startup to Mastercard in 2009 and was asked by CEO Ajay Banga to help forge the company's path into the digital future.[1] We saw in chapter 1 how Banga had inherited a risk-averse, consensus-driven company—ill-equipped to work with emerging technologies, let alone create them. At Banga's behest, Mastercard's board had begun acquiring firms to bring in new technology and, more importantly, new talent who understood innovation. "Garry Lyons really piqued our interest," said Martina Hund-Mejean, chief financial officer at the time. "He spoke a hundred miles an hour, and his brain probably worked even faster."

Lyons, a serial entrepreneur, hadn't expected to stay at Mastercard be-yond two years. "But then, Ajay came along," he explained to us with a smile. Lyons was hesitant to accept Banga's offer at first, having seen how legacy businesses often mishandle innovation: "I told Ajay, 'If you want me to move the needle next year on the P&L, I'm the wrong guy. If you want me to do innovation theater, I'm the wrong guy.'" But Banga assured Lyons he wasn't interested in theater. "Don't do innovation the way cor-porate America would traditionally do it. Do it the way you think it should be done," he told Lyons, granting him a budget and autonomy to spend it as he pleased.

For his part, Banga saw in Lyons not just a visionary entrepreneur but a *bridger*. Lyons deeply appreciated the power of Mastercard's incumbency—its scale, customer base, and trusted brand—and could convey how cutting-edge technologies would translate into tangible opportunities for the company. Richard Haythornthwaite, board chairman at the time, agreed:

> Garry was trusted from the outset. . . . [He] had taken an idea through scale [his startup Orbiscom], and had been very sen-sible on his own journey, very process-minded, and could ex-plain very clearly how he did it. . . . He was one of the most commercially astute technologists that I had come across.

Energized by Banga's trust and tenacity, Lyons took the job. In 2010, he became Mastercard's executive vice president of research and development—and he had his work cut out for him. Recall from chapter 1 that, at the time, employees ranked "innovation" as the *twenty-sixth* most important factor (out of twenty-seven) for the company's future. Lyons recognized this reality and set out to change it. As he saw it, his mandate was first and foremost to change how Mastercard's employees, customers, and investors thought about technology and the possibilities of innova-tion. He would do this by showing them the "art of the possible."

Lyons assumed the role of "priming the core" and the market—preparing Mastercard's employees, investors, and customers to embrace innovation and new digital technology. He did this by building Mastercard Labs (Labs), an entirely separate R&D arm to show internal and external stakeholders the art of the possible and provide them with methodologies and capabilities to drive digital transformation. When Ken Moore succeeded Lyons as head of Mastercard Labs, the company was well on its way to transforming from a payments company to a "technology company in commerce," as he put it. His task was to build a more tightly integrated process between Mastercard Labs and the core product organization focused on repeated, systematized execution and delivery of innovation.

Envisioning a Digital Future

When Lyons began his new role, the first iPhone was hardly three years old. Still, he imagined that in the imminent digital world, every connected device (from PCs to wearables) could be a vehicle for commerce. "We were just barely emerging from an analog world at that point," Haythornthwaite recalled. "And here was Garry penciling out what a digital-first world was going to look like."

Lyons believed that Mastercard's possibilities for growth in the digital economy were practically endless, and he saw his first task as getting his colleagues to believe this too. For many at Mastercard, "technology presented danger," said Banga. "People thought that the transition to electronic and digital would kill us rather than be our biggest opportunity," a colleague added.

In one of his first initiatives, Lyons posted a high-energy video on YouTube titled "Mastercard by the Numbers." In it, he exclaimed that while the tech media was "enamored" with Facebook at the time, the platform didn't even have a billion users. Mastercard's network, in contrast, already included 1.9 billion cards and 35 million merchants in 210 countries and 150 currencies.[2] As Lyons described, Mastercard's payment infrastructure, trusted brand, and global scale presented a "phenomenal starting point" to grow and compete in the digital economy.

While appreciating their advantages, Lyons and Banga were aware of the challenges a legacy institution could present. "Installed infrastructure is the enemy of innovation," said Banga. "It makes you fat, dumb, and happy—stuck where you are." Both agreed that any effort to experiment with new ideas within the core business came with risks and great responsibility. "Innovating inside a big company . . . was challenging in many respects because we had so much to lose," said Lyons. He understood that the reliability of Mastercard's network (running with 99.999 percent uptime) was paramount for maintaining trust in the marketplace. "We had to be very thoughtful about innovation," he added. "We could not damage the Mastercard brand or customers' trust, but equally, it couldn't be an inhibitor."

Recognizing the need for a safe space to experiment, Lyons decided to launch Labs in Dublin, where he was living at the time. This specialized R&D unit would be ring-fenced from the core product teams and focus on creating "disruptive, breakthrough solutions to launch Mastercard's next phase of growth."[3] Lyons and his team would *curate* partnerships with venture capital firms and make small investments in early-stage technology companies—purely for learning rather than return on investment. Once they identified a promising technological trend, they would *translate* these opportunities into the payments context. This meant prototyping and incubating new solutions, which they would then transition to Mastercard's new emerging payments team—responsible for diversifying the company's products and services—before *integrating* them into the core business as full-scale solutions.

Lyons hired a small cadre of engineers, technologists, and user-experience specialists with expertise in prototyping and agile product development methodologies, a far cry from Mastercard's usual banking and consulting hires. As Lyons recalled, he and his team "had many theories about where [they] thought technology would go and how it was going to impact payments." Among Lyons's early investments was a company specialized in electrocardiogram authentication. The insights gained led his team to launch a research stream on biometric wearable payments (years before the Apple Watch hit shelves).

In addition to biometric-enabled payments, Lyons and his team became the first within Mastercard to experiment with the cloud, digital identity, and blockchain, among other technologies. From the beginning, Lyons made every effort to ensure his team's innovation efforts met Mastercard's strict security and trust requirements. Banga was working to foster a sense of urgency and thoughtful risk-taking across the company, yet he always stressed the need to "care about unintended consequences. We had to take responsibility for that on our shoulders."

Although the technology was in its early stages at the time, blockchain particularly interested Lyons because of his experience with virtual card numbers and tokenization at Orbiscom. Lyons knew it was risky to run experiments with sensitive payment-related data on a public blockchain. But rather than letting this deter his team, he hired specialized talent to build a private blockchain for experimentation. "There weren't many people with [a blockchain] skill set back in those days," observed Deborah Barta, senior vice president of provenance and strategy at the time. "The allure was, 'Treat [Labs] like a startup. Come, run fast, and build great stuff.'" Lyons's choice to bring this talent in-house allowed his team to begin learning about blockchain and the opportunities it presented for Mastercard early on. It didn't matter that the purpose wasn't yet clear; Lyons brought the right mix of curiosity and foresight to trust that this experimentation would soon pay off.

Priming the Core Business to Embrace Innovation

While Labs was the company's epicenter for innovation in the short term, in the long term, Lyons and Banga agreed that Labs should be a "stepping stone" to the future.[4] (See principle 8 in figure 7-1.) To help Mastercard's employees become independent innovators, Lyons would start by exposing them to new ideas and technology from outside the company. As he often said, "Every company is either a technology company or needs to become one." Lyons firmly believed that everyone within Mastercard—junior-level employees, executives, and board members alike—should understand technology and embrace innovation in their roles. The problem, however, was that "people weren't thinking about where technology was going," he said, and they were unwilling to invest time and resources in noncore activities as a result.

Bridging Senior Leadership

Lyons leveraged his relationships with senior leaders to begin upskilling Mastercard's executives and board members, many of whom did not have a basic understanding of technology. "The company didn't even know

FIGURE 7-1

Mastercard: Eight guiding principles

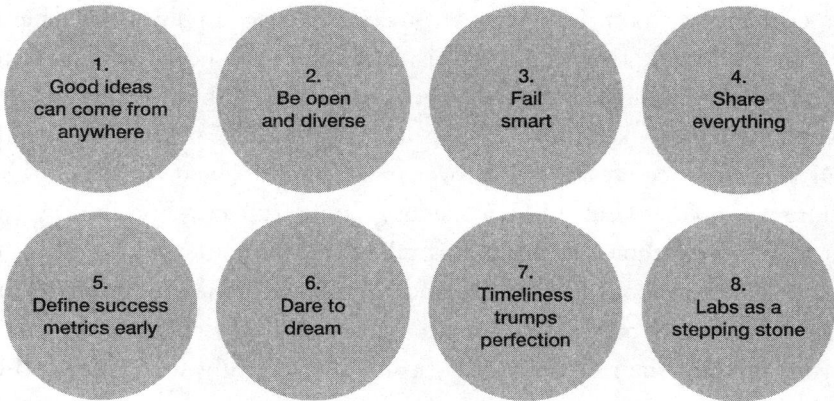

1.
Good ideas
can come from
anywhere

2.
Be open
and diverse

3.
Fail
smart

4.
Share
everything

5.
Define success
metrics early

6.
Dare to
dream

7.
Timeliness
trumps
perfection

8.
Labs as a
stepping stone

how to spell *digital* at that point in time," said Hund-Mejean. This, to Lyons, needed to change urgently: "A lot of companies fail with innovation because they are not able to understand the impact of technology at the most senior levels; hence, it doesn't get the buy-in that it should."

As a bridger, Lyons believed that the best way to develop people's understanding of technology was by *showing* them what was possible—by translating abstract technological concepts into tangible prototypes that others could see and feel for themselves. Moreover, as part of this translation work, he always made an effort to frame these prototypes in terms of their practical business applications.

During the company's annual executive leadership program, Lyons decided to run dedicated technology sessions where he presented the Labs' work and introduced his colleagues to new technical vocabulary. "As directors," said Haythornthwaite, "we were desperate for that exposure because it was all a new language." Lyons arranged for the leadership team and board to visit Labs regularly. He even invited his colleagues to participate in strategic decisions he was making surrounding Labs, instilling in them a sense of mutual commitment and influence in their work.

As Lyons interacted with his colleagues, he realized that their level of comfort with technology varied, and some needed more support. He took the time to meet with individual leaders one-on-one to explain technological trends and insights from the venture capital community in language they could understand, always empathizing with their level of expertise. "Garry didn't alienate the people who had been there for a long time," noted Hund-Mejean. "He utilized their thinking, their background, their experience to take the best forward—to make them feel good."

Above all, Lyons and Banga worked together to maintain healthy relationships between those working on the core business and the Labs team working on "the new." As Haythornthwaite reflected, "Garry and Ajay were able to do this without ever getting into an 'old world, new world,' or a 'second-class, first-class' citizen type of environment. And it became a very, very healthy springboard for all the ideas that were there." Together, Lyons's and Banga's efforts set the tone for integrating innovation more broadly into Mastercard's daily operations.

Bridging at the Operating Level

Just as Lyons bridged the present and future on the senior leadership team, he built an innovation management function within Labs to do the same for junior employees and middle management. This team was responsible for convening and communicating with employees (curation), teaching them the language of technology (translation), and building a sense of mutual influence and commitment to innovation (integration). As Lyons explained:

> Innovation was not one person's or one team's job. We did a huge amount of evangelizing. I wasn't trying to get everyone to focus on creating new products. I was trying to get them to think about doing their own job differently—to improve the way they thought about efficiencies. Could they apply technology? Could they tell the story differently? Were they continually trying to find a better way? Were they inspired by the work that people around them were doing?

Lyons and his team launched a host of internal initiatives to "unearth game-changing ideas" from Mastercard's employees, as he put it, including competitions, rapid prototyping sprints, offsite hackathons, and an online platform where anyone could submit proposals. Lyons's choice to offer direct exposure to senior management and large cash prizes for competitions caught people's attention. In one contest, sixty-two employees received sponsorship and training to incubate an idea and pitch it in front of the whole company for the chance to win $250,000. All Mastercard employees were invited to vote on the finalists, and the majority chose to participate. "Ajay had a single vote," Lyons explained. "Everybody had a single vote. It was completely democratic."

Like the competitions, Labs' innovation sprints were hugely popular. In forty-eight hours, Lyons and his team helped employees convert their nascent ideas into tangible prototypes that were then presented to customers. As one leader observed, people "queued up to be part of these teams." Not only did employees leave the sprints with concrete deliverables, but they also learned prototyping skills through hands-on practice.

Complementing these applied experiences, Lyons and his team delivered workshops and trainings to raise awareness about emerging technologies and innovation methodologies. While these were initially ad hoc, as soon as human resources caught wind of them, they partnered with Labs to expand and standardize the trainings across the company. Together with HR, Labs even began hosting Innovation Weeks featuring global webcasts about internal innovation initiatives and external technology trends. Edward McLaughlin, president and chief technology officer, noted that "innovation is like ethics: it has to pervade the organization. . . . Innovation Week helped bring everyone into it and make sure they were a part of it." To further democratize ownership of innovation, Lyons worked with the legal team to make it easy for anyone at the company to file a patent.

Through their various internal engagement initiatives, Lyons and his team sought to spur a conversation about innovation internally, one in which all employees could play a part. They helped embed new vocabulary, mindsets, and skills like agile thinking and development. Of course, risk-taking and new ways of working did not come easily to all. "There were some challenges and frictions," said an executive vice president. "It wasn't all rainbows and butterflies." Lyons decided to shut down some competitions along the way because the ideas they produced were too similar to those that typically emerged on the core product teams. However, a colleague observed that ultimately the events became "less about the innovations themselves and much more about creating innovators in the process."

Simplify: Overcoming Implementation Challenges One Step at a Time

After a year focusing on experimentation and internal engagement, Labs had developed plenty of promising prototypes. Though unfinished, Lyons was not shy about presenting them to Mastercard's largest customers and shareholders—a risk that initially made his long-tenured colleagues uncomfortable. "People probably looked at me like I had two heads," said Lyons, "but I actually think people related to that." Frequent "innovation showcasing," he believed, was necessary to begin changing customers' and investors' perceptions and expectations of Mastercard in the marketplace (applying pressure to innovate within). At a 2011 investor day, Lyons and his team presented a vending machine with embedded payment capability and even provided the three to four hundred attendees with smartphones to let them experiment with virtual payments. "When people could see it for themselves," Lyons said, "it made sense to them."

Lyons decided it was time to incorporate commercial talent to get products and services off the ground. To help with bridging, he recruited Barta in 2012, who was then leading Mastercard's fraud-management product development, to further develop an idea that had emerged in a Labs innovation contest. "I was the first businessperson to join Labs," Barta recalled. "I was brought in to bring a little bit of the commercial muscle and a little bit of the flair in terms of showing, internally, that we could do things more quickly in a way that didn't affect the core systems."

Within six months, Barta and the team built Simplify Commerce (Simplify), a platform that enabled SMEs to easily accept digital payments. Simplify blazed new trails by targeting a customer segment Mastercard did not yet serve; it was also the first Mastercard product built in the cloud and designed to be API-first (prioritizing interoperability in the software development). While Lyons had originally hoped that Simplify would be handed over to the emerging payments group and then the core products group, its transition was far from linear. The hope was that "the body would accept the organ," as Barta recalled, but "I presented this beautiful creature that we had built, and the [core business] said, 'Who wants this? What do we do with it? Did we buy this? Is this an acquisition?' It was very difficult to show the tie back into the core."

Lyons's team was encountering the very same problem Nicole Jones had worked so carefully to avoid at Delta: having a promising, innovative offering dismissed by its recipients because it strayed too far from the company's core activities. "There was a lot of skepticism," said Lyons. The other challenge was incompatible technology. Michael Miebach, the head of the Middle East and Africa at the time, explained, "In the Labs, we had the coolest development tools and the coolest people to play around with them. But our network and our [core] tech infrastructure wasn't the coolest because it had grown up over fifty years. So solutions needed to jump from environment A to environment B."

The key learning, in Barta's words, was to "take the organization with you for the journey. Because if you do this on an island, or in a vacuum, you don't gain the buy-in." In the end, Simplify's product, technology, and marketing components were broken up and handed over to their respective homes in the core business. Lyons decided to send Barta along with it to make sure "that the tissue grafting actually took hold," in Barta's words.

By 2013, it was clear to Banga that Lyons had moved the needle on the development of digital products and services *and* something far more important in his estimation: culture. Lyons and Banga had agreed early on that measuring the impact of Labs would be crucial. While revenue and profits were not yet viable metrics, the innovation management function collected employee engagement metrics for each of its events. A group of employees, it found, applied to participate in every one of its competitions and sprints; as the number of Labs events increased, so did participation. Moreover, when surveyed, employees now ranked "innovation" the number one factor most important to Mastercard's future. "People were getting excited about innovation and working at Mastercard," said Lyons. Banga expanded Lyons's responsibilities as chief innovation officer to include digital transformation and digital payments.[5] (See figure 7-2.)

FIGURE 7-2

Mastercard's innovation metrics

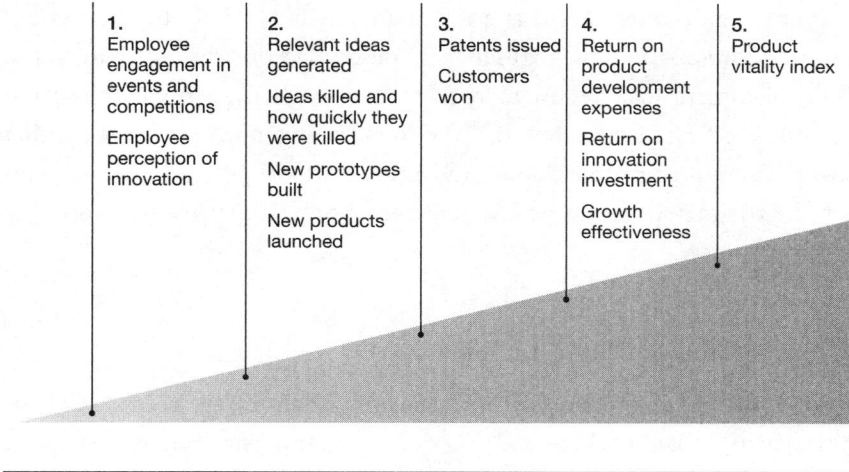

1.	2.	3.	4.	5.
Employee engagement in events and competitions	Relevant ideas generated	Patents issued	Return on product development expenses	Product vitality index
	Ideas killed and how quickly they were killed	Customers won		
Employee perception of innovation			Return on innovation investment	
	New prototypes built			
	New products launched		Growth effectiveness	

Deepening External Partnerships

By 2014, the payments industry was changing rapidly as smartphones and e-commerce became ubiquitous. With Labs' help, Mastercard too had begun to transform. All the experimentation with blockchain that Labs had done early on enabled the launch of Mastercard's digital enablement service—a tokenization engine that facilitated secure, digital transactions. A pivotal moment came in 2014 when this engine was selected to power both Apple Pay and Android Pay. McLaughlin reflected, "The real breakthrough there was, for all their capabilities, [Apple and Google] felt the best way to serve their customers' interests, and bring commerce onto their platform, was to use Mastercard technology as the underlying foundation." This deal made billions of devices compatible with Mastercard's network.

As Mastercard continued its digital innovation, Lyons and his colleagues observed that many of the financial institutions they relied on to distribute their new products and services weren't innovating at the same pace. The problem was Mastercard's business-to-business-to-consumer business model. Revenue depended on usage by end consumers, but

Mastercard did not interface with them directly. Thus, as much as the company innovated, one manager explained, "We were then stuck with the capacity of our partners to deliver."

Lyons began to see that this was a challenge his team of bridgers could help to address. At Labs' regular technology demonstrations, banks and other customers had begun to request help with their own innovation projects. At first, Lyons noted, "We kept saying no, because we didn't have thousands of people doing innovation at the time, and I didn't want us to be distracted. But it suddenly dawned on me that we were missing an opportunity."

Partnering with Customers: Labs as a Service

In 2014, Lyons collaborated with Mastercard Advisors, the company's consulting arm, to launch Labs as a Service—an immersive innovation sprint hosted at Labs' headquarters in Dublin. A member of the leadership team explained, "Because we were having success internally, because Labs worked for us, we made it an external product. . . . The idea of packaging innovation was something very novel at the time." Together with Lyons and his team, customers would cocreate a working prototype ready for user testing, a go-to-market plan, and a board-friendly video presentation in just five days.

The most frequent customers of Labs as a Service were senior leaders in legacy banks and financial institutions charged with digitally transforming their businesses. "These guys had tough, board-level responsibilities in the C-suite," one Mastercard leader remarked. "Labs as a Service helped them create the thinking on a regular basis." Lyons reported to the executive team that one client hired Labs for twenty engagements in a period of eighteen months: "Why is that interesting? Not because we were making a huge amount of money, but because it changed the conversation with that customer. Innovation was helping to move the needle with lots and lots of customers."

By providing innovation as a service, Labs not only helped Mastercard's ecosystem partners accelerate their digital transformations. Mastercard quickly came to be seen as bringing more value than its competitors when bidding for deals. Haythornthwaite described that when he would go meet with customers, "The first thing they said was, 'We had an amazing trip to Dublin.' . . . It became this extraordinary way of deepening our relationship with people."

Partnering with Startups: Start Path

Lyons believed Mastercard could learn more about emerging technology trends if Labs scaled and strengthened its relationships with startups, especially fintechs (who many incumbents saw as threats to the industry). Going beyond ad hoc investments, Lyons and his team launched an accelerator program within Labs called Start Path. The intention was to attract the best and brightest startups to Mastercard and convert select relationships into formal R&D partnerships.

To Lyons, Mastercard's value proposition to budding enterprises was clear. In addition to data and mentorship, joining Mastercard's network allowed startups to scale their offerings to more than 80 million merchants in 210 countries and territories.[6] At the same time, Lyons's own experience as an entrepreneur made him sensitive to startups' potential fears—ones we witnessed in Al Mazrouei's work in The Hive. He remarked:

> A big company that wants to work with a small company will generally throw in a legal team, a big NDA, a confidentiality agreement, and a fifty-page engagement contract. And the small company will be thinking, "They're coming to steal my IP." I understood that a big company could cripple you without meaning to.

Lyons made every effort to earn startups' trust and assure them that their relationship with Mastercard would be one of mutual influence and trust. Advocating on their behalf, Lyons convinced Mastercard's legal department to limit the Start Path contract to two pages. When interacting with entrepreneurs, he shared his own stories of building Orbiscom and why he chose to partner with Mastercard. Ultimately, he understood each startup's needs were different and asked explicitly how Mastercard could serve them: "Tell us the four things you want us to do," Lyons recounted.

Over time, Haythornthwaite explained that Start Path became a "very significant venturing operation. . . . We started seeing ourselves after a while as a magnet for what was happening in the industry." Lyons and his team even began brokering partnerships between the Start Path startups and Mastercard's core product teams when opportunities for cocreation arose. "We were the professional dot connectors," Barta noted. "It was about strategic value combining together."

To ease collaboration with startups and other external partners, however, Mastercard's approach to technology development had to become more open over time. Lyons and his team championed new internal policies and practices around APIs. They helped launch Mastercard Developers, a set of APIs and tools that allowed others to innovate in an integrated way with Mastercard's network. Eventually, Miebach noted, "The way we constructed products was API-first. It was a lot more transparent. It was a lot more modular. So, our ability to take something and plug it in somewhere else was much easier than before."

Bringing Innovation Closer to the Core

As Labs expanded its scope, Lyons made sure to continue involving his colleagues in strategic decisions. In time, he observed that his efforts to bring Mastercard closer to the startup community improved the company's ability to make acquisitions.

In 2015, the board and leadership team had a series of tough conversations before agreeing to purchase Applied Predictive Technologies, a provider of business analytics software to support Mastercard's foray into a new space. Less than a year later, in February 2016, Miebach, now Mastercard's chief product officer, went before the board proposing the acquisition of Vocalink, an automated payment-clearing firm. "We had one hour planned," Miebach recalled, and the decision to acquire was made in five minutes. "The last fifty-five minutes was about 'How could we do this [the acquisition] fast enough?' It was clear the board had also internalized the company's notion of thoughtful risk-taking, and it completely changed the conversation."

Mastercard's nearly $1 billion acquisition of Vocalink was its largest to date, and it aligned with the company's new strategy to provide consumers with more choice of *how* to pay (account-to-account, digital currencies, cards).[7] By acquiring Vocalink's infrastructure, Mastercard could expand the range of payment flows it facilitated in the short term, enabling it to innovate its core payments platforms at a less risky pace.

Meanwhile, to support this re-platforming, Banga and the board had decided to restructure Mastercard to better align the products, operations, and technology organizations. Lyons and other innovation champions were promoted to lead the effort. "It was incredibly organic," said Haythornthwaite. "The board spent a lot of time thinking about how to get the transfer through the organization through the movement of people."

In his new role, Lyons would lead both Labs and a new digital payments organization—to serve as the bridger who could, in his words, further integrate "the development and delivery of emerging digital payments solutions to ensure a high-quality consumer and merchant experience." But at the same time, Lyons expressed to Banga that this would be his final chapter at Mastercard. "I had to scratch an entrepreneurial itch again. I certainly wouldn't have left other than that," said Lyons. He was proud of the company's progress on its culture and in the marketplace, but it was time for him to return to his roots.

Passing the Baton

By 2018, Garry Lyons had stepped down as Mastercard's chief innovation officer to launch Shipyard Technology Ventures, a venture-building company that helped large corporations create ready-for-scale products and services. Banga asked Lyons to continue to consult for Mastercard, Shipyard's anchor investor. It was an unusual arrangement, Banga recalled: "People thought I was mad, but I wanted more people to do that. Having more friends on the outside creating and innovating was part of our whole approach to innovation."

Before leaving, Lyons had many thoughtful discussions with the executive team about the future of Labs. As Miebach recounted, "Labs needed to be a source of innovation. It needed to be a cultural driver, but at the same time, it couldn't be the answer that every idea only came out of Labs." Lyons had carefully considered the type of bridger needed to tie Labs more closely to the core business. He passed the baton to Ken

Moore, executive vice president of Labs and self-identified "practical innovator." Moore had founded Citibank's first innovation lab in 2009 and grown it into a global network of collaborative centers. "I did innovation in a corporate bank at a time when nobody cared about innovation," Moore described. "Had I taken moonshots at everything and had everything been a four- or five-year bet out into the future, we would have been dead. Instead, we took a balanced, results-oriented approach."

When Moore first joined Mastercard in 2016, he said, "[Labs] was seen as edgy." In his first year, Moore had helped Lyons expand Labs to several sites across the globe and build out a network of Tech Hubs. Although separate from Mastercard's main offices, these hubs were convening places where engineers from the core business could experiment together with customers and the Labs team. They were sleek, modern workspaces equipped with the latest digital tools, and they accelerated Mastercard's ability to attract top talent. "We were becoming more and more known as a place that you would want to come versus the Facebooks and the Googles," said Ron Garrow, Mastercard's chief human resources officer at the time. Haythornthwaite added, "We started being able to recruit whoever we wanted. . . . We were getting 500,000 CVs a year for 3,000 open posts."

Moore understood that Lyons had originally built Labs to awaken employees' and customers' sense of imagination. Labs was "exactly what it needed to be at that point in time," he reflected. But Mastercard had now begun to "look and feel" quite different: "We started to think of ourselves as a technology company in commerce." In Moore's view, Labs' role was no longer simply to "inspire the company to a different tomorrow, but to execute on that tomorrow as well."

Bringing Labs Closer to the Core

One of Moore's first moves as the new executive vice president of innovation was to reframe Labs' strategy to facilitate closer collaboration with the core business. The company was consolidating its core products, digital payments, Labs, and processing activities under Miebach, chief product officer at the time. Labs' new identity, Moore explained, would center on executing and scaling new solutions as a de-risking service for the core products organizations. To deliver, he would align Labs' operating model more closely to that of the core business and introduce a more disciplined approach to risk management.

Moore restructured Labs around vertical and horizontal innovation portfolios, which were defined in partnership with the products organization and mapped directly onto its goals. In addition to specifying technological priorities, these portfolios outlined short-, mid-, and long-term horizons for innovation, which allowed Labs to be responsive to the business's needs over time. For example, if the company needed to find short-term revenues, Labs directed its resources toward projects with short-term yields.

Moore also formalized a shared process for innovating with the core business called "the funnel." Ideas entered the funnel only if an executive sponsor inside the core product organization vouched for it. Labs led the initial research, concept, and prototyping phases, but as projects progressed toward market testing and commercialization, management responsibility shifted to the core business. To build a sense of shared urgency and commitment, Moore implemented a new guideline that prototypes had to be tested in the marketplace within eight weeks of entering the funnel. In cases where the core product team did not have the resources or capacity to absorb and commercialize a solution, it became best practice to "[graft] people to go with it so some of the tribal knowledge could be embedded into the individual product team," said one leader.

Over time, Moore also developed and introduced a risk assessment framework—DFV (desirability, feasibility, viability)—to help Labs and the core business jointly determine if innovations should enter the funnel. First, they defined an innovation's *desirability* in relation to the relevant pain point for customers: How tangible was the pain, and how many customers felt it? Next, they defined *feasibility* in terms of the various channels by which they could pursue a solution—whether through acquisition, partnership, or internal development—and the practicality of each. Last, they defined *viability* in terms of the link between Mastercard's business rationale and the value-add for customers: Did the value proposition to customers fit with Mastercard's overall business model?

With DFV, Moore aimed to help both his team and those in the core business think holistically about the contingencies surrounding an innovation and its implementation. "People often used 'prototype' to refer only to technology," he said. "I didn't believe in that. We needed to prototype all three lenses." Moore and his colleagues were pleased to see that "DFV risk" quickly became part of Mastercard's innovation vocabulary. "We became much more mindful of the fact that the go-to-market was more important than even the idea," an executive observed.

By establishing shared goals, language, and processes, Moore helped shorten the bridge between Labs and the core business—preparing it to absorb not only new products but entirely new ways of working. In 2019, after years spent upgrading its technology stack, the products group adopted the Labs' funnel methodology as its standard operating model, naming it "Mastercard Studio." Anyone could submit an idea to the products organization through the studio, and then agile squads would guide it through the entire product development life cycle—from prototyping to commercialization—just as Labs had formerly done. "There was a growing-up aspect we needed to learn as part of our Labs journey," Miebach remarked. "Labs codified agile, lean-startup-type thinking into Mastercard's way of working." Soon, Mastercard Studio would allow dozens of Labs prototypes to transition seamlessly into the core business for commercialization each year.

From Building Partnerships to Catalyzing Ecosystems

By 2019, Moore and his colleagues recognized that the rise of open banking, central bank digital currencies, cryptocurrencies, and other financial services and technologies was fundamentally transforming their industry. In this new world of payments, "you partner or die," said Linda Kirkpatrick, Mastercard's president for the Americas. "[None] of us, if we operated in a vacuum, could succeed in the world that we were living in. . . . Smartly partnering was absolutely the name of the game."

In this new context, Moore began to feel his leadership role at Mastercard was expanding. He increasingly felt the need to not only build bridges across boundaries but to be a catalyst of innovation at the ecosystem level—sparking opportunities for multiparty cocreation at scale. His colleagues on the leadership team agreed: "Everybody had a little piece of the pie that they could contribute to make one plus one equal three," said

Kirkpatrick. Mastercard's executives also appreciated that this would require a more systemic approach to innovation. "It takes more creative thinking," reflected Jessica Turner, global head of open banking and API. "How would this innovation affect this person, this person, and this person in the ecosystem? Why would all these other parties want to participate in [innovation]? What's in it for them?"

Moore decided to scale Labs as a Service through several of Mastercard's business units, including its growing Data and Services group. It quickly became "one of the most sought-after of all of our services" at the company, he said. Through these engagements, Moore observed that many merchants, corporations, and banks continued to struggle to keep up with new nimble, more risk-tolerant competitors. So, he and his team added a brokering service, Mastercard Engage, to their Start Path accelerator, where they matched startups with Mastercard clients who were eager to innovate with more speed. "Rather than seeking to disintermediate us, [fintechs] were increasingly looking to us to be a partner," remarked one leader. As Labs became a convening force over time, Moore and his team began orchestrating more complex R&D networks across broader sets of partners, including Microsoft, IBM, and Verizon. One initiative sought to bring 5G technology to the global payments network.

By 2020, when Covid-19 hit, Labs was prepared to innovate systematically with internal stakeholders and a whole slew of new digital-first partners (e.g., Stripe, Square, and PayPal) to accelerate the adoption of digital payments. In the first quarter of 2020, Mastercard processed more transactions through digital channels than plastic cards, painting a picture of how quickly consumers were adopting contactless payment.[8] By mid-2020, Mastercard even made a major acquisition to expand the company's role in the fast-growing open-banking world. By then, acquisitions had become a "one-meeting decision" for the leadership team, according to Haythornthwaite. "That would never have happened in my view if we had not created the culture and the confidence, via Labs, and in turn, really built up the confidence at the board that we knew what we were talking about."

By the time Michael Miebach became Mastercard's new CEO in January 2021, taking the reins from Banga, Moore's team had earned a reputation for getting results.[9] Labs as a Service had executed 430 engagements with 230 clients across industries. Start Path had been selected as the

World's Best Corporate Accelerator. Ten innovative products had been transitioned and integrated into the core businesses per year on average and fifty-four new products and services were being developed.

Amid these material successes, Moore, who had been promoted to chief innovation officer in January 2021, said that he and the leadership team "didn't even think that the name 'Labs' was appropriate . . . anymore." Together, they decided to rename Labs "Mastercard Foundry." As Moore explained, "When you think of a metal foundry, you think of the smelting of metals—a destructive yet creative process where something old is broken down and something new is created, and an assembly line of products comes out at the other side." Labs, now the Foundry, had transformed Mastercard into an "engine for digitization" along the way, said McLaughlin. "If it's Amazon and e-commerce, Apple and digital media goods, Uber and mobility, all of those innovations were powered by our commercialization. . . . In the shift to digital, we became the essential ingredient that allowed all of this innovation to be unleashed."

Lessons from a Decade of Bridging

Why are some innovation labs and corporate accelerators able to deliver when others cannot? Because they have the right kind of leadership—bridgers like Nicole Jones, Raja Al Mazrouei, Garry Lyons, and Ken Moore who build quality relationships across organizational boundaries and, in doing so, forge paths between the present and future.

Similar to the APIs that allow different technical systems to communicate and work together, bridgers are the "social APIs" in organizations who build the social connections necessary for people to innovate across boundaries. In tracing Lyons's and Moore's roles over ten years, we see that the work of bridgers is deeply contextual. Just as technical APIs must be upgraded as systems evolve, bridgers' efforts to curate, translate, and integrate must constantly adapt to the changing needs and capabilities of the partners they connect.

Starting in 2010, Lyons's focus was inspiring Mastercard's employees, customers, and investors with the possibilities of tomorrow. While he built relationships externally, he and his team spent much of their time priming internal stakeholders to embrace ideas, tools, and methods from the outside. They translated the opportunities of technology into language that resonated with their colleagues and created engagement programs that fostered participation and ownership in innovation. Later in his tenure, Lyons also established channels—Labs as a Service and Start Path—to interact and build trust with customers and startups in new ways.

By laying the groundwork for Mastercard colleagues and external stakeholders to cocreate, Lyons enabled Moore to then introduce shared rhetoric, tools, and processes that allowed for more integrated innovation across boundaries. Labs and the core product organization learned to innovate "hand in glove," as one leader described, systematically turning concepts into full-scale commercial solutions. When the core products business fully absorbed Labs' operating model, cocreation between the two groups, external customers, and partners became more efficient and effective. This integration came just in time for the Covid-19 pandemic, when demand for rapid digital innovation exploded.

Over ten years, Lyons and Moore built the connective tissue for diverse parties inside and outside Mastercard to realize the future of payments. Bridging took time, effort, and deep respect for the needs of the legacy organization and its partners, but these future-thinking leaders ultimately helped transform Mastercard into an innovative machine. Before long, Moore recast his own leadership role to reflect the company's growing ambition. The purpose of Mastercard Foundry became driving innovation across the broader payments sector—a global ecosystem of over a hundred million merchants and tens of thousands of banks.[10]

Like Moore, the leaders who would shape Mastercard's future would be those who could "stitch partnerships and ecosystems together," as one executive put it—a talent quickly becoming indispensable to compete in an ever more dynamic global economy. We call these leaders *catalysts*.

THE CATALYST

PART THREE

CATALYST

Building Movements

What if your ambition requires mobilizing stakeholders across an industry, sector, nation, or even the globe to innovate? To drive genius at this scale, it's not enough for leaders to shape culture and capabilities in-house or to build partnerships to the outside. Audacious business and societal challenges demand *catalysts*—leaders who drive innovation at the ecosystem level.

Catalysts galvanize and nurture strategic movements to harness the genius of those far beyond their immediate reach, often several degrees removed. They activate innovation in key stakeholders close to them and empower those stakeholders to carry that energy forward and invite others to join the movement.[1] While catalysts frame collective possibilities and encourage multiparty cocreation, they are masters of letting go. They do not impose collective agendas; they create the conditions for them to emerge. Catalysts share not only the learning and value created with all involved, but also the sense of progress and possibility that fuels the movement's forward momentum.[2] As our stories in part III will show, the best test of a catalyst leader is whether the movement is sustained without them.

Catalysts build movements through three interrelated functions: *mapping*, *seeding*, and *cultivating*. As explorers forging new paths, catalysts begin by *mapping* their ecosystem's complex social terrain and locating themselves within it. Leveraging their personal networks and actively building new ones, they ask: What are the contours of the problem I hope to solve? Who are the key stakeholders? Where are these stakeholders? What relationships—and power dynamics—shape their interactions? What are the barriers to cocreation, and what are the facilitators? Catalysts are deeply aware that their organizational resources are limited relative to the scale of their ambitions. Mapping helps focus their time and attention to maximize impact.

Catalysts activate movements by *seeding* opportunities for others across their ecosystem to innovate. Seeds are tangible interventions designed to inspire and invite stakeholders to participate. A seed could be almost anything: an idea, a technology, or even an introduction to a new partner. Seeds make new possibilities for innovation visible and are stepping stones for action. They spark imagination, allowing stakeholders to think and work in ways, individually and with others, that they may not have thought possible before. Catalysts craft these opportunities deliberately so that in pursuing them, stakeholders advance their own local purpose *and* collective ambitions. They also place these seeds deliberately, leveraging the contextual intelligence gained from mapping to channel their energy where cascading effects are more likely to unfold.

But catalysts recognize that seeding opportunities for innovation is not enough; they also nurture them to increase the odds that they will bloom, a process we refer to as *cultivation*. Catalysts embed the technical and social support systems needed to help their seeds take root, including building digital capability and repairing dysfunctional stakeholder relationships so multiparty cocreation can emerge and endure. As collective action bears fruit, it encourages further participation, fueling the movement's momentum. Catalysts' ongoing mapping efforts allow them to monitor the pulse of their momentum, adapt their mindset and behavior to support its continued evolution, and identify new ways to accelerate cocreation across the ecosystem.

The previous chapters illustrated the architect's role through legacy companies and the bridger's through separate innovation units. For our catalysts, the common stage is entrepreneurship. All of our leaders are values-driven businesspeople, with some establishing social enterprises to improve our collective future. Each built a new team, company, or nonprofit to facilitate their movement-building efforts.[3] They devoted significant time and attention to developing high-energy change agents in their organizations—who could then activate others in the ecosystem. Once again, we'll see our leaders harness the power of digital technologies to foster and sustain these catalytic interactions at scale.

CHAPTER 8

Unleashing the Power of Movements

Akira Fukabori and Kevin Kajitani at avatarin

> *We are creating an avatar movement, but it is not our concept.*
> *[It] is a shared concept that everybody has ownership of. We are*
> *always thinking about what the win is for society and for every*
> *player involved. It's a novel way of doing business.*

—**Akira Fukabori and Kevin Kajitani, cofounders of avatarin**[1]

In 2016, Akira Fukabori and Kevin Kajitani—two young aeronautical engineers at All Nippon Airways (ANA)—stumbled upon a baffling statistic.[2] In an age of accelerating globalization and digital connectivity, how was it that only 6 percent of the world's population flew on commercial airplanes each year?[3] As they dove into the data, they realized the other 94 percent represented a major new customer segment for the ANA of tomorrow. It was also a "grand challenge" in their eyes that, if solved, could impact billions of lives.

Based in Japan, the robotics capital of the world, Fukabori and Kajitani began imagining a future in which ANA provided "an alternative mode of travel" to billions of underserved people. It was a new type of global infrastructure consisting of general-purpose robots (avatars) that facilitated the two-way transfer of sight, sound, taste, touch, and smell over the internet. Using a sharing economy model like Uber's and Airbnb's, individuals across the globe could rent and remotely embody these robots for a wide range of tasks, even missions, in distant physical environments. Defusing a bomb, performing life-saving surgery, exploring the old town of Barcelona, preparing meals for the elderly in their homes—when it came to use cases for avatars, "the limit was one's imagination," said Kajitani.

As for the limits of Fukabori's and Kajitani's imaginations, there were none: their initial intention was to pursue actual physical teleportation. But after consulting dozens of quantum physicists across the globe, they learned, disappointingly, that the technology was at least 150 years away. In one discussion, however, a physicist helped reframe the opportunity, pointing out that people had been using telephones, the internet, and video conferencing to figuratively "teleport" themselves for decades. "So we started with that," Fukabori said. "We came up with the idea to teleport human consciousness and skills rather than bodies." To many, that still sounded like science fiction.

Fukabori and Kajitani recognized that neither they, nor the entirety of ANA, had the talent and technologies to turn this dream into reality. What they and their organization did have, however, was an appreciation for systems thinking and managing complex logistics: how to bring together disparate tasks from different organizations into a safe, high-quality travel experience that no single organization could deliver on its own. Like an airline, a new industry of avatar-enabled mobility would depend on numerous stakeholders innovating and playing their part. It would require highly specialized expertise in a wide range of advanced emerging technologies: haptic sensors, artificial intelligence, robotics, cloud, and telecommunications (among others).[4] Some of these capabilities were distributed across startups, corporations, and universities around the globe, while others didn't yet exist.

Led by Purpose, Not Position

Fukabori and Kajitani, both of Japanese descent, grew up on opposite sides of the Pacific Ocean (Tokyo and Seattle, respectively), but each discovered early in life a passion for solving global problems. As boys, they both attended Montessori schools, where they were encouraged to act on their curiosity and entrepreneurial impulses. Fukabori launched recycling programs for milk cartons and chopsticks in grade school and, as a teenager, built an online platform to connect nongovernmental organizations with social entrepreneurs. Kajitani founded his own startup early in his career, before landing his first engineering job at Boeing.

Fukabori, also an engineer, joined ANA because he admired its entrepreneurial history and hoped the company would provide him with opportunities to impact society. After all, within just three decades after World War II, ANA grew from a startup with two helicopters into a massive international airline. Although Fukabori enjoyed his engineering work, he devoted his evenings to designing Blue Wing—a program he hoped to launch at ANA that would subsidize airfare for social entrepreneurs and nonprofits. Energized by the concept, Fukabori talked about it to anyone who would listen. But after years of pitching, Blue Wing still hadn't won any leadership support. In Kajitani, he found a sympathetic listener.

The two met for the first time in 2010, while working on the Boeing 787 Dreamliner project. Kajitani was new to Tokyo and ANA, and they quickly bonded over their mutual fascination with space and questions about "life's bigger purpose," as they put it. "At heart," Fukabori recalled, "we shared values that motivated us to launch programs to drive global action."

In the spring of 2011, a 9.1 magnitude earthquake and tsunami struck Japan, leaving almost twenty thousand people dead.[5] In the wake of that unspeakable disaster, Fukabori observed that Japanese corporations were exhibiting a reinvigorated interest in addressing social causes. He wondered whether this was a window of opportunity in which ANA's executives might be more receptive to a proposal like Blue Wing. Fukabori began researching tactics of social movement organizers and decided he would zero in on people at ANA who believed in the idea, regardless of where they stood in the organizational hierarchy. This initial coalition of the willing, he hoped, would generate a groundswell of support that might convince ANA's executives to give Blue Wing a chance.

Fukabori tapped into an after-hours, employee-led innovation program at ANA and recruited twenty-six volunteers to the cause—the first of whom was Kajitani. The two then traveled to ANA headquarters and began knocking on the doors of company marketing leaders. The prospect was daunting, Kajitani recalled: "There was this rift between headquarters and the airport where we were located. We had different ID badge lanyards, and people saw us and thought, 'You don't know anything about headquarters or marketing.'"

Their tenacity soon caught the attention of Shinya Katanozaka, ANA's senior executive VP of marketing and sales at the time. Instead of leading with a social impact argument, Fukabori and Kajitani pitched Blue Wing as an opportunity to expand ANA's global brand awareness. They already had a team working on the idea, they explained; all they needed was startup capital to develop a proof of concept. Katanozaka had been on the lookout for entrepreneurial talent that could "break down walls" at ANA. He decided to allocate a modest budget for the team to pilot Blue Wing. "Akira was a young man working in operations," he explained, "and he came to me suddenly with a proposal. He very passionately described Blue Wing and . . . how he wanted to spread and enhance the value of ANA globally. This was very refreshing."

After many after-hours meetings with their volunteers, and with Katanozaka's continued support, Fukabori and Kajitani turned Blue Wing into a full-fledged marketing program within ANA. The duo were rewarded for their efforts with promotions to the company's corporate marketing team—a move that was practically unheard-of for ANA engineers. Fukabori would run Blue Wing full-time on the promotion and advertising team, while Kajitani was transferred to the database marketing and AI forecasting team. As luck would have it, their new desks were right next to each other.

From Side Gigs to Moonshots

After learning how to attract the volunteers and resources needed to implement a new initiative within ANA's corporate labyrinth, Fukabori and Kajitani set their sights on their next project: to launch a crowdfunding platform at ANA to help "reinvigorate innovation in Japan," as they put it. Over dinner in early 2016, they identified all the ways the Japanese market discouraged the startup impulse and mapped out what ANA could offer—funding, sales channels, and distribution support. The next day, with the same approach they used in championing Blue Wing, they began putting themselves on executives' calendars to pitch their crowdfunding platform, which they came to call WonderFLY. "I was very surprised when these two young people just made an appointment in my Google Calendar to propose something," said Yoshiaki Tsuda, ANA's head of corporate strategy. "I chose to support them because of their passion, rather than the business model itself."

Shortly thereafter, in a conversation with Tsuda and Katanozaka (who by then was CEO), Fukabori and Kajitani learned of ANA's plans to launch a new innovation department, the Digital Design Lab. The two immediately asked to be transferred to the lab to work on crowdfunding. Kajitani was allowed to transfer and dedicate himself full-time to the initiative, but Fukabori's request was denied.

Fukabori kept his eyes open for other ways besides crowdfunding to drive impact. Through a serendipitous ANA marketing event, he learned that the US nonprofit, XPRIZE Foundation, was hosting a first-ever summit: companies would compete for the opportunity to choose and sponsor their next moonshot technology prize. Fukabori didn't hesitate; he knew he wanted to participate on behalf of ANA, and he brought Kajitani in on the plan.

The duo knew the competition would be a hard sell to ANA's leadership. They would need to persuade their bosses to allow them to take three months off from their day jobs—and pay a six-figure entry fee. "When you're in a big company," Fukabori explained, "you're asked to create new business, not to create big solutions to tackle global agendas." Still, the two were undeterred. They'd already learned to frame bold, far-fetched ideas in terms of short-term wins, and they had earned credibility with key company executives like Katanozaka and Tsuda. When they pitched the XPRIZE to Tsuda and the deputy director of human resources, they framed it as a matchless opportunity for global brand-building (a win for marketing) and talent development (justification for HR).

To their surprise, they won over both Tsuda and HR. Right then and there, Kajitani recalled, "I blurted out, 'Thank you so much for this opportunity. We're going to win this prize.'" Now they just needed to figure out what ANA's XPRIZE entry should be.

A Winning Idea

After three months of consulting with physicists, technologists, and engineers worldwide, the two leaders and their team of XPRIZE advisers landed on a moonshot technology: avatar robots through which humans could teleport their five senses over the internet. At the October 2016 XPRIZE Visioneering Summit in Los Angeles, the ANA Avatar team introduced this technology as the pathway to "perfect mobility for 7.5 billion people." David Locke, XPRIZE executive director of prize operations, was struck by the presentation: "It was very brave for a conservative Japanese airline to propose a prize that would disrupt not only their business model, but potentially their entire industry."

But the audience didn't share Locke's enthusiasm—not at first. At the end of the first round of voting, Fukabori and Kajitani's idea was ranked last against eight other teams. Not easily discouraged, the duo was determined to change their fortunes. They decided to keep their information booth open until 3:00 a.m. each night of the summit. They spoke to every visitor who was willing to listen, one-on-one, figuring out how to make their avatar vision tangible and personal. Visitors from the healthcare sector learned, in vivid detail, how avatars could allow surgeons to operate on patients ten thousand miles away. Academics listened to the two men explain how a single robot could connect a remote community to the world's best educational institutions. Scientists understood that previously unexplorable aspects of the sea or outer space could be studied with avatars—and all this could be done without disturbing local cultures and environments.

By the end of the summit, Fukabori and Kajitani had managed to unleash attendees' imagination and convert the nonbelievers. ANA won the chance to sponsor the next XPRIZE! As excited as they were, Fukabori and Kajitani had little time to celebrate—their crowdfunding initiative WonderFLY was due to go live the next day. Meanwhile, Tsuda, who was also in the audience, hadn't considered the possibility that Fukabori and Kajitani might win. That night, he boarded a 1:00 a.m. flight back to Tokyo with no expectation of sleeping: he needed to prepare a pitch to convince Katanozaka that ANA should fund the $22 million competition.

Back at ANA headquarters, when Tsuda announced the victory, Katanozaka recalled:

> I felt like saying congratulations. But then . . . I began to think—this meant they needed a budget. . . . At that time, it was unknown what this would become, but I did feel that there was a big potential there. When I was a child, I was passionately interested in the idea of time machines, so the concept of teleportation was something that I could relate to strongly.

Convincing a Japanese board to invest in a California technology competition was another story, and Katanozaka insisted that Fukabori and Kajitani should make the pitch themselves. They were a charismatic pair, and with Blue Wing and WonderFLY, they'd earned a degree of credibility with the board. "Individually," said Katanozaka, "Akira and Kevin had strong capabilities, but it was like 0.1 as individuals. . . . When they were together, their capabilities were 10."

Fukabori recounted that the board "knew who we were and actually cared about what we said. But we were two guys coming to talk to them about a teleportation business. Naturally, they laughed at us. Others worried about cannibalizing the airline." Winning the XPRIZE summit, the two argued, had already earned ANA $9 million in media coverage in the United States—nearly half the cost of the prize. Moreover, a partnership with the globally renowned XPRIZE could be an unparalleled opportunity to reinvigorate the airline's identity as an innovator. In the end, Fukabori and Kajitani managed to win over the decision-makers yet again. Although ANA's contract negotiations with XPRIZE would take months, the two men began immediately charting a path toward the avatar future.

Mapping the Avatar Landscape

After the summit, invitations to conferences and meetings began pouring in. Fukabori and Kajitani accepted every opportunity to spread the word about avatars and the future of mobility. They delved into technical challenges with academics and explored partnerships with telerobotics startups. With every interaction, they gained greater clarity of the state of the technology and the points where innovation was most needed. And they did all of this on top of their day jobs.

At the end of 2017, just as the XPRIZE contract was being finalized, HR allowed Fukabori to join Kajitani in the Digital Design Lab; the two were now authorized to dedicate themselves full-time to their avatar project. The team at XPRIZE was elated. "When I found out that I'd be working with Kevin and Akira, it was a dream come true," Locke recalled. "These two very young guys were the change agents who disrupted the conservative culture at ANA to bring the program together."

But Fukabori, impatient by nature, now believed that "sponsoring an XPRIZE was not enough." After all, technology competitions tended to produce "museum pieces" that "wouldn't see the light of day," he said. Prizes alone couldn't guarantee a market for the technologies, nor could they ensure that the cost of components wouldn't be prohibitive for future innovation. Determined to avoid this fate, Fukabori and Kajitani decided they could do more as leaders to increase the chances that the ANA XPRIZE would improve billions of lives within a reasonable time frame.

In the short term, they would accelerate the development of an avatar service industry—to catalyze an "avatar movement," as they put it—and create a runway for the XPRIZE technology to land. To build future demand for avatar services, they would raise public awareness and educate users about the technology and its use cases. Simultaneously, they would employ this user demand to boost the supply of avatars outside of the XPRIZE. They would encourage corporations, universities, and other investors to fund research and development, increase the scale of production, and thus decrease the cost of components. Finally, they would work proactively with the government to shape a regulatory framework to maximize use cases and safeguard the long-term viability of the technology.

Meanwhile, Fukabori and Kajitani knew they needed to create a digital platform to integrate these various pieces and facilitate avatar services over the internet. To reach a billion people, the platform would have to prioritize accessibility. Any robot in their network should be able to interface with their software, hardware, cloud, telecommunications, and machine learning technology, and any user should be able to connect to the avatars, no matter the strength of their internet connection. To facilitate the real-time, virtual transfer of human senses, the biggest challenge would be to innovate a new type of internet infrastructure—one that could transmit, download, and store significantly greater volumes of data than even Google could.

It quickly became clear to Fukabori and Kajitani that they were embarking on a business journey that couldn't live forever inside ANA. The technical and human problems they faced couldn't be surmounted by them alone, not even with strong backing from the airline. Their initiative would eventually need to spin out and become an independent startup. They decided to give themselves until autumn 2022—the conclusion of the ANA XPRIZE competition—to launch their platform business, which they began calling "avatarin."

Fukabori and Kajitani knew they were taking on a leadership challenge unlike any they'd faced before. Though they may not have known it at the time, there's no question that the duo was beginning to think and act like *catalysts*. They knew they'd have to find ways to convince myriad actors to play their part in cocreating the avatar future. It would require a whole new business paradigm: avatarin would not serve as a gatekeeper to the emerging avatar ecosystem, optimizing for its own value capture; rather, it would foster and sustain innovation by sharing value with others. As Kajitani explained:

> It would be arrogant for any single organization to think that the people right in front of them were the only ones who could solve certain problems. In today's world, it was about network[ing] to find the right people to solve [a] problem and making sure that there was a benefit for everybody involved.

To increase their odds of success, the duo decided they would meet, talk, and work with anyone interested in their vision of an avatar future—whether they be a technologist, researcher, local government official, or small business owner. They would embrace people with diverse ideas and motivations, help each understand how they could contribute, and bring them along on the journey.

Seeding an Avatar Movement

Just as they'd done with Blue Wing and WonderFLY, Fukabori and Kajitani formalized their project, calling it "ANA Avatar," and recruited thirty-seven spirited volunteers from across the company to develop it. The two leaders intuitively understood a key aspect of the catalyst's job: giving people space to pursue their priorities. "The limits of the possibilities were yet to be defined," said Kajitani, "and we didn't want to limit ourselves to what we already knew." They invited their team to begin brainstorming avatar use cases and contacting organizations for field tests. ANA's brand helped them secure meetings with companies, though "many struggled to understand the concept at first," one volunteer noted; "they thought avatars were the same as teleconferencing systems." Fukabori and Kajitani didn't limit their outreach to the commercial sector. To their surprise, cultural institutions like museums and aquariums were the most receptive and willing to experiment with avatars at the outset.

Turning Competitors into Collaborators

With the official launch of the ANA Avatar XPRIZE planned for March 2018, Fukabori and Kajitani had to move quickly to attract top technologists to their movement. Until then, most robotics R&D was focused on creating autonomous robots that performed specialized functions, such as painting an auto part or opening a door. In contrast, the ANA XPRIZE would convene hundreds of teams from across the globe to innovate tele-operable, general-purpose avatar technology—which posed a slew of technical challenges.

Although XPRIZE teams normally saw one another as competitors, Fukabori, Kajitani, and XPRIZE executive Locke agreed they would have to get the teams to combine their specialized expertise—to cocreate—if they hoped to produce a viable general-purpose avatar by the end of the competition. Together they designed "team pitch" events to encourage startups specialized in virtual reality and sensor and haptic technology, among others, to network and come together organically. Though it wasn't customary for sponsors to participate in XPRIZE events, Fukabori and

Kajitani showed up at the team pitches regularly, to motivate the teams face-to-face and instill hope that there would one day be a market for their innovation. They presented the latest updates of their avatar platform, use cases they were discovering, and general trends they were tracking in relevant technology. These efforts, Locke observed, encouraged "new ideas to start hatching" across teams in ways he had never seen before with XPRIZE.

Making Long-Term Goals Tangible Today

Fukabori and Kajitani believed that major Japanese corporations such as ANA would one day play important roles in the avatar ecosystem—not only providing R&D investment and large-scale robot manufacturing but also ensuring demand for avatar services in the long term. But when they met with big companies, they found most were unwilling to make investments in noncore business opportunities with no immediate payoff.

In a chance run-in at a conference, an official from the Japan Aerospace Exploration Agency (JAXA), Naoko Sugita, told Fukabori and Kajitani that she'd seen that same corporate risk-aversion before. It had stifled Japan's efforts to build a commercial space industry for years. Sugita had been charged with launching a new public–private partnership focused on developing space technologies that would have near-term business applications. When she learned of the avatar concept, she said, "It was love at first sight." Fukabori and Kajitani had been deeply investigating avatar applications in the space industry: avatars, they explained to Sugita, could help JAXA and its industry partners thread the needle between long-term investments in space and short-term applications on Earth. "If a robot worked in space," Fukabori said, "it could work in radioactive areas, deep sea contexts, and other dangerous situations."

Just as the XPRIZE partnership had attracted startups and robotics experts to their movement, Fukabori and Kajitani thought a partnership with JAXA might attract Japanese corporations while also helping the government deliver on its new space agenda. In 2018, with executive support from Tsuda, the duo partnered with JAXA to convene an "Avatar X Space Consortium." Representatives from over thirty-one of the most influential Japanese companies would brainstorm business models and use cases for avatars on Earth and in space. By 2020, each participating company would have a tangible, personalized stepping stone to the future—a "road map to space"—which the companies could then choose to invest in. Fukabori explained the design choice: "We wanted to make sure that we were propelling the vision but also doing something concrete at the same time. This was a valuable learning from the XPRIZE Foundation. They taught me how to think humanity-scale big but to use existing technologies to prove that the vision was meaningful in the interim."

Testing Use Cases to Show the Art of the Possible

Meanwhile, to inspire the XPRIZE and Avatar X participants, Fukabori, and Kajitani, began working with government partners to test off-the-shelf avatar robots and use cases in the field. "The message we communicated to the government was, 'We can't do this as a single company, or even as a consortium of companies or an ecosystem,'" said Kajitani. Their appeal was heard by the governor of Oita Prefecture, on Kyushu Island. The working-age population was sinking faster in Oita than anywhere else in Japan; maintaining basic services was becoming an urgent problem. "We felt that AI and robotics could provide solutions to the challenges that would emerge," said one Oita official.

In their tests, Fukabori and Kajitani weren't surprised to see that both school-age children and the elderly gravitated to the technology. Unlike many Western countries where robots were often viewed as threats, robots were deeply embedded in Japanese culture and sensibility. The Japanese "understood that there were underlying societal issues that required autonomous systems and robots to help sustain society," Kajitani explained. As he and Fukabori observed the robot–human interactions, they reaffirmed their commitment to "a wildly human approach" to robotics, as they put it. They weren't interested in replacing humans with autonomous systems, but rather focused on tools that would, in Kajitani's words, "expand humanity": "When Akira and I imagined being an elderly person being cared for by sterile, white, autonomous robots, we started to question the meaning of life. . . . We already had the technology and the societal need. The missing element was the human factor."

One inspiring example was a field test in an Oita restaurant. Avatars bused tables and earned wages—all while being controlled remotely by bedbound amyotrophic lateral sclerosis (ALS) patients from their homes. Kajitani noted, "Avatars gave the ALS patients a new body to mobilize them, which also enabled them to reintegrate into society." Fukabori and Kajitani were energized when their field-test partners proposed new avatar use cases and business models that they couldn't have imagined, such as a fishing-pole avatar that enabled users to catch fish from their homes or offices. Not only could users feel the haptic feedback of the fish pulling on the line remotely, the next day, ANA shipped the fish to their doorstep. "It was like a new farm-to-table concept," Kajitani noted. "It was very user-generated and spontaneous—people were seeing new connections. It was reflective of the world we hoped to create."

As Fukabori and Kajitani gained a clearer view of the underlying data processing and deep learning infrastructure needed to power avatar user experiences, they became increasingly aware of the legal and ethical implications of their work—including potential unintended consequences. For example, if someone living in Tokyo is waiting tables in New York through an avatar, where do they owe taxes? And what about unethical actors? How could they be identified and removed from the platform? The two leaders began attending ethics and technology forums and sought open dialogues with regulators in different regions. They were always eager to respond to governments' requests to learn about their AI models and their approach to personal data protection. "We wanted to design our platform so that each individual would be the steward of their data," Fukabori emphasized. "That's the web that we wanted to create."

By the end of 2018, press coverage was mounting about ANA's avatar program. Katanozaka and Tsuda convinced the board it was time to move the project out of the Digital Design Lab and make it a stand-alone department. In another first for ANA, Fukabori and Kajitani became the first nonmanagerial staff ever to run a new department, complete with a full budget and five full-time employees.[6]

Cultivating the Avatar Movement

As their various streams of activities progressed, Fukabori and Kajitani learned that they needed to be deliberate about maintaining momentum across their budding avatar ecosystem. They started to always keep their passports with them; at a moment's notice, they would drop everything and fly to attend their partners' robot tests. Face-to-face interactions, Kajitani said, "helped with creating the movement, energy, and momentum, and maintaining the relationships over long distances."

Yet even with this regular interaction, some partners struggled to stay committed. As catalysts, Fukabori and Kajitani soon recognized that their partners would need to find their own drive. "Otherwise, the growth of the ecosystem was going to depend on how quickly we could scale, which should not be the case. We wanted to create an organically, constantly growing ecosystem," said Kajitani. Perhaps because the leaders expressed this intention, some partners simply stopped communicating with the two, which they came to accept as a kind of "natural selection."[7]

Maintaining the Avatar X Consortium's momentum required Fukabori and Kajitani to be more hands-on than expected. Once they had grouped the participating companies by industry, they had assumed the companies would be able to cocreate their road maps together. But many struggled to "commit to something where they weren't sure what the return on investment would be," said Kajitani. He, Fukabori, and their collaborators from JAXA actively facilitated weekly meetings of the companies and cultivated "tribal knowledge," as they put it, across participants to help enable collaboration.

When two competitors struggled to work together, Fukabori and Kajitani decided to split them into separate working groups and encourage each to pursue its own avatar road map. "We didn't want to box anybody in," Kajitani explained. "There wasn't only one vision for avatars in space, and we didn't want others to just follow ours. We wanted to make sure that everybody was actively creating their own vision." Finally, to inspire the consortium participants to be bolder in their ambitions, Fukabori and Kajitani led by example: they committed to installing an avatar on the International Space Station before the companies' road maps were due in 2020.

Through their various activities, Fukabori and Kajitani found themselves developing a bird's-eye view of the state of avatar technology. Startups had begun approaching them for strategic advice about which technological opportunities would help them gain market share, and shared challenges were becoming increasingly visible. The duo soon realized they were uniquely positioned to accelerate innovation at the industry level. It was time to move beyond raising awareness, Fukabori explained: "We needed to find the breakthrough points in the industry and put our money on the best minds to . . . bring the industry along."

Among the most pressing industry bottlenecks was tele-operable hand technology, which enabled a human to receive real-time haptic feedback from a robotic hand they controlled remotely (essentially enabling a remote sense of touch). In 2018, Fukabori and Kajitani contacted three leading startups in haptic gloves, sensors, and dexterous hand technology and offered to fund a collaboration among them. With 10 million yen (US$100,000) from ANA, Fukabori and Kajitani gave them the autonomy to organize the partnership. One of the entrepreneurs, who was initially skeptical of working with corporations, noted, "Akira and Kevin had a big-picture idea and were very open to how to accomplish it. They didn't know every step it would take to get there. They were really open to working with a lot of creative people who had ideas that worked toward that vision."

While Fukabori and Kajitani were careful not to infringe on the startups' autonomy, they found it wasn't always easy to let go when they were the ones making the investment. As one entrepreneur noted, "Trying to architect the relationship so it satisfied everyone's needs was pretty tricky. . . . At one point, I spoke up to Kevin and Akira and said, 'Guys, this is a team effort, not a you-guys' effort.' We had honest conversations about it, and we worked through it because we all cared about the vision."[8]

Fukabori and Kajitani took the lesson to heart and refocused on figuring out ways to help the startups work more effectively. They stayed in regular contact with the team, introduced them to others in their fast-growing network, and provided them with publicity and marketing opportunities. Another engineer involved in the partnership explained that Fukabori and Kajitani "wanted to get the best product possible without burdening us with restrictions on how to do it. That allowed us to come up with some really unique solutions."

Within two years, the startups had solved one of the long-standing issues in their industry: they delivered a bimanual hand system prototype, which they debuted at the 2019 Amazon Mars Conference. To Fukabori's and Kajitani's pleasant surprise, a video and GIF featuring Jeff Bezos using the hand system quickly went viral. It was successes like this that kept the XPRIZE teams and Avatar X Consortium energized, aligned, and hopeful about the avatar industry's future.

By mid-2019, Fukabori and Kajitani identified another glaring industry bottleneck. The lack of low-cost robots was delaying large-scale field testing of their avatarin platform. Until a cost-effective solution was available, the broad-based adoption of avatar technology would be limited, as would demand for avatar services. Although they feared that building their own robot might undermine trust from their many startup partners, Fukabori and Kajitani decided to develop and manufacture a simple, low-cost "tablet on wheels" called "newme." In one-on-one conversations, they carefully explained their decision to partners. They insisted that they were in a unique position within ANA where they didn't have the same strict budget and development timelines as other robotics startups. Ultimately, they stressed that this step was in service of the entire industry.

The Movement Accelerates

In October 2019, Fukabori, Kajitani, and the ANA Avatar team debuted their flagship robot newme at Japan's Combined Exhibition of Advanced Technologies trade show. Katanozaka delivered a keynote announcing that ANA's service platform, avatarin, would go live in April 2020: a thousand newme robots would be deployed to a hundred businesses, including ANA, which would begin offering avatar services.

Tens of thousands of attendees visited the avatarin booth, including government ministers and the leaders of Japan's biggest companies, and ANA walked away with a major award. In January 2020, the Japanese government launched a "Future Technology Fund," and avatar technology was selected from a pool of eighteen hundred ideas to receive $1 billion in R&D investment. "Japan finally got the picture," Kajitani reflected, "all of these things together were creating a snowballing type of effect."

As fate would have it, just as Covid-19 lockdowns began taking effect worldwide, the avatar movement took off. "We had been promoting and talking about avatars for the last four years," Kajitani recalled. "The

speed and breadth of the understanding and the mindset shift around
the technology caught us by surprise." While several planned newme
deployments were canceled, including some for the 2020 Olympics,
Fukabori and Kajitani pivoted to deploy avatars to hospitals, schools,
and other settings as needed. When one of their early test partners, the
owner of a small family-owned cake company, asked if avatarin could
urgently provide a newme robot for his elderly father who was hospital-
ized, Fukabori personally delivered the robot free of charge in his own
van the next day.

In April 2020, after months of negotiation with ANA's board, "avatarin, Inc." became an independent startup.[9] It was an unusual move for a
Japanese company and wouldn't have happened without continued support from Katanozaka and Tsuda. "If avatarin was a plant," said Katanozaka, "it was like the buds had just come out." He had no expectation of
profit, or even revenue, in the short term. But in his view, ANA's support
of Fukabori and Kajitani had already begun to pay off:

> I learned from Kevin and Akira . . . that if the top people can
> express the vision, then employees will be able to work on their
> own to create new business. As Kevin and Akira proceeded
> with their work as entrepreneurs, there would be many em-
> ployees of ANA who would want to follow in their footsteps.
> This would trigger further innovation and foster a culture of
> innovation within ANA, which I think would be most valu-
> able beyond anything else.

Many from Fukabori and Kajitani's original team of ANA volunteers
joined them at avatarin, along with a number of their long-standing
ecosystem collaborators. One of their academic partners explained that
he signed up because he was excited about the avatarin vision to "change
society from a technical *and* behavior perspective." One of their first
acts as co-CEOs of their new independent company was to articulate
their values—the twelve be's—that would guide their exhilarating but
arduous journey ahead: be human; be open; be bold; be friendly; be different; be fast; be healthy; be positive; be honest; be fair; be a team; be
the top.

Today, Fukabori and Kajitani are delivering on the promise they made to ANA's board back in 2016. In Haneda Airport, one of Tokyo's largest, you see travelers of all ages approaching avatarin robots, receiving customer service from remote ANA employees. Fukabori, Kajitani, and their partners at JAXA did install an avatar on the International Space Station by their May 2020 deadline and subsequently launched a "Space Avatar Project" to explore possibilities for avatar-enabled space travel, operational support for astronauts, and other experiences.[10] Even some of Japan's largest companies, including Mitsubishi, are now investing in avatarin's technology.[11] And as for the ANA Avatar XPRIZE—the springboard of this avatar movement—a German robotics company called NimbRo took the $5 million first-place prize, with teams from France and the United States following in second and third place.[12]

Though teleportation is still a few generations off, an avatar-connected world is already becoming a reality thanks to the catalytic leadership of two unassuming young idealists at ANA.[13]

Catalysts and the Power of Movement Building

The story of Akira Fukabori and Kevin Kajitani vividly illustrates that a leader doesn't need to be CEO to be a catalyst. This pair were values-driven engineers, determined to use ANA's platform to create a positive impact on the world. They were undeterred by their own lack of formal authority and resources. Instead, they dared to try; within just a few years, a global ecosystem of startups, technologists, corporates, nonprofits, and governments was actively innovating toward an avatar future. Above all, Fukabori's and Kajitani's insistence on cocreation, and bringing people along the journey, sets the tone for what it means to be a catalyst, as does their approach to technology. For them, technology was never an end in itself. It was a tool and strategic enabler, a means for achieving greater, human ends—together.

Fukabori and Kajitani teach us that leaders shouldn't shy away from bold, ambitious ideas, regardless of where they stand in the organizational hierarchy. Catalysts build movements that generate energy and momentum, attract believers, and leverage their slices of genius for large-scale collective outcomes. Essentially, their role is to initiate action—to get the snowball rolling—toward a future they can neither see nor begin to realize without enlisting the collective genius of others.

While Fukabori and Kajitani were quite deliberate about their movement-building efforts, they remained open to the possibility that innovative ideas could come from unexpected places. They started by articulating a purpose that was "big enough for everyone," as Fukabori likes to say. When a purpose is broad enough to resonate with diverse people, it can become a platform for others to contribute their personal passions and areas of expertise.

Movement building for Fukabori and Kajitani was *not* about telling people what to do or ignoring dissenters. Rather, it was about inspiring and mobilizing others to participate. Masterful storytellers, they brought their passion and energy to every conversation. They insisted on framing their ambitions in language that was local and personal to each stakeholder—be they the head of marketing or the board of ANA, a startup or their government partners at JAXA. They transformed inspiration into action by creating tangible opportunities for others to cocreate with them. They planted seeds for collective action through strategic investments and forums like the XPRIZE and JAXA consortium. They cultivated those seeds through continuous dialogue: by sharing learnings, celebrating partners' contributions, and—perhaps most importantly—connecting all stakeholders' individual priorities to their emergent global agenda.

Note that the journey of avatarin is a cross-generational story within ANA. None of it would have been possible had Katanozaka and Tsuda not trusted the two young engineers, and provided them with the support and protection to try something no one had done before—something that would be difficult to measure by typical KPIs. "We were young guys that nobody knew trying to do something inside a big corporation," Kajitani reflected, "We didn't have the experience, connections, or the ability to convince middle management to support us. Luckily, we had the cosign of upper levels of management."

What was clear to Fukabori and Kajitani when they first began their avatar journey is now clear to us all: an idea—if inclusive, inspiring, and relatable—can become a movement, and that movement can drive innovation at incredible scale and truly "expand humanity." As we've seen in this chapter, however, even when others in an ecosystem are *willing* to innovate toward a grand challenge, they might not yet be *able* to do so, given their own constraints. But here too, catalysts can help create the conditions for success. In the following chapters, we'll dig into each of the catalysts' movement-building functions—*mapping, seeding,* and *cultivating*—to understand how catalysts increase the odds of success.

CHAPTER 9

Mapping Uncharted Territory

Ndidi Okonkwo Nwuneli at African Food Changemakers

In traditional African communities, we get together and sit around in a circle. This is our heritage. Technology allows us to create those circles and to scale.

—Ndidi Okonkwo Nwuneli

Growing up in the Nigerian state of Enugu, Ndidi Okonkwo Nwuneli spent her childhood wandering through her neighborhood, picking fresh guavas, mangos, and avocados off the trees and sharing them with anyone and everyone in need.[1] "There was abundance for the whole community and beyond to enjoy," she recalled. But when Nwuneli moved to the United States at the age of sixteen, she discovered that others in the world had an image of the continent that was very different from the lush, bountiful garden she had known. To Western media and her peers in school, the face of Africa was a starving child.[2]

Nwuneli was not naive; she understood Africa's significant political and economic challenges. But she insisted that the West's narrative did not reflect the complete picture. Nor did it represent the enormous potential of Africa's people, who officially comprised the world's fastest-growing population.[3]

In her early twenties, after earning her BS from Wharton and MBA from Harvard, Nwuneli set out to change the global narrative of Africa—starting with the underlying problem of hunger. With no clear path to realize her ambition, she charted her own course—actively *mapping* the terrain she traversed to identify where to focus her limited resources to drive innovation and change.[4] At every turn, Nwuneli was guided by her personal values: a generous view of human beings, a deep sense of service, and a steadfast belief that "when you pull up one person, who pulls up another person, who pulls up another," as she put it, "it turns into a force." Only with time and experience would Nwuneli discover her role as a catalyst, helping entrepreneurs across the continent forge the path to Africa's future with her.

Mapping the African Agricultural Landscape

Early in her career, Nwuneli worked with McKinsey in the United States and Africa, where she came to understand the impact, both positive and negative, of multinational corporations on the African agricultural industry. As she gained an appreciation for Africa's position in global food and agriculture supply chains, she learned a startling fact: although Africa had 60 percent of the earth's arable land and grew much of the world's food, the continent still struggled to feed its own people.[5] "What was going wrong?" she wondered.

In 2002, Nwuneli returned to Nigeria full-time as the pioneer and executive director of the FATE Foundation—Nigeria's foremost business incubator and accelerator. For the first time, she worked hands-on with local businesses. "Many of these entrepreneurs struggled for survival in exceedingly difficult and often hostile environments," she observed. She heard countless stories of how impossible it was to find new, consistent sources of demand—let alone secure financing, build strong brands, develop a reliable supply chain, and identify and develop talent. Yet she found herself deeply inspired by the entrepreneurs' creativity and resilience. Rather than viewing them as victims who needed charity, she came to see these individuals as a talent pool that could be the source of radical transformation for Nigeria—and even Africa as a whole.

Still, in her conversations with the entrepreneurs, Nwuneli heard their discouragement after struggling—often for decades—to earn a livelihood. She also noticed a glaring gap in the entrepreneurial landscape: the absence of young people and women, who she knew could be pivotal in turning around Africa's agricultural future. Women in particular seemed to lack the confidence to found agribusinesses.

This mindset was familiar to Nwuneli, who had also lacked confidence as a young businesswoman. She remembered arriving in the United States feeling like a complete outsider, wondering what she had to contribute. But she recalled how some of her professors had encouraged her, helped transform her self-image, and build her confidence. "Instead of seeing a poor African student, they saw something in me," she said. Now her dream was to help spark that same confidence in other women and young people. She wanted to help them believe they could be part of a movement for change in Africa, and she made her next career choices with that intention in mind.

Nwuneli left the FATE Foundation to launch two nonprofits. The first, LEAP Africa (leadership, effectiveness, accountability, and professionalism), aimed "to inspire, empower, and equip a new cadre of principled, disciplined, and dynamic young leaders in Africa."[6] The second, Ndu Ike Akunuba (NIA), which translates to life, strength, and wealth, supported female university students in Nigeria. As the daughter of a professor, Nwuneli had an overarching strategy for both organizations: to use education to prepare the next generation of entrepreneurs to innovate on African solutions to African problems.

Establishing these organizations required Nwuneli to begin mapping out the landscape of relationships she needed to move forward. She began developing a broad set of partnerships with local businesses, the government, educational institutions, and civil society leaders. Reflecting on this process, she said:

> You don't have to be an extrovert. You just have to be someone who values people and doesn't see relationships as transactions. . . . That's the secret sauce. You're not thinking about how this person is going to help me—but this person is a human [who has] value. I see them, they see me. What values do we share in common, and how can I cultivate a genuine relationship?

As Nwuneli's networks grew, so did her personal reputation in Nigeria as a leader with integrity, purpose, and humility. At the same time, her diverse interactions helped her gain a more holistic view of the problems in African agriculture. She observed that smallholder farmers were producing enough staples and specialty products to feed people in their region and beyond. But something was preventing food from getting to where it was most needed. Nwuneli identified two related probable causes: food waste and government policies.

Nwuneli attributed the problem of food waste to systemic failures—from broken or nonexistent distribution chains to fragmented markets—that made it difficult to get products from farms to distribution centers, let alone to tables. This meant that incredible quantities of homegrown food were going to waste, for example, an estimated 40 to 60 percent of fruit harvested by local farmers.[7] As a result, small-scale farmers hesitated to plan for growth, let alone invest in it. And so, the inevitable occurred: local food processors—where they existed—took the easier path of sourcing raw materials from *outside* their home country.

The second related problem was government policies, which were inconsistent and sometimes counterproductive. Could farmers and small businesses count on subsidies, and under what conditions? Would trade deals reduce export tariffs enough to spur international demand, or would they lower import tariffs, further undermining local producers trying to sell to their neighbors? Importing powdered milk, for example, was a full 15 percent cheaper than sourcing it locally due to trade policy alone.[8] And even if infrastructure improved, was anyone poised to promote local products to regional buyers, whether through marketing campaigns or economic diplomacy?

As the pressures on the food and agricultural sector became clearer to Nwuneli, so did new opportunities for her role as a catalyst within it. Nwuneli knew she needed to remain flexible and responsive to where to invest her energy; from day one, she had built LEAP and NIA to "outlive her," as she put it. Knowing that she couldn't focus her time and attention on these initiatives indefinitely, she had the foresight to establish strong successors and boards of directors that could carry their missions forward. As she described, "This is where being an enabler is important. How do I build a team where I don't have to be everywhere at the same time? If other people can do it, I don't have to be there. . . . Finding mission-driven high achievers who share the values, share the vision . . . , and hold you accountable is really important."

After delegating management and oversight of LEAP and NIA to two trusted boards, Nwuneli set her sights on tackling the next problem she'd stumbled upon. Rather than create another nonprofit, she decided the time had come for her to become a food entrepreneur herself.

Illuminating the "Hidden Middle"

In 2009, Nwuneli and her husband, Mezuo, launched AACE Foods (AACE). It was a for-profit "social enterprise," as she called it, which sourced local ingredients (chilis, turmeric, and maize) from "smallholder farmers"—food-growers who operate on just a few acres of land.[9] AACE would process those raw materials into products (spices, seasonings, and cereals) for local markets and export. For Nwuneli, building AACE Foods was "painful," an eye-opening experience to the difficulties African food and agriculture entrepreneurs confronted regularly. As she described:

> We were ill-equipped to fully understand the magnitude of the hurdles that others faced until we started our own agribusinesses. . . . You [couldn't] pick up the phone and say, "Oh, I'm looking for a supplier of ginger," and there are twenty that have been vetted. They say they can help you, but they absolutely can't. You have to map out the farmers and then teach them how to weigh their ginger and remove the stones.

Around the same time, Nwuneli and her husband launched Sahel Consulting, a management consulting and investment firm committed to tackling institutional barriers in Africa's food and agriculture landscape, including policies, limited access to capital markets, and lack of financial and operational expertise.[10] As with LEAP and NIA, Sahel was built from an ecosystem of partnerships. Working closely with global development finance institutions, foundations, governments, international development agencies, and academic institutions, Sahel focused on helping Nigerian SMEs raise capital, develop market-entry strategies, hire leadership, develop talent, and establish financial and operational structures.

Based on her practical experience at AACE, Nwuneli began to fill in the map she was sketching of the agriculture ecosystem. When she identified key barriers, Nwuneli activated the consultants in Sahel's "catalytic ventures" arm dedicated to developing innovative interventions. For example, when AACE struggled to find spice distributors, Nwuneli and the teams from AACE and Sahel launched a program for women to become distributors, training them in bookkeeping, sales, and logistics.

By 2016, the partnership between Sahel and AACE Foods was paying off. AACE was sourcing products from a network of ten thousand smallholder farmers—a scale Nwuneli could never have predicted.[11] The company employed 150 people, many first-time job seekers, and offered them benefits from health insurance for their families to adult literacy programs. Nwuneli noted that the company held a "graduation" for the literacy students during the annual Christmas party. "Last year, forty women who [formerly] didn't speak any word of English put on their caps, and they had a graduation ceremony," she said. "It just brought tears to my eyes."

Nwuneli's bold jump from the nonprofit to the business arena taught her a critical lesson: the lifeblood of the African agriculture ecosystem was neither the multinationals nor the smallholder farmer, where so many international development resources were committed. Instead, it was the SMEs—the "hidden middle," as Nwuneli came to call them, "that are doing the heavy lifting to connect the dots."[12] Building a single SME like AACE could mean empowering dozens, if not hundreds, of employees and thousands of smallholder farmers from whom they sourced their raw materials.

A Cure for the "Crab Mentality"

In 2018, Nwuneli shifted her attention to addressing the needs of SMEs and figuring out how to leverage them to catalyze innovation in the food sector. She interviewed more than eighty founders of food and agricultural SMEs to discover why they struggled to scale.[13] The lack of knowledge, tools, data, and investment were well-known. Yet Nwuneli uncovered another barrier in her interviews that was never discussed: the lack of trust among the entrepreneurs. "It became clear to me that we were so fragmented—we didn't know each other; we weren't working together," said Nwuneli. The main problem, she described, was that in "resource-constrained environments, you have the crab mentality"—a mindset of secrecy, withdrawal, and competitiveness. "How can people work in isolation and get anything done?"

Nwuneli's diagnosis led her to reframe her challenge: for the African agricultural ecosystem to realize its potential, she needed to drive cocreation among SMEs. Given Africa's projected population growth, she estimated that if everyone were to spend just $1 a day on food, that alone would create an $876 billion annual market; ratchet that up to $10 a day, and the market was worth $9 trillion.[14] How could she unleash generations of entrepreneurs, today and tomorrow, to create this future? Her answer was to leverage digital technology to give SMEs the chance to interact and, over time, build trusting relationships as they witness for themselves the power of cocreation.

Nourishing Africa by Convening Entrepreneurs

After working in the agricultural sector for nearly two decades, Nwuneli had became a trusted authority on agribusiness and food production.[15] Acquaintances and strangers alike approached her for thoughts on anything from crop rotation to marketing, for opinions on trade and climate policy, for contacts, endorsements, and back-of-the-envelope investment advice. Over time, these organic interactions crystallized into a vision of real change in Africa: it was precisely this kind of exchange that needed to be scaled. She imagined a digital "community circle" that brought together food and agricultural entrepreneurs across the continent to share their learnings and innovate together.

Nwuneli began by hiring a small team of young tech talent: software developers, digital communicators, and entrepreneur engagement specialists. They were under thirty—digital native millennials and GenZers—and for many, it was their first job. Nwuneli's goal was to attract high achievers who "wake up every day excited and energized to make a difference. It's not a job. It has to be a calling."

In 2019, after her new team had been trained through Sahel's catalytic ventures arm, Nwuneli launched Nourishing Africa, a digital platform that she endeavored to grow into "a home for one million entrepreneurs." It was a website designed to aggregate information as a "one-stop shop" for African entrepreneurs of all sorts—from farmers and food processors to retailers, chefs, and agriculture technology companies. The platform would offer access to knowledge, trainings, connections, and other resources. Nwuneli intended that Nourishing Africa would accelerate the ability of SMEs to connect with trusted partners, grow their businesses, and build a $1 trillion food and agriculture industry by 2030.[16]

Entrepreneurs would be the platform's main content creators: they would publish detailed public profiles about their businesses, which would become searchable for others. As with all platforms, Nwuneli recognized that the value of Nourishing Africa would depend on scaling it—increasing the number and diversity of participants. Yet she insisted on forgoing quick growth in favor of uncompromised quality of both platform participants and the content they provided. Paramount for Nwuneli was to craft an environment where entrepreneurs could say to one another without reservation: "I can trade with you, I can invest in you, I can partner with you," as she put it.

Rather than making the platform open to everyone, Nwuneli opted for a membership model with significant barriers to entry. "In the digital world," she explained, "people use masks to appear to be something they are really not. We were very worried about having those types of bad eggs enter our world. If there is one big scandal, that can automatically destroy the membership, and anything associated with it." Because Nwuneli was committed to reaching underserved SMEs, she decided that charging a membership fee did not align with Nourishing Africa's mission. Instead, she approached membership from the perspective of establishing a social contract of sorts based on reciprocity: members should be just as eager to *give* to the platform as to get. To gauge potential members' commitment, she imposed a lengthy application and vetting process to weed out bad actors. She also required that members post and participate regularly in community events (in-person or online), which discouraged free riders. Moreover, as members experienced the value of the platform, they were encouraged to recruit other SMEs to join.

Nwuneli thought carefully about designing a business model for Nourishing Africa that aligned with its mission of serving SMEs. She relied on her deep local and global networks to recruit companies to become paid partners and contribute content and resources to the platform. Many partners were willing, even eager, to pay to connect to the population of Africa's SMEs, which were otherwise often hard to reach. These included potential sources of financing (banks, accelerators, incubators, private equity and venture capital funds, and sponsors of prizes or challenges), foundations and nonprofits, government agencies, industry and trade associations, knowledge partners (business schools, training groups, and research organizations), media outlets, and, of course, corporations looking for SME suppliers. Although these partners wouldn't be platform members, they enriched the Nourishing Africa ecosystem by providing education, data, services, and connections for the SME members.

In addition, Nwuneli insisted on creating opportunities apart from the digital platform for members to meet face-to-face. "While tech is a huge enabler," she said, "it can also be a destructive force if there is no regulation or ethical fiber holding us back from taking advantage of people. . . . You can actually tell somebody's character if you get to see them."

Building Trust by Modeling Values

As with her previous initiatives, Nwuneli took deliberate steps to prepare Nourishing Africa to outlast her. She established a board, hired co-CEOs, and worked ardently to instill a sense of values in her team that would guide their decisions as they built out the ecosystem. She saw the members of her team as essentially guardians of trust: vetting candidates, brokering partnerships, and managing the platform and community-building events.

For a culture of trust to thrive, Nwuneli recognized that it must be accompanied by an uncompromising stand on quality:

> When I ran my first nonprofit, if you asked me at the time, I wanted to be loved. . . . But now I'm very okay not being loved. I just want to be respected. Because, at the end of the day, it's about the work. And it's bigger than every one of us. This is such important work; we can't afford to do it in a shoddy manner.

At times, Nwuneli's hard-nosed attitude rubbed some of her team members the wrong way. But one thing was never in doubt: she always had the long-term benefit of the entire ecosystem in mind. And when the inevitable misstep occurred, she would not dwell on the mistake but simply say, "How fast can we fix it?"

Another way in which Nwuneli prepared her team was by sharing her contacts with them so they too could become effective catalysts. Again, this generous approach to leadership came with high expectations: "I want them to say, 'This is my relationship, too—and I'm going to show up and deliver,'" she said. Nwuneli also gave her team members opportunities to represent Nourishing Africa in industry meetings, media events, SME gatherings, and international conferences. "These are opportunities to learn and grow, and build their own personal networks and reputation," she said.

Nwuneli also taught her team the importance of listening to stakeholders and responding to their emergent needs, a key catalyst principle. Nourishing Africa, she insisted, had to be a *living* platform if it was to maintain trust and build momentum over time. "If you have the trust, the credibility, and you're responsive to the needs of people," she explained, "they will give and they will get. And it will become more enriching for you." She insisted that her team use surveys to constantly take the pulse of the platform, and innovate in response to feedback. "The ecosystem changes every day," she said. "If you're not ready to be responsive, how can you be relevant?" By modeling these core values, Nwuneli imparted the mindset and skills her team would need to continue building relationships—one by one—and gradually nurture a robust, innovative ecosystem.

Prioritizing Digital Resilience

The Covid-19 pandemic in 2020 devastated Africa's agricultural communities, and Nwuneli felt this impact deeply. Millions of consumers were spending less, buying only the essentials.[17] Food processors and distributors were forced to cut costs, leaving upstream SMEs with no sales channels. When Nwuneli's team surveyed the members of Nourishing Africa, fully half could not imagine their businesses reopening.

But Nwuneli began to see a glimmer of hope in other industries from which her organization might take some cues. SMEs in other consumer sectors, like apparel, were pivoting to WhatsApp, Instagram, and LinkedIn as sales and marketing channels, swiftly creating online marketplaces and shifting to direct-to-consumer models. Clearly, digital solutions were the path forward for Nourishing Africa's SMEs to survive the pandemic. "The smallest entrepreneurs didn't know how to pivot," recalls Nwuneli, and "the impact of them dying affects ecosystems . . . and communities."

As she continued immersing herself in the problem, Nwuneli explored ways to accelerate digital innovation—and, in turn, resilience—for Nourishing Africa's member entrepreneurs. She and her team scanned the landscape of potential partners to bring in critical capabilities, and they found that many international organizations were developing training programs to help SMEs go digital. Nwuneli's team decided to initiate a series of partnerships, including one with a global foundation, to help its members adopt digital technologies.[18] "We should have started this much earlier," Nwuneli admitted. "Covid was a wake-up call." The two organizations partnered to cocreate a training series to teach agricultural entrepreneurs how to use digital tools.

When they launched the program, however, no one signed up. At that point, Nwuneli said, her team had to forge what for them were "unusual relationships" with local and state governments, community and faith-based organizations, and trade and women's associations. These were groups the SMEs already trusted but that Nwuneli and her team had largely neglected to date. "We had to really find the grassroots organizations that could convince [our entrepreneurs] to get involved," she explained.[19]

In the meantime, Nwuneli and her team were also working proactively to match SMEs with agriculture technology companies that could help them. With Nourishing Africa's support, thousands of small agrifood businesses began collaborating. For example, with the help of tech start-ups, farmers began using sensing technologies to monitor crops remotely during lockdowns. App-enabled motorbike drivers (who used to carry people) began delivering food products to local farms and shops, becoming key links in the agribusiness supply chain. This was exactly the type of cocreation that Nwuneli had hoped to unleash through Nourishing Africa. "The whole ecosystem was evolving," she reflected.

Nwuneli finally saw the seeds of a movement beginning to sprout, unexpectedly bolstered by the pandemic. And the critical role SMEs played in economies became even more stark. As she and her team encouraged Nourishing Africa members to share their innovation stories on their platform, she noticed that, "We were able to build momentum very quickly because people did need that support and that information."

To Nwuneli's surprise, a whole new roster of partners began approaching Nourishing Africa—all offering to fund e-learning, among other programs, for SMEs. "Not only are SMEs drivers of innovation and job creation," Nwuneli explained, "but they are small enough to pivot during periods of crisis. They are oftentimes more agile than large companies and closer to the grassroots." For example, the Nigerian Export Promotion Council approached Nourishing Africa about developing and implementing a program to help five thousand Nigerian entrepreneurs create capacity to export food products to the rest of Africa and the world.

By 2022, Nourishing Africa had provided services for over ten thousand small businesses and had grown to two thousand members. As momentum built, Nwuneli identified two new potential revenue streams for the platform: advertising and data. SMEs were still a hard-to-reach population. Big organizations, including multinationals, were offering to pay Nourishing Africa significant money to get the attention of their SMEs, and even more for the information the platform collected. Nwuneli was deeply protective of Nourishing Africa's entrepreneurs and conducted due diligence on all potential partners. She and her team were conservative about the deals they entertained, assessing each one based on the value it added to the SMEs. With such opportunities, Nwuneli always considered, "Who sees your entrepreneurs as prey versus productive assets and communities?" For example, one large company proposed a multimillion-dollar project that would have generated useful information for the SME community, but in exchange, it wanted access to Nourishing Africa's email list. Nwuneli immediately deemed this a step too far and vetoed the arrangement.

Maintaining Momentum When Trust Is Broken

In 2021, the partnership between Nourishing Africa and the global foundation moved into a new phase. The foundation provided funds for an e-learning program to help entrepreneurs pivot following the devastating impact of Covid; it also agreed to offer grants of 3 million Naira (about US$3,000) to 125 of the roughly 1,000 companies that would be selected for the program.[20] To qualify, company owners had to present a pitch describing their business and show how the funds would help them address the challenges of recovering from Covid. Independent judges would also visit the businesses to verify stories and confirm eligibility.

About 30,000 entrepreneurs applied, 1,000 were selected and completed the e-learning, and 300 went on to apply for grants. The pitching and evaluation processes ran smoothly. The 125 winners were selected, but before the grants could be distributed, an official from the foundation called Nwuneli. "We've received an anonymous email claiming there is some kind of fraud happening at Nourishing Africa," she said. "The list of grant recipients is supposedly phony." It was Nwuneli's worst nightmare, exactly the kind of trust-shattering event she had worked so hard to prevent.

Nwuneli launched an immediate investigation with the help of forensic auditors, and it emerged that a Nourishing Africa employee had received bribes to tamper with the results. What was worse, when two other team members had heard rumors and raised questions, they'd been satisfied by vague reassurances from their colleague. If not for the anonymous whistleblower, the scheme might have succeeded. Working closely with Nourishing Africa's board, Nwuneli moved swiftly to minimize the damage. She fired the dishonest employee and brought legal charges against him; the team members who had turned a blind eye were also let go. The grant program was canceled, and the money immediately returned to the foundation.

The experience shook Nwuneli and everyone at Nourishing Africa, as well as the team at the foundation. The hundreds of entrepreneurs who had applied for the grant program were disappointed and angry. Nwuneli turned inward to draw lessons from the episode. The attempted fraud showed her just how fragile trust can be, and how even a single bad actor can threaten an ecosystem of thousands, painstakingly built over years. She learned she had to focus even more time on talent development, doubling down on efforts to instill values and judgment in her team. Going forward, she made sure every meeting started with a review of organizational values and a discussion of how they should play out in daily work.

While Nourishing Africa had faced a major setback, Nwuneli refused to let the actions of a few spoil the movement that was beginning to transform the lives of thousands of entrepreneurs and their communities. In 2022, she decided to convert Nourishing Africa from a for-profit business into a nonprofit and merge it with another initiative she'd launched during the pandemic—one focused squarely on raising global awareness and demand for African food.

Turning Crisis into Opportunity

The new organization, named African Food Changemakers (AFC), unified two long-running strands in Nwuneli's career: building Africa's food supply ecosystem and changing the world's narrative of it. With this merger, Nwuneli and her colleagues reaffirmed AFC's conviction that "connections made through food are a powerful way to change narratives."[21] Almost all the community-building programs Nourishing Africa had pioneered would be part of the new portfolio of activities managed by AFC.

In forming her new organization, Nwuneli brought with her the lessons learned from the attempted fraud at Nourishing Africa. To prioritize trust, she stressed that the nonprofit would *not* participate in any program involving direct distribution of funds to entrepreneurs:

> We now realize how dangerous it can be to get into giving out money. We'll connect our entrepreneurs to private equity [and] venture capital. They can search for funding opportunities on our site. So, we'll give knowledge, data, access, linkages, a community. We'll be a bridge to funders, but we're not touching the money.

Going forward, Nwuneli reaffirmed that AFC would be "so relevant to their members' needs that they would want to stay connected, and draw more people into the community to make it even richer." To lead the young organization, Nwuneli brought in Ruth Egbe, an engineer with twenty years of experience in human resource management and organizational development. As AFC grew, Egbe introduced new structures and processes. Too much reliance on remote collaboration was leading to "an erosion of value," as Nosa Obano, one staff member, remarked.[22] He was put in charge of recruiting what they referred to as "ambassadors" across the continent—SMEs who could assist in mapping out local ecosystems and delivering activities tailored to their specific communities. Nwuneli and Egbe also established rich monitoring and evaluation systems, encouraging the team to leverage data-informed insights to progress on four impact metrics: empowerment and growth of SMEs, job creation and economic impact, community building and collaboration, and innovation and sustainability.

Entrusting Egbe with AFC operations on the ground allowed Nwuneli to pivot her focus to her original passion: "creative storytelling . . . about Africa's contributions to the global food ecosystem, its culinary heritage and exciting future." Inspired by Japan's and Korea's national efforts to export culture through foods like sushi and Korean barbeque, a member of the AFC team, Bushirah Abdulrahaman, was charged with doing the same for dishes such as jollof rice, a staple in Nigeria and Ghana. AFC began using various media channels to introduce new ideas about African food into global culture. It collaborated on a Netflix series about African American cuisine in America, founded an annual food festival, created a podcast, and produced a stream of documentary videos.[23]

AFC's aspirations are high but not out of reach. "I have a dream that someday jollof rice will be more popular around the world than sushi," said Nwuneli. "Imagine a symbol on food packages like the one that says 'Gluten free'—but with the words 'Sourced from Africa.'" She continued:

> I want American consumers to buy chocolate bars that say "Made with cocoa from Ghana" on the package. I want them to realize that the best spices like turmeric come from Nigeria. When people realize that the sesame bagel they love is made with sesame from Sudan, it changes the way they see Sudan. And over time, African farmers will benefit.

AFC's efforts to change the African narrative abroad have also pushed the team to double-down on changing mindsets on the continent. At a trade fair in Cairo, AFC held a cooking competition where chefs tried to outdo one another with their takes on jollof rice. It was a wild success, but later Nwuneli learned that plantains for one recipe were sourced from Costa Rica; no one had asked AFC members whether one of them could provide plantains, but she was certain someone would have raised their hand. "It goes back to trust," she says. "People need to trust our community to step up when there's a need. That's why we created the community!"

AFC membership has grown to more than 6,600 SMEs based in forty-eight of the fifty-four African countries.[24] This community is split equally between SMEs who work directly with farmers and other players in the food industry, such as food processors, retailers, and chefs. More than fifteen hundred food entrepreneurs have been trained through AFC's workshops and programs.[25] Coalitions of SMEs have formed, both organically and with AFC interventions, to address specific challenges, such as advocating for changing tariff policy on dairy products or sharing smart-climate practices. These connections are having a real impact on previously disconnected African entrepreneurs. "When they find out about this community," Nwuneli said, "it blows their mind. They're like, 'Oh my gosh, thank you for this support. I don't feel like I'm doing this by myself anymore.'"

Nwuneli's original goal of including one million members in AFC is within reach—so long as she and her team hold fast to their practice of forging strong, values-centered connections with the people they serve. Perhaps most rewarding for Nwuneli, she reflected, is how entrepreneurs have come to identify with the AFC community: "People meet me now all over the world and they say, 'I'm an African Food Changemaker.' And that just makes me so proud and excited. When you have that, a movement, a community is evolving."

How Catalysts Map Their Ecosystem

When Nwuneli first set out on her journey, she didn't see herself as a catalyst; she gradually discovered her role—and how best to fulfill it—by mapping the problem, and opportunities, over the course of her career.

For catalysts, mapping is itself a process of discovery-driven, experiential learning. It involves getting out of their organizations, immersing themselves in on-the-ground realities, and being curious about the people whom they seek to activate. As much as catalysts like Nwuneli conduct research into the issues they see, they fundamentally learn through their interactions with others. By forging broad networks of trusted relationships, catalysts fill out the contours of problems and opportunities, who the key stakeholders are, how they relate to one another, what barriers they face, and what enablers (like emergent coalitions) can be leveraged.

Nwuneli's insights were cultivated over more than two decades of hands-on experimentation. At first, she thought that African entrepreneurs struggled to scale their businesses because of a lack of leadership, institutional barriers, and fragmented supply chains. But only after she herself became an actor in the industry, and grappled with the obstacles firsthand, did a fuller map of the underlying social problems emerge. Ultimately, Nwuneli uncovered an otherwise hidden issue in the African food and agricultural landscape: the inability of SMEs to collaborate— which came down to a lack of trust. Quite simply, since the individual entrepreneurs didn't even know one another, they wouldn't risk sharing their scarce resources.

Through iterative mapping and remapping, catalysts zoom in and out between the problems they discover on the ground and the purpose they aspire to fulfill. As Nwuneli did so, she gradually learned where innovation was most needed—what conditions she needed to put in place for an innovative agricultural ecosystem to take root. Her interventions included leadership development, trust-building, and digital resilience, to name a few.

Charting uncharted territory can be daunting, involving missed turns, detours, and dead ends. For Nwuneli, it was her purpose and values that gave her the tenacity and resilience to pioneer. With each organization she founded, she insisted on leveraging the human potential and ingenuity that already existed, culminating in AFC—a digital community, energized by trust, that empowers African entrepreneurs to shape their own destiny.

In 2024, having entrusted the operations of AFC to Egbe and the team, Nwuneli moved to Washington, DC, to become the president and CEO of the nonprofit ONE.[26] There, she leads a global movement advocating for equity and justice, and the investments to ensure economic opportunities and healthier lives in Africa—a natural continuation of her catalyst journey. Among many other things, the move has given her new insight into her own gifts: "I [began to] see myself as a destiny helper," Nwuneli said. "I bring people together and say, 'You guys should know each other. If all I did this morning was to make sure you knew each other, that's great for me.'"

CHAPTER 10

Seeding a Global Culinary Revolution

Massimo Bottura, Lara Gilmore, and the Francescana Family

Alone, I am Massimo Bottura. Together, we are Osteria Francescana.

—Massimo Bottura

It's not just about our value; it's about the ecosystem's value.

—Lara Gilmore

The dynamic duo behind Osteria Francescana—twice named best restaurant in the world[1]—may have seemed like an unlikely pair on paper.[2] Massimo Bottura was an aspiring young chef from Modena, Italy, whose best childhood memories were "at the feet of the women [he] loved most," eating tortellini freshly rolled by his mother and grandmother. When he wasn't in the kitchen, he was out "racing around" with his brothers in Italian cars or riding motorcycles across the hills of Emilia-Romagna. Lara Gilmore, born in Washington, DC, studied art history in college and began her career working for a photography magazine and apprenticing at contemporary art galleries. In the spring of 1993, they both found themselves in New York City, starting part-time jobs at an Italian café in SoHo.

As their diverse worlds collided in that small café, neither would ever be the same. Massimo shared his legendary stories about growing up in a big family and his antics back in Modena, while Lara introduced him to theater, contemporary art, and artist studios on the Lower East Side. He was fast and impulsive, while she was pensive and attentive. They had little in common, and yet, in conversation after conversation, they discovered more about themselves than when conversing with anyone else. At that time, neither could have envisioned that within two decades, they would become catalysts for a global movement, bringing the culinary culture of Modena, Bottura's hometown, to the world.[3]

The "Francescana Family"—as they call their venture—encompasses two worlds that rarely meet: high-end dining and community kitchens, the realms of the elite and the underserved. This global ecosystem includes not only Bottura and Gilmore's network of restaurants, but dozens of chefs they've trained; scores of volunteers, entrepreneurs, artists, businesses, and governments they've partnered with; thousands of diners who book once-in-a-lifetime food experiences months in advance; and hundreds of thousands from all walks of life who are served through their social enterprises.

This chapter follows Bottura and Gilmore's very personal journey of building the Francescana Family, this time showcasing the critical function of *seeding*: how they activated and empowered a generation of chefs to drive innovation in local communities across the globe. True to their ethos of "using values to create value," Bottura and Gilmore leveraged quality food, culture, and community to scale their family business. Throughout their journey, they created "canvases" for their chefs to live these values, express their individual slice of genius, and cocreate a more just and sustainable food future with their local partners.

The Culture of Modena: Slow Food, Fast Cars

In 1995, two years after meeting, the couple took over an *osteria* in the heart of Bottura's hometown and opened a contemporary Italian restaurant in its place. Although "osteria" was the most casual category of Italian restaurants, they decided to keep the former restaurant's name—"Osteria Francescana." It was an "interesting contradiction," they noted, given their ambition was to one day earn a Michelin star. Three months later, the couple married and, as Gilmore has cited on numerous occasions, "First I married the restaurant, then I married the chef, which meant that I married the project."

Modena is a small city in the Emilia-Romagna region, known for some of Italy's most iconic food treasures, such as balsamic vinegar, Parmigiano Reggiano cheese, prosciutto, and mortadella. "Centuries of culinary traditions secure[d] Emilian ingredients a noble place in the Italian pantry," noted Gilmore.[4] Family businesses of all sorts dot the region, some of which have become iconic global brands. Most notably, Ferrari began as a family venture and surged into a global sensation, inspiring other brands like Maserati and Lamborghini, and spawning a vast network of local automotive suppliers. Reflecting on this history, Gilmore noted, "There is a sense that you can come from nothing and make yourself into something here." Bottura put it simply: "There's the American dream here in Modena."

Yet Bottura was troubled by how much of that dream had been lost since his childhood, with the "decline of family-run farms and the rise of industrial agriculture."[5] Bottura's culinary training turned him into a proponent of the Slow Food movement, started in 1986 by Carlo Petrini, an Italian food activist and writer. With the goal of ensuring access to good, clean food at fair prices, the Slow Food movement resisted the rise of fast food with a call to preserve regional cuisines and support sustainable farming and food consumption.[6] In building Osteria Francescana, the couple would remain grounded in the tenets of Slow Food, coupled with another pillar of regional culture—fast cars. "It's in my mind all the time . . . the way I think, the way I move around," Bottura mused.

From Theory to Practice: *Festina Lente*

With their unique blend of talents—Bottura the culinary wizard and Gilmore the artistic visionary—they imagined they could do something unprecedented with Osteria Francescana, and they were willing to risk everything to give it a try. Unlike most of their Italian peers, who focused on perfecting renditions of the national cuisine, Bottura sought to create a once-in-a-lifetime dining experience that combined tradition and innovation. He had a catchphrase to guide this work that he coined back in 1998: *tradition in evolution*. "I break tradition all the time," Bottura said, "because I love to look at the past in a critical way, not a nostalgic way."[7]

Among his first recipes to attract attention was "Tortellini Walking on Broth." Instead of serving the tortellini in rich capon broth, as was traditionally done, Bottura lined them up in a thin veneer of broth thickened with agar. The dish symbolized his fond memories in the kitchen growing up—not only with his mother and grandmother, but also with Lidia Cristoni, a local villager and mentor who first taught him to make pasta. The tortellini's placement on the plate was an intentional provocation by Bottura: "Are you paying attention to what you are eating? Do you understand the value of the five-hundred-year-old tortellini tradition?" Another early Bottura original was "Five Ages of Parmigiano Reggiano." Bottura dared to transform the Parmigiano, usually grated on top of pasta, into the protagonist of the recipe. Made with cheese alone, the dish became symbolic of Bottura's ability to imagine and create the multiple facets, textures, and flavors of Modena.

Yet the innovation went well beyond the cooking. "We always thought of what we were doing as hospitality," said Gilmore. "Instead of considering the experience a four-hour moment of hospitality, we wanted [it] to begin the moment that you made your reservation." Gilmore and Bottura choreographed the dining experience, to surprise and even disorient diners. They sculpted an intimate and contemporary space: avant-garde artwork from their private collection adorned the walls, while more traditional plateware and crystal graced the tables. The kitchen played with classic Italian flavors, adding clever twists and word plays that reimagined tradition while still honoring it. Meanwhile, the serving staff used their storytelling acumen to share each dish's deeper meaning—often going beyond the ingredients into the world of ideas.

Modena locals and the Italian public did not initially take to Bottura's modernist spin on Italian cuisine. "It's very dangerous to play with the classics," Gilmore summarized. She continued:

> It can be the most exciting thing because you understand them fully when you've played with them, but it can also be the riskiest. There are three things that are critical to the book of Italian culture: Don't speak negatively about the Pope. Don't criticize the Italian national soccer team. And never mess with your grandmother's recipes.

"Slow food, fast cars" was the couple's guiding principle as they navigated "slow resistance to change." Every day, their team at Osteria Francescana worked with local farmers, butchers, and cheesemakers to source the best ingredients for their evening service. Bottura and Gilmore insisted on showing genuine empathy, respect, and trust when they did business with their neighbors. Perhaps unwittingly at first, they adopted an ecosystem mindset as they grew roots in Modena, seeing Osteria Francescana as a platform to showcase their community's treasures. They spotlighted local artisans and producers on their menus and encouraged guests to visit them. Their marketing materials always promoted Modena and the Emilia-Romagna region more broadly. "This simple landscape of farmers and earnest, hard workers and hearty food could be a magical combination," Gilmore noted. Local attitudes began to shift little by little.

As travelers and gourmets began making the pilgrimage to dine at Osteria Francescana, some of the harshest skeptics began softening their view of the trattoria's breaks with tradition. Then, in 2001, serendipity sealed their fate. A prominent Italian food writer stopped to eat at Osteria Francescana while traveling between Milan and Rome. A week later, he published an article about the unexpectedly delicious lunch and in just a few months, the restaurant was awarded its first Michelin star.[8]

Despite these early glimmers of fame, Gilmore and Bottura remained humble and focused on creating long-term value for their region. "There's a Latin expression," Gilmore noted, "*festina lente*, which are two opposite words. *Festina* means to go fast, and *lente* means to go slow. It translates to 'hurry, slowly.' For us, this means, how can we take everything that we do every day and bring more long-term value to it?" In practical terms, *festina lente* translated to scaling through empowering people—both inside and outside the restaurant's walls. Bottura began to see Osteria Francescana as a vehicle for cultivating relationships among local stakeholders and driving regional growth:

> One of the biggest steps to make Modena a destination was to build bridges—build bridges between Lamborghini and Ferrari; build bridges between Parmigiano, Lambrusco, Balsamico, and Prosciutto. . . . It's not Ferrari or Lamborghini; it's Ferrari *and* Lamborghini. All together, we have a very powerful voice.

Stars Are Made Not Born

After receiving their first Michelin star, Bottura and Gilmore began to strategize about what it would take to reach the pinnacle in their field: three Michelin stars. They knew they couldn't get there alone; they needed to leverage cocreation in their kitchen.

Bottura structured his kitchen with the "brigade model," typical of gourmet kitchens, with stations of lead chefs who report back to the executive chef. Bottura, however, saw himself less as the general and more as the head mentor. He and Gilmore sought to create a community, where chefs were not simply *on* the team but *played* as a team. Before the evening service, they gathered the entire staff around a communal table to break bread, laugh, reflect on experiences from the night before, brainstorm new ways of doing things, and iron out any last details.

Bottura and Gilmore delighted in developing all their talent at Osteria Francescana. One sous chef described how Bottura actively sought diverse opinions while creating in the kitchen: he would ask "someone who is twenty years old who's never cooked a piece of meat before to really understand and to feel it the way [the rest of us] feel it and see it." Bottura "has to have a dialogue with someone with zero experience," the sous chef went on to explain: "He'll put together a plate of venison . . . and find someone who has nothing to do with venison in the kitchen, and they taste it together. They discuss it. 'How do you feel about the cooking? What do you feel about the sauce?'" In this way, Bottura avoided a trap so many experts fall into—sticking to what they know, instead of questioning basic assumptions and experimenting.

To help his chefs develop independent identities as culinary innovators, Bottura implemented an exercise called "Who are you?" This took twenty-one-year-old Bernardo Paladini by surprise when he first joined the kitchen. When Bottura approached him and asked, "Who are you?" a confused Paladini answered, "I am Bernardo." But once he caught on, Paladini described it as "the most beautiful exercise I've ever done. I still remember the dish I made—a *raviolo*, putting together all the flavors of my city, Rome." As Allen Huynh, co–sous chef, explained, "We challenge all our chefs to represent themselves in any fashion they want on a plate, and they can use any of the materials and resources in the kitchen to sum up their gastronomic experience or voice in some way."

Osteria Francescana received its second Michelin star in 2006, which Bottura and Gilmore attributed in large part to cocreation with a trio of young chefs: Taka Kondo and Yoji Tokuyoshi, both from Japan, and Davide Di Fabio. Di Fabio grew up in a rural village in Abruzzo, Italy, and had joined the kitchen directly out of high school at eighteen years old. As Gilmore explained:

> In the kitchen, it's never about one chef. Taka, Davide, and Yoji, who arrived around the same time, became the heart and soul of the kitchen. They ran the kitchen with Massimo. He couldn't have gotten the second Michelin star on his own. He needed a team around him to help him express his ideas, and these three key players developed the recipes, the ideas, and executed them every night.

When Bottura began receiving invitations to cook at restaurants and events across the globe, he insisted on bringing the young chefs with him. "He was very proactive about giving them opportunities," Gilmore said. "He told everyone, 'This is my trio, the ones I work with.' He brought them forward from behind the kitchen to the front stage from the beginning." Bottura was adamant he was no solo genius; he thrived on diversity of thought.

Despite its growing global reputation, Osteria Francescana continued to face external resistance from local naysayers, who continued to disapprove of the restaurant's willingness to play with tradition. As Gilmore described:

> To change anything, especially hundreds of years of culinary tradition, takes a lot of effort, willingness to take risks and determination to hang in for the long run. For Massimo, this meant being prepared and ready to hold on during a storm, taking the time to know who he was and what he wanted to be, to invent and reinvent.

To help the team cope with the ups and downs and encourage a sense of resilience, Bottura used a catchphrase in his kitchen: "Be like a tree.

Grow slowly." His team continued to strive for perfection in their kitchen, Bottura made clear that mistakes were a critical part of collaborating, experimenting, and learning together. Amid a busy evening service, Kondo accidentally dropped a finished tart on the kitchen floor, splattering the impeccably plated dessert. The kitchen fell quiet, awaiting Bottura's reaction. He walked over to a mortified Kondo and, upon seeing the mess, shouted, "Taka, it's so beautiful! Don't you see?"

With the broken tart as his guide, Bottura instructed Kondo to take the remaining lemon tarts, break them, and arrange them on new plates. The result was an iconic Osteria Francescana dessert: "Oops! I Dropped the Lemon Tart," which concluded the seven-course "Come to Italy with Me" menu they were serving at the time. It was a tribute to the flavors and ingredients of southern Italy, without which the Italian kitchen could not exist. Gilmore described how "the dish combined everything that a three-star Michelin restaurant should be: flavor, technique, quality of the experience, and quality of the storytelling from the front of house. In its broken form, the lemon tart captured the essence of Southern Italy far better than a perfect tart ever could."

In 2011, Bottura and Gilmore received their third Michelin star, and that year Osteria Francescana was named the fourth best restaurant in the world.[9] Bottura had an intriguing insight about where the star came from: the mistake Kondo had made in the kitchen.

The Kitchen as an Innovation Launchpad

Catalyst leaders see talent as seeds for growth and nurture them as best they can.[10] But catalysts also know that when these seeds sprout, they must step aside to give them space to grow.

After the third Michelin star, Bottura's kitchen began to undergo what he called "a revolution" in redefining its identity. It started when one of Bottura's star chefs, Yoji Tokuyoshi, was ready to move on, followed by Davide Di Fabio. "It was hard for Massimo to let them go," Gilmore recalled. "But he understood why they had to leave. . . . They needed their next project, one where they could shine." If his chefs were to spread the slow-food, fast-cars movement, they too needed to become catalysts for innovation in their new homes. Tokuyoshi opened a restaurant in Milan, and Di Fabio became the chef in a restaurant closer to his hometown. Perhaps unsurprisingly, they both soon earned their own Michelin stars.

As they learned the difficult art of letting go, Bottura and Gilmore also had to be more deliberate in attracting and preparing the next generation of chefs to lead. One such person was Canadian chef Jessica Rosval, who arrived at the end of 2013. She credited her joining the team to Gilmore's efforts to buck a long-held prejudice in the industry. "I have a lot of respect for her," said Rosval. "She was the one that found the women on the team an apartment in the center of the city, next to the restaurant. She was responsible, in a way, for planting that seed with Massimo, constantly telling him that he needed to bring more women on board."

From her first day in the kitchen, Rosval rose to the challenge. "I had been managing an entire kitchen before [in Canada], and then I was given just a station," she admitted. "On my first day, I had two Italian chefs working with me, and I had to teach them a menu that I didn't even know, in a language that I didn't speak." Gilmore remarked that "learning was Jessica's first superpower—not just the culinary technique, but the deep thinking and the conceptualizing. She had this concept of excellence and quality in everything." Within a few years, Rosval found herself by Bottura's side, traveling the world to cook at prestigious events.

Planting Seeds for the Future: From Local to Global

In 2012, two massive earthquakes devastated northern Italy, killing dozens of people and displacing tens of thousands. Many buildings were damaged, including the warehouses that stored the exclusive and slow-to-process Parmigiano Reggiano. In the aftermath, 360,000 wheels of cheese were damaged, which could have resulted in losses as much as $50 million and threatened many of the region's oldest artisanal family businesses.[11] "When the earthquakes occurred," Gilmore explained, "we used our voice to help save the dairy farmers. And then, we just started becoming more and more active about making sure our actions were not only about the earthquake, but about other social issues. We didn't want to just buy the cheese from the dairy farmers—we wanted to activate bigger changes."

One of those big changes was triggered by Bottura's rendition of a typical dish, *cacio e pepe* ("cheese and pepper"), which economically used all parts of the Parmigiano wheel and substituted rice, a more common ingredient in the world, for pasta. Bottura promoted the recipe in a virtual event that attracted more than forty thousand viewers worldwide. "From Argentina to South Africa," Bottura said, "people started buying incredible amounts of Parmigiano Reggiano. It was unbelievable." The intended result was realized: the boost in cheese sales meant that no local cheesemakers lost their jobs, and "Parmigiano Reggiano Day" was created by the Consortium of Parmigiano Reggiano.[12]

In the wake of both great tragedy and great success, Gilmore stood in their home staring at Bottura's chef jacket—now with three Michelin stars embroidered on it. As Gilmore recounted:

> We had this realization, as we were looking at it, that the value of the long journey to achieve three stars rests in what you do with them once you get them. . . . We were working for seventeen years for that benchmark, but when we got there [we] realized that we've been not just working but creating value, capacity, and agility. In that moment, we flipped it around and started thinking about projecting outwards, sharing all our learnings to help people grow.

It was then that Bottura and Gilmore affirmed their calling: to "plant seeds for the future," as they said. Both were highly influenced by German artist Joseph Beuys, who authored a popular phrase in his work: "Never stop planting." At a pinnacle in their careers, with learnings from the past in tow, they agreed to focus their time and energy to "never stop planting ideas in every action, word, recipe, structure, restaurant, and community activity" throughout the Francescana Family ecosystem. This way, they knew, they would be able to impact a broader talent pool and clientele who would, in Gilmore's words, "carry the seeds of impact" on a global scale.

Food for Soul: Feeding the Planet in a New Way

In 2015, Bottura and Gilmore initiated a project during the World Expo in Milan, themed "Feeding the Planet, Energy for Life." They seized the opportunity to address the twin challenges of food waste and food insecurity that, as restaurant owners, they were keenly aware of. Bottura and Gilmore resolved to expand beyond their roles as restauranteurs and cofounded a nonprofit cultural association called Food for Soul.

Bottura and Gilmore modeled Food for Soul after the type of dining experience they knew best. They would use perfectly good surplus food from the Expo, categorized as "waste," to create a dignified dining experience primarily for unhoused or low-income people—a clientele that restaurants like Osteria Francescana would never reach. They would create a new model for addressing the "absurdity," in Gilmore's words, that nearly one-fifth of food produced globally is thrown away while nearly one in ten people are undernourished.[13]

Leveraging the social capital they developed in the previous decades, Bottura and Gilmore approached several local Italian stakeholders—a Catholic relief agency, academic institutions, high-profile chefs, even the Vatican—to see how they could work together to increase Food for Soul's scale and impact. With these partners, they transformed an abandoned theater in an impoverished Milan suburb into a *refettorio* (community kitchen).[14] They installed a professional kitchen and decorated the dining space with work by some of Bottura and Gilmore's favorite world-renowned artists. "It was an experiment," said Jill Conklin, director and strategic officer of Food for Soul:

> It was about redefining the art of service, through all the wonderful, amazing experiences that they had learned over the years at Osteria Francescana, and also [redefining] who they are as social entrepreneurs coming from a place like Italy and Modena, where tradition and culture means so much. It was about taking those same principles and putting them into [a new] social space.

More than sixty internationally renowned chefs, including one of Bottura's mentors, the iconic Alain Ducasse, joined the initiative at the Milan Expo. Bottura invited his closest colleagues to embrace and demonstrate that "chefs can be more than the sum of their recipes," in his words. Bottura and Gilmore knew the Milan refettorio was not a "give back"; rather it was conceived to provide a rich gastronomic experience for a new clientele, while reimagining what surplus food could become. "Food for Soul is not a charity project," Bottura emphasized, "it is a cultural one." He said:

> What really makes the difference in Food for Soul is the service, the power of hospitality, and the beauty all around. When people walk in, we tell them, "Welcome, come in, we will take care of you." They sit at the table, and we ask them, "Do you prefer sparkling or still? . . . Here is the appetizer, the main course, and the dessert. Take your time."

When the World Expo in Milan ended, Bottura recalled thinking, "It's over, and we are going to leave the refettorio to the city of Milan as our heritage." Little did they know they had sparked a movement. Not long after the Expo, the phone rang very early one morning and Bottura got out of bed to answer. When he returned, Gilmore asked who was calling so early. "The mayor of Rio de Janeiro," he told her.

"What does the mayor of Rio de Janeiro want from you?" she asked.

He had requested a refettorio for the Rio Olympics the following year. Bottura's answer: "Why not?"[15]

The Cocreation Model Spreads: Refettorio Harlem

Over the next few months, business and government leaders from around the world reached out to the couple to bring the refettorio model to their own cities. What started as a one-off cultural project in Milan activated a global food justice movement driven by Francescana Family values. Bottura and Gilmore scaled Food for Soul to thirteen cities (and counting), from London to Mérida, Mexico.[16] The two leaders knew they personally lacked the contextual knowledge in many places, so they recruited on-the-ground stakeholders to cocreate a localized extension of Food for Soul. "Each refettorio partner has their own unique experiences," Conklin described. "We like to say that we're globally inspired and locally rooted."

By 2018, Food for Soul had officially touched ground in the United States. The nonprofit received a grant from the Rockefeller Foundation, and their first project together would be a refettorio in New York City. Bottura and Gilmore loved the idea of planting seeds back in the city where their relationship and vision for Francescana Family had first begun.

The couple decided that Refettorio Harlem would be established sometime in 2019 near the Emanuel AME Harlem Church—a historic hub of the civil rights movement. The church served as Food for Soul's site partner, collaborating with Bottura and Gilmore to transform a community hall into a refettorio space. Another critical partner was Free Food Harlem, a local organization that served "anyone in need of food assistance and social connection."[17] Roxanne Jimenez, then Food for Soul's social impact and sustainability manager, recognized the importance of partners who had "boots on the ground" and could help codesign solutions that fit their communities.

Bringing together organizations across a local ecosystem often requires hands-on time and attention. Gilmore and Bottura would usually visit early in the development of a new refettorio to ensure the design was inclusive and welcoming, and tap their vast professional network for resources. In Refettorio Harlem hangs an enormous photograph donated by one of the couple's favorite artists and good friends, JR, who shared their belief in "art as social change." The image in Refettorio Harlem depicts the US–Mexico border in 2017 to remind all that come to the refettorio of their aspiration to break down both physical and metaphorical borders through food, culture, and community. Gilmore noted the importance of art in their ecosystem:

> For us, art is our landscape of ideas. Since arriving in Modena, we have built relationships with artists and those relationships continue to this day. Our relationships have always informed our decisions and growth as well as distinguished the depth of Massimo's thinking behind the culinary creations.

After paving the way for Refettorio Harlem to open its doors, Bottura and Gilmore entrusted local chefs and volunteers to shape the dining experience, from prepping the surplus food to greeting guests at the door with a smile to refilling their water glasses. Jimenez, who was based in New York City but helped oversee the refettorios globally, spoke to their relationship-building approach with staff in each city: "What can they teach me right now? What wealth of knowledge do they have as a refettorio partner or operations manager or chef that we can tap into? You put all this knowledge together, and that's what Food for Soul is."

Within the first few years of being in Harlem, the momentum generated by the local stakeholders paid off: the refettorio would grow to deliver more than 27,000 meals, save 52,000-plus pounds of food, and serve 3,300 guests.[18] "I remember watching this interview with Massimo," reflected Ellen Port, a volunteer at Refettorio Harlem, who said:

> He's very passionate and infectious. He said he wanted to create ten thousand refettorios around the world. I think this is very possible. This is very scalable. It's like a whole ecosystem of win-win here. . . . I've only been to three [refettorios]. I'm on a mission to go to all of them. I'm on a mission to spread the word. I am on a mission to open ten thousand refettorios around the world with Food for Soul.

Casa Maria Luigia: Another Platform for Cocreation

In 2018, Bottura and Gilmore told their team back in Modena they were planning to purchase a 250-year-old farmhouse in the Emilian countryside. They named it Casa Maria Luigia, after Bottura's late mother, and set out to transform it into a twelve-room (and growing) luxury guesthouse amid corn fields and vegetable gardens, complete with an *acetaia*, a traditional balsamic vinegar cellar. Their guiding mantra in creating the guesthouse was the Modena sensibility: *Buongiorno, benvenuti, venite, ci prendiamo noi cura di voi* ("Good morning, welcome, come on in, we will take good care of you"). They wanted it to be "a home away from home" in Modena—a place where guests traveling to visit the region and dine at Francescana Family businesses could experience the unique stories, recipes, and hospitality of the Emilian countryside. They decorated with contemporary art pieces from their personal collection—from a Warhol in the kitchen to an Ai Weiwei in the main entryway.

They set up a "record room," where guests could enjoy Bottura's collection of over a thousand vinyl records, and a "playground" that housed exercise equipment and Bottura's collection of Italian sports cars and motorcycles. Guests were encouraged to wander about, help themselves to a fresh snack or glass of wine in the communal kitchen, or poke their heads into the guesthouse's quirky nooks and crannies. No two rooms were the same. "We were not looking to make a hotel with a homogenous style," Gilmore remarked. "We wanted to create a sense of discovery when entering a room, and an invitation for fantasy."[19]

Some were skeptical about their move from restaurateurs to hoteliers, but for Bottura and Gilmore, their work was grounded in their determination to contribute to the long-term development of the Modena region. "This has always been my dream to bring people to Modena," Bottura said, "and share the unique charm and world-class ingredients. But it isn't about us anymore—it is about . . . building the foundation for more generations to discover Modena."[20]

Jessica Rosval, like others within the Francescana Family, was one of the skeptics about the project, but she soon began to imagine the possibilities it represented:

> When they started setting up the kitchen and the dining room space, I was coming here a lot because there were private events happening, and at that time, I was the events chef. I started bringing things in, . . . feeling the space. I started getting attached. . . . When Massimo and Lara started talking about bringing in other chefs, I started getting a little bit protective.

Rosval's engagement did not go unnoticed, and when Bottura and Gilmore offered her the position as head chef, she readily accepted. On May 1, 2019, Casa Maria Luigia officially opened, and within a month, Rosval led her new team in their first dinner service of "Francescana at Casa Maria Luigia," an experience that honored the most iconic dishes of Osteria Francescana that were no longer served at the flagship restaurant. People who had been waiting for ten years to get a table at the trattoria now had another venue where they could experience the Francescana Family dishes and hospitality.

The Movement Takes on a Life of Its Own

Inspired by Bottura and Gilmore's example of living their values, Rosval wanted to provide opportunities for a growing migrant population in Italy to find meaningful employment. In 2020, Rosval colaunched the Association for the Integration of Women with Caroline Caporossi, a former intern with Food for Soul. This social enterprise provided resources for migrant women to participate in a culinary training program, share food traditions from their own cultures, and establish roots in Modena. The initiative soon led to the birth of Roots in 2022—an eatery and coworking space, where many of these same migrant women were responsible for delivering a diverse menu showcasing dishes and stories from their home countries.

"Roots was so successful as a social restaurant," Bottura explained, "because Jessica and her team were thinking deeply about who the women are that are a part of their program. These chefs were involved in a social process, one that translated ideas into food." Indeed, Rosval and Caporossi's work as budding catalysts themselves would be recognized with a Champion of Change award from The World's 50 Best Restaurants.[21]

A few years after Rosval first moved to Casa Maria Luigia, Gilmore and Bottura approached her with yet another "artistic challenge." "You are going to start painting with your own food to express yourself," Bottura recalled telling her. "And we are going to create the most amazing background." He continued, "Scaling the business happens when there is need to scale *talent*. What we did was build a new place, and we told [Rosval] it could be her canvas." And so, in the fall of 2023, Rosval became the head chef at a second restaurant at Casa Maria Luigia—Al Gatto Verde—where she would earn her first Michelin star and first Michelin food-sustainability star.[22] That same year, Casa Maria Luigia received three Michelin keys, the highest honor for businesses in the hospitality industry.[23] "This is what has always kept me here," Rosval later reflected. "You always feel like you're building."

Tirelessly Sowing More Seeds of Opportunity

As the Francescana Family ecosystem continued to grow locally and globally through new restaurants and refettorios, Bottura and Gilmore thought carefully about how to distribute their chefs across venues in a way that would empower them. "Behind the curtain, they have some tricks up their sleeve," was how one team member described the duo's continual efforts.

"Which chef should we send to create the next venture?" Gilmore would ask Bottura. "How can we keep the Francescana Family identity and also give people freedom and the ability to be creative, grow, and build their own reputations?" Bottura knew that they wanted to give the opportunity "to these amazing, talented chefs to express themselves," adding, "To be truly successful, you need to move people around who are all a part of your community. And my chefs are all a part of the community."

When Bottura was looking for the head chef of their first restaurant partnership with Gucci, he thought of Karime Lopez. Lopez was a Mexican chef who had a background working at one of the best restaurants in Lima, Peru. She had come to Modena when she married Taka Kondo, and instead of placing her in the Osteria Francescana kitchen, Gilmore asked her to work with her on testing and writing recipes for a book. Bottura proposed to Lopez: "I have a project for you. It will be in Florence with one of the most beautiful companies that we have here in Italy." Bottura and Gilmore never looked back; it was the right choice. Within two years, Lopez received her first Michelin star, becoming the first female Mexican chef ever to be awarded one. Eventually, her husband, Kondo (one of Bottura's first hires), joined her in Florence, where the two became co-executive chefs in 2022. As Lopez remarked, "We are the most important restaurant in one of the most important *piazzas* in Italy, and it is run by a Mexican woman and a Japanese man."

Gucci Osteria was a hit, and excitement quickly mounted among their cadre of chefs. The next location would be Los Angeles—far-flung from the local Italian scene. Bottura and Gilmore sought to embrace the jump overseas without sacrificing the Modena-style quality and character. The man for the job, they determined, was Mattia Agazzi, who was then training as a sous chef under Lopez. Reflecting on Bottura's mentorship over many years, Agazzi put it simply: "Massimo helps you to be the next protagonist for whatever project there is. . . . Sometimes you don't agree, or you don't share the same ideas. But of course . . . based on how much you believe in Massimo, you just listen to him."

And like his mentor, Agazzi would bring with him the two Francescana Family pillars of impeccable quality and community immersion. Just weeks after becoming head chef at Gucci Osteria Beverly Hills, he and his team began collaborating with the Hollywood Food Coalition, a nonprofit focused on food insecurity. Volunteering in neighborhood soup kitchens, Agazzi's staff served about ten thousand meals in just two months.[24] "They started teaching the cooks there how to make pasta, how to clean fish," Bottura described. "They became a part of the community." Gilmore concurred. "[Great] chefs show more than the sum of their recipes. They ask themselves, 'What can I do with this skill that I have? How can I be a part of society, not just thinking about my own career, but others?'" And as for the new restaurant, it earned its first Michelin star in 2021, less than two years after opening.

Despite the exciting expansion of the Francescana Family, Bottura and Gilmore continued cultivating chefs at their home base and training ground in Modena. After the Covid-19 lockdown ended in Italy, Bottura asked his chefs at Osteria Francescana to return to the kitchen, with one caveat—before they did, each had to listen to *Sgt. Pepper's Lonely Hearts Club Band*, an iconic Beatles album, and then create a new dish. Gilmore explained his reasoning: "He said, 'This is what I'm going to do to keep everybody connected.' . . . They will listen to the songs and take a magical journey with their minds."

The entire team was all in—all inspired by different songs on the album, but unaware of why they had this peculiar assignment. The first days back in the kitchen were chaos, blending messy experimentation and excited energy all in one space. Shortly before Osteria Francescana reopened, the team finally understood: their new dishes would make up a new tasting menu. Bottura named the menu after a song on the record, "With a Little Help from My Friends." Rosval reflected on the experience:

When do you ever see a great chef like Massimo telling his cooks, "Now you make the menu" . . . in our three-Michelin-star restaurant? Massimo has that confidence, the willingness to share even his success, his spotlight. He looks inside people; he sees how hard they work, how hard the team works because we believe so much in what we're communicating. We believe so much in the family we have here.[25]

Lessons from a Seeding Success Story

Reversing a well-known maxim, "think local, act global" captures the heart of the culinary movement Bottura and Gilmore have catalyzed. Thirty years after its founding, Gilmore and Bottura still refer to Osteria Francescana as "the beating heart" of their work. For them, all roads lead back to Modena, whether from a Michelin-star restaurant in Tokyo or a refettorio in Sydney. It was there that they reimagined the Italian kitchen, balancing innovation with tradition. It was there that they learned how to build the social fabric required to help fortify the economy of Emilia-Romagna. It was there they could spark a domino effect with Osteria Francescana, establishing Food for Soul, Casa Maria Luigia, and other social enterprises to accelerate their work. Most importantly, it was there that they used their "values to create value." They seeded opportunities worldwide for their first-rate cadre of chefs and social entrepreneurs—each with their unique skills and passions yet steeped in the slow-food, fast-cars mindset. They all believed that social connections through food and culture could be a powerful force multiplier for positive impact.

In June 2023—nine years after Osteria Francescana received its third Michelin star—the American Academy in Rome presented Bottura with a McKim Medal, a "UNESCO intangible heritage" award for his achievements in Italian cuisine. Addressing the crowd in his acceptance speech, he said, "We recognize ourselves as a family that shares the same values that characterize our own sense of responsibility, because this is where awareness leads: it leads us to be responsible for each other, within the same group and outside, to our community." He paused for a moment, then repeated the four values at the heart of his leadership philosophy, values he believes all chefs need today: "Culture. Knowledge. Awareness. Sense of responsibility."

By the end of 2023, the Francescana Family employed 206 talented people in Modena, a rise from 140 people before the pandemic, and 500-plus people globally. Between all their ventures, there is a combined total of seven red (culinary) Michelin stars and two green (sustainability) Michelin stars. Since its inception, more than 150,000 volunteers have been involved in Food for Soul's refettorios, with more than 3.5 million meals served to a million-plus guests around the world.[26]

In Bottura and Gilmore's story, we've seen two leaders working side-by-side tirelessly to activate an innovation ecosystem by opening doors—creating canvases for others to express themselves—and keeping the door open for the unexpected. They've relied on a unique approach in doing so: if you keep searching, you will find more future around the corner. For catalysts like Bottura and Gilmore, the work of seeding is anchored in passing on their deeply held values to others and giving them freedom to grow and prosper. Leveraging food and culture, they launched a regenerative movement committed to food dignity and sustainability.

CHAPTER 11

Cultivating Frugal Innovation at Scale

Vineet and Anupama Nayar at Sampark Foundation

Sampark . . . was envisioned as an open-source organization. Others can borrow it, institute it, and replicate it. We don't have a problem with that. Our purpose of existence is to reach 20 million children. How we get through to them is a means to an end; it's not an end in itself.

—Vineet Nayar

We put ourselves in the teachers' shoes, in front of a class of disadvantaged children who had no one to help them at home, no place to go, and had little exposure to the world. We had to figure out how to bring the world to them.

—Anupama Nayar

In August 2014, Vineet and Anupama Nayar pulled into a school compound at the edge of a village in rural Punjab, India—the first of ten schools they would visit that day.[1] A decade earlier, the husband-and-wife team, together with Vineet's mother, had founded Sampark Foundation, committing $100 million of their personal wealth toward improving public primary education in India. But so far, Sampark had not accomplished what they had hoped. "We had been cutting checks, supporting

NGOs, experimenting with ideas, but nothing was happening," declared Vineet.[2]

In 2013, Vineet had stepped down from his CEO role at HCL Technologies, where he led the company's dramatic turnaround into a world-leading IT services business. Since then, Vineet had gotten more hands-on with Sampark and assisted in launching its biggest initiative yet: a partnership with the Punjab government and a local NGO to introduce a kit of teaching materials in five hundred schools. The materials were counting blocks, game boards, and other tactile tools intended to disrupt India's "factory model of education," too focused on rote learning.

On that hot August day, the Nayars were eager to see their program's impact on the ground. When they walked into the first classroom, they found a teacher reading words and phrases aloud from an English textbook to a crowded room of over thirty children. The students were sitting on mats rather than at desks. The dark room had no electricity, and its concrete walls were bare, except for a single chalkboard at the front. When the teacher asked the children to repeat the English words aloud, some responded in the same rote style; others didn't even bother.

Anupama herself was a teacher, and Vineet the son of a teacher. What they saw in that classroom was not what learning was supposed to look or feel like. The teaching kit their partner NGO had supplied was nowhere to be found. Later, the Nayars learned that it was tucked away in the principal's office, unopened, along with a stack of books and two computer tablets. The principal explained the teachers' fears that if the kits went missing or were damaged, they'd be held responsible by the local government officials. The principal added that as much as he appreciated the Nayars' interest, he had bigger problems on his mind: nearly half of the school's students and two of the teachers hadn't shown up that day. He and the remaining teacher were covering three classrooms, over a hundred students in total.

Having attended government schools in villages at the base of the Himalayas, the Nayars were not surprised by the school's visible resource constraints. They knew that the passage of India's 2009 Right to Education Act had led to rapid growth in enrollment that had further strained the system.[3] Teacher and student absenteeism were also known challenges, especially in poorer communities where parents often chose to send their children to work for money instead.

At the nine other schools they visited that day, the Nayars were similarly startled by the colorless classroom atmosphere and the children's dispirited participation. Vineet lamented, "The capacity of the teacher to teach was not there. The motivation of the parents to send children to school was not there. And hence the child was not interested. . . . We were teaching music to people who didn't understand the notes."

As they drove home, Vineet turned to Anupama and asked, "Just what are we attempting to do?" Like countless NGOs before them, Sampark was failing to make any meaningful impact on children's education. "We were happy," said Vineet. "We were covering five hundred schools; we were spending so much money. We were fooling ourselves. Our entire vocabulary was efforts, not outcomes." They needed to find another way—a systemic approach to tackle the problem. The stakes were simply too high: the 144 million children enrolled in public primary schools held the future of India in their hands. Above all, Vineet insisted that their solution must be large scale. "Everybody is working in these small pockets here and there," he said, "and everybody is thinking, 'I'm doing good for the society.' But if we don't address the masses, this is never going to get solved."

Vineet would remember Sampark's disastrous pilot in 2014 as "the year of many mistakes." This chapter tells how the Nayars and their team not only turned Sampark around but pumped new lifeblood into India's public education system. We'll see how the Nayars, like our previous catalyst leaders, map out their key stakeholders and seed a movement with disruptive yet frugal product innovations. But the lessons of Sampark go further because its mission goes further: to help millions of children harness their dignity and unleash their self-determination. Sampark built a wildly popular education movement by *cultivating* the capacity of millions of students, teachers, government officials, and community members to regenerate and sustain this movement on their own.

Mapping Out the "Value Zone"

From their 2014 pilot, the Nayars concluded that the problem with education in India was not simply the lack of resources, but a lack of inspiration. The government was spending more money on education every year.

Yet six out of ten children in grade five could not read grade two texts. Eight in ten could not do simple math sums. And while 96 percent of school-age children started first grade, more than a third dropped out of the system before finishing primary school.[4] Communities blamed teachers for the poor results; parents who could afford it moved their children to private schools. Not only were teachers overwhelmed with administrative duties; they were often responsible for teaching subjects, like English, that they had little mastery of themselves. Even the most well-intentioned educators could barely keep afloat.

The more Vineet contemplated their situation at Sampark, the more he was reminded of HCL in 2007. He joined the company as CEO when it had been stymied by a lack of motivation, commitment, and—as a result—innovation. As the IT outsourcing industry was transitioning from hardware to services, the "value zone" (where value was created at HCL) was shifting from internal R&D teams to the interface between frontline employees and customers. To transform HCL into one of India's leading IT services businesses, Vineet radically "inverted the organizational pyramid." Frontline employees, previously thought by all as the base, were moved to the top of the pyramid. The managers' role was no longer to direct and control the front line, but rather to "enthuse, enable, and empower" them to innovate on the customers' behalf. Vineet's provocative mantra "Employees First, Customers Second" became HCL's ethos. His radical approach was wildly controversial at first but eventually paid off. By the time Vineet stepped down in 2013, HCL's "value portal"—a platform where employees cocreated solutions with clients—had generated more than seven thousand innovations with an estimated impact of nearly $1 billion.[5] Revenues had grown from $700 million in 2005 to $4.7 billion in 2013, and HCL had scaled from 30,000 to 85,000 employees across thirty-two countries.[6]

It wasn't until Sampark's failure in Punjab that Vineet identified the true value zone in the education system: the relationship between the teacher and the child. *Teachers* were the frontline innovators Sampark needed to activate. But they were embedded in, and accountable to, a government bureaucracy administered by hundreds of thousands of officials who did not see the slices of genius in teachers. As Vineet considered how to ignite innovation in classrooms across the country, he reframed their challenge: "Could we be a catalyst of change, so that the government's investment would begin to yield more promising results?"

Anupama was hesitant. Taking on the task of catalyzing change in the government sounded impossibly slow, complex, and frustrating. But after many debates, the Nayars agreed: Sampark's purpose was not only to bring quality education to millions of children today but to secure the same opportunity for future generations. The only path to a scalable and sustainable solution was to bring the current government system along, converting teachers into innovative change agents and government officials into their empowering enablers. Vineet recognized the leadership task he was taking on: "At HCL, I inspired employees. In 'Teachers First,' the regional (and local) administrators were in a command-and-control position, and our outreach to the teachers could only be through them. This would be ten times more difficult yet ten times more powerful."

Since Sampark's founding, Vineet had insisted that he would not be its leader, even though he had agreed to be more involved with the Punjab experiment. But once he and Anupama understood the challenge they were taking on, he said, "The pretense of not being operational vanished. It was clear I needed to be the CEO of Sampark Foundation." The new vision was to transform Sampark from a philanthropy into a "disruptive design shop," as he put it. Vineet knew from the corporate world how a single innovation at the right price point could have rapid, large-scale impact across industries and societies. Sampark would adopt the same tactic: introduce disruptive products into classrooms that encouraged and spread innovation across the education system—and made it contagious. By necessity, these products had to be what they called "frugal innovations" if they were to reach thousands of classrooms.

The Nayars committed to a concrete goal: improve learning outcomes for 20 million children by 2025—at which point they would hand off all their materials and other intellectual property to the public education system, and Sampark would cease to exist.[7]

Seeding the Ecosystem with Technology

The Nayars knew they couldn't follow the path of other NGOs and simply drop iPads into schools with no electricity. True to the meaning of *sampark*—"connections" in Hindi—the Nayars agreed that Sampark's products should nurture emotional bonds between teachers and students and improve relationships between teachers and government. But they should also inspire government officials to invest in the classroom experience, compel parents to encourage their children's learning, and ultimately, make education a pillar of India's communities. Technology would be essential, but only insofar as it enabled the human experience. As Vineet explained:

> If Sampark could help make the classroom transaction exciting, the teacher would take credit for that . . . , the children would start coming back to school, and the whole system would be encouraged. The [product] innovation had to put the teacher at the center and be such that it was easy to understand, easy to digest, easy to execute, fun, and ignited the classroom dynamic. . . . If a child said, "I love you" to his teacher, it would be so contagious that it would revolutionize everything.

Product innovation would be Anupama's domain. Over decades of teaching, she had developed a deep appreciation for the psychological and social aspects of children's learning—too often overlooked in Indian education. After painstaking research into global best practices, and speaking with teachers in rural classrooms, Anupama and a small team developed Sampark Smart Shala. This math and English program for grades one to five had four parts: a pedagogy, a kit of physical teaching materials, teacher training, and a monitoring system. While the teaching materials from most NGOs added more work for teachers, Sampark's were tailored to states' required curricula and designed to make the teachers' jobs easier.

At the heart of Sampark was its pedagogy, which aimed to help teachers shift from rote-based learning to fun, activity-based learning. Its premise was to follow children's natural cognitive journeys: start with concrete, real-world examples and then move to abstract concepts. Anupama also insisted that their materials resonate with children in their specific contexts:

> We could not use an ice cream cone for reference—the child, not in their wildest dreams, knew what an ice cream cone was. To teach fractions, pizza was out of [the] question. To teach

vocabulary, there was no furniture in the home—there was no table, there was no chair. We had to get down to the level of what was in their specific environment.

Although it made their job significantly more time- and energy-intensive, Anupama's team tailored every poster and game board to the specific linguistic, cultural, and environmental context where they'd be used—for example, teaching counting in one state with pictures of mangoes and guavas, while another state might use images of plums and peaches.

Implementing Sampark Smart Shala

The operational task of bringing Sampark Smart Shala into schools was Vineet's domain, and it required formal permission from state governments. Vineet understood officials' sensitivities toward NGOs. "[They] come in and say that they're going to do X, Y, Z, and then they disappear," said an official from Uttarakhand.

To initiate a partnership, Vineet focused on building trust at the top of the education bureaucracy's chain of command. His personal brand as a former CEO opened doors to meetings with senior officials, and his years of leading innovation in the private sector taught him to stimulate demand for behavioral change. It was Vineet's ability to speak "the language of votes, the language of the officials," as he put it—to articulate *how* improving educational outcomes would translate to the ballot box—that made many willing to listen.

Vineet insisted that "if you want somebody to do something, make it easy for them." Sampark, he explained to officials, was more than a world-class product tailored to their state context. His team would train the teachers, distribute the materials, and monitor the program in every school in the state. And while Sampark would cover the costs of this end-to-end solution in the beginning, Vineet insisted the government over time would need skin in the game as well.

In 2014, Vineet secured partnerships with the states of Chhattisgarh and Uttarakhand to roll out Sampark Smart Shala in more than forty thousand schools. (In his years in business, Vineet had developed a habit of agreeing to impossible goals—and then figuring out how to deliver later.) The joint secretary to the chief minister of Chhattisgarh, Rajat Kumar, recalled:

> Sampark's commitment was so much more than what we generally saw [from NGOs]. They understood that we didn't want islands of great results, but that we wanted intervention across all schools in the state. They brought the funding, the materials, the training, and their own accountability structure, which demonstrated to us their sincerity of purpose. We were not disbanding or changing our schools or teachers; their proposition was just to add value to the existing system.

Vineet knew that the buy-in he secured at the top of the education bureaucracy would not simply trickle down to local communities. It had to be cultivated intentionally by his team at Sampark, which he called the "Sparks," the term he had used to refer to front-liners at HCL.[8] With a long-term view of transferring the program to the government, Vineet insisted that Sampark's field presence remain asset-light. He hired only one Spark per district, each responsible for distributing kits, training teachers, and monitoring implementation in about a thousand schools. Vineet knew this was an impossible task for any one person to handle, but that was by design: he intended for the Sparks to be the change-making CEOs of their district, finding innovative ways of engaging officials, teachers, and community members to help them meet their numbers.

Sampark started small and phased its releases—beginning with five hundred schools. To build demand for its program at the local level, Sampark hosted inaugural launch events in each district attended by press, teachers, and community members. "Vineet Nayar showing up signaled to us that their commitment to this work was real," said one official.

Inventing Sampark Didi

Just months after launching the program, Vineet received feedback from the government of Chhattisgarh: the math materials were great, but could Sampark provide an English teaching program as well? They wanted a program they could launch at an event three months away. Without hesitation, Vineet accepted the request. Anupama and her pedagogy team were in disbelief—the math program had taken them years to refine. But after just weeks of iteration, they developed a small orange speaker with preloaded English lessons narrated by a playful fictional teacher called Sampark Didi—*didi* meaning "sister" in Hindi. Drawing inspiration from Bollywood, Didi taught English through hundreds of stories and songs designed to capture children's hearts and imaginations. It was powered by a rechargeable battery, so it could work in schools with no electricity.

Through Sampark Didi, children would learn five hundred new words and be able to form a hundred new sentences in one year's time. Alongside them, teachers would learn proper pronunciation and gain the confidence to teach English. Best of all, Sampark Didi's English lessons built to a climax: a play called *My Family* that students were to perform in their village squares. "Few in the audience would be able to understand anything," Vineet observed, but "when parents heard their child talking about them in English, it told them something meaningful was happening at school."

Activating the Catalyst in Others

Soon after the launch in Chhattisgarh and Uttarakhand, Vineet realized he'd "made a blunder" with some of the Sparks he hired. Those from India's top universities were not up to the task of working in areas of extreme poverty, with no access to food or plumbing. "They had a vision of education," Anupama explained, "and they had great ideas, but they didn't want to do the dirty work."

For the Spark role, the Nayars soon decided they would worry less about academic credentials and hire for attitude. Their next cadre of Sparks were people "who [knew] themselves what it [was] like to sit in those classrooms," said Anupama. The Nayars committed to training each Spark personally. They recalled one instance when a new Spark traveled three days on foot, after landslides in his village disrupted transportation, just to attend the training. "He sat down straight in the training," Anupama recalled, "without washing his face." Vineet added, "He had not eaten, he had not drunk anything. I actually folded my hands and said, 'I wish I had that in me.'"

Instead of just imparting skills, the Nayars awakened the Sparks' passion and hunger for self-improvement. They encouraged new hires to connect their personal values to Sampark's purpose and articulate what they hoped to learn in this job. Then, Vineet explained, "We [threw] people into positions they had never done before." The Sparks pulled all-nighters to prepare presentations on topics they knew nothing about, and Vineet provided rigorous feedback, reminding them, "I can only enable—I cannot make you succeed." As one of Sampark's Sparks described, "He was a very tough boss, but he always challenged us to do wonders. He always motivated us and inspired us to do big work in life." Vineet made it known that the Sparks were free to opt out of this training at any time, but none ever did.

Vineet and Anupama transformed the Sparks into cohorts of catalysts who were confident, autonomous self-starters. By setting the stage for them to achieve something they never thought possible, the Nayars helped the Sparks raise their expectations of themselves and learn to do the same for others. "When you come back and say, 'Even I can do this,' you will start leading," said Vineet. "It's an agonizing process. You need to have patience for that. But after that, it's magic."

Activating Teachers and Officials

The Sparks determined on their own how to transform teachers and officials in their districts into change agents. Teacher trainings were their first opportunity to shift teachers' mindsets—and for many Sparks, it was their first-ever public-speaking experience. In stark contrast to the usual government workshops, the Sparks used songs, dance, and games in their sessions to show teachers what joyful, empowering classrooms *could* feel like. They were careful to introduce Didi as the teachers' "creative pair." Sarita Devi, a principal of a school in Gorakhpur, agreed: "Didi does not, in any way, replace teachers. Emotions and culture are developed by human beings, not the machine. . . . Without the teacher, there is nothing."

After training, the Sparks built trust and momentum with teachers through in-person school visits. Although they were tasked with monitoring the use of the pedagogy and materials in classrooms, the Sparks explained to the teachers that their role was "to help you . . . simplify your day-to-day work," as one put it. If a teacher was jumping straight to abstract concepts or not pausing to check student comprehension before moving on to new lessons, the Spark nudged gently. As Anupama explained, "We couldn't say, 'You just move aside, and we'll tell you how to teach.'"

For every school, Vineet decided that Sampark would provide one Smart Shala kit and train one teacher. While this was an operational necessity, the scarcity took on a dual function with careful tending from the Sparks. As trust was built, the Sparks asked teachers about their own ideas for new teaching materials, encouraging them to act on these ideas and invite others in their schools and communities to do the same. "Teachers had a lot to say and felt like no one listened to them," explained one Spark, Sandeep Kumar. "Listening to them made them willing to listen to us." Reena Dobhal, a teacher in Uttarakhand, described Kumar's first visit to her school: "He was so energetic. He demonstrated the kit with the children. I was inspired to be more energetic as a teacher [and] to create new kinds of materials." Over time, Dobhal regularly shared her ideas for new tools with Sandeep for feedback "because of the faith and trust built with him."

In addition to engaging teachers, the Sparks worked arduously to transform local officials into advocates. Getting on officials' calendars could take weeks, sometimes months. There were days when Sparks waited five hours in officials' offices for five minutes of face-to-face time. They learned to use these waiting times to turn the officials' assistants into thought partners, asking them about their views on education and informing them about Sampark.

Still, many new Sparks feared speaking with officials. But after hours of practice delivering pitches to each other and their managers, they learned to seize every moment they got. The Sparks always brought Sampark's kits and printouts of their monitoring data and third-party assessments to meetings, so officials could touch and feel the materials themselves. Many officials were immediately impressed with the product, as well as the data. "I visit schools frequently and I can be more specific and targeted when I go," said one official. "I am able to ask better questions about what teachers need from us." Another official commented on the Sparks' role as enablers: "The government is the backbone of any education initiative that tries to get started here in India. In the past, other NGOs have not understood that, but Sampark does."

Election cycles were a constant challenge for Sampark as the entire chain of education functionaries could be replaced at once. Even between cycles, officials rotated in and out of their roles every year, if not sooner. When a key government champion moved out, it completely disrupted Sampark's momentum in a state. This meant that for the Sparks, relationship-building never stopped. One official from Varanasi applauded their commitment:

> Sampark is not just an NGO that comes into schools and takes pictures and then leaves. They want to make change. They recognize how their role is to implement and celebrate the success of teachers, teachers that are inspiring because they work day and night to create impact. In other words, Sampark understands how teachers are a critical part of the change exercise.

It became best practice for the Sparks to invite every new official in their district to join them on their school visits. "Faith is something that's built over time," one senior official remarked. "When I entered this role . . . I didn't know Sampark. But then I interacted with them, visited schools myself, and saw the teachers and students recognize them. I felt the energy . . . this made me a believer."

Over time, the Sparks became a trusted source of insights and ideas for officials. "When I talk to [the Sampark team], listen to them, my capacity builds. From morning to evening, we see files. But Sampark tells us what teachers and students need. It's like learning a new language and seeing the problem and solution in a new way," said an official from Uttarakhand.

Building Momentum by Learning and Adapting Together

Vineet expected everyone in his organization to constantly seek ways to improve their work. Sampark, he explained, was a "learning place, not a place for a career." As Priya Pandey, Sampark's human resource colleague, explained, "He looked at employees beyond their defined job responsibilities. If he saw capability in someone, he assigned tasks that seemed impossible at first, but which enabled learning and encouraged growth." Instead of trying to retain talent, Vineet actively encouraged everyone to move on as soon as their learning had stopped: "Instead of being afraid of their leaving, we decided to celebrate it. I told them I would be their reference. If they went for an interview, we would train them. The Sparks were surprised by this."

By cultivating constant learning and growth in his team, Vineet infused the organization with unstoppable momentum. Sampark, in his words, was a "high-energy, self-run organization"—one where every employee, even those in the head office, was "continually in motion." Recognizing that one good product wasn't enough to keep teachers and officials energized and engaged over time, the organization continued collecting feedback and responding to stakeholders' evolving priorities. "Every methodology will become obsolete in a year's time," Vineet told his team.

Sampark's product innovation was an iterative dialogue across the whole organization and its external stakeholders, much of which occurred over WhatsApp. The Sparks—Sampark's eyes and ears in the field—constantly fed feedback from teachers and officials into WhatsApp groups to inform decisions on the pedagogy, creative, and operations teams in Delhi. As Ulhas Shah, state head of Maharashtra, said, "If things from the ground are not communicated, things cannot be improved from the top."

Vineet and Anupama insisted that every new product idea be subject to rigorous debate and scrutiny. When their perspectives differed, the couple weren't afraid to have fiery debates in front of the team; they sent the message that friction was welcome and necessary for innovation. "I get excited about scale, execution, people, implementation," said Vineet, who often was biased toward speed. Anupama complemented this view as the guardian of quality and empathy: "He sees the big picture. But I don't let him move forward without the details being covered." Vineet firmly believed that "if you can have conflict up front, then execution is easier."

The founders encouraged employees to think of every new product or decision as "working hypotheses" rather than fixed initiatives. "If you launch a decision as an initiative," Vineet noted, "people wait for it to fail. If you launch it as an experiment—indicating that you will reverse it if it doesn't go right—people participate in shaping it. They own it." There was always, however, one final bar to meet: "We do not implement any-thing without the approval of the Sparks," said Vineet.

In addition to expanding their teaching materials into new subjects and grade levels, Sampark used design thinking to cocreate a host of new digital tools. In 2016, when smartphones and broadband access began to spread to rural areas, the organization launched Sampark Baithak—an app with hundreds of hours of cartoon videos bringing Didi to life. Anupama's pedagogy and creative teams added QR codes to Sampark's student workbooks that linked to these videos, so students could continue their learning from home. Students had to ask parents for their phones to view the videos, engaging entire families in children's nightly homework.

Embedding Support Systems

Vineet was encouraged when more states began contacting him for meetings; it meant Sampark's innovations were drawing attention. But as we've seen already in part III, the issue of *sustaining* momentum is a key one for the catalyst. Once the seeds of innovation are sown, who will water them and provide sunlight and nutrients to grow? In other words, once a catalyst has initiated mindset and behavioral changes, what can they do to make them endure?

As catalysts, Vineet and Anupama needed to build support systems to empower key stakeholders to cocreate without them.[9] Vineet had special concern for the Sparks in the field: "How could we create an environment where people were constantly getting validation, despite not being in the same physical space?" This is where digital tools could play a big role in maintaining a "culture of togetherness," as Vineet put it. In Sampark's WhatsApp groups, he and Anupama encouraged everyone in the organization to share their stories. "When I, or a state head . . . liked a comment on WhatsApp," said Vineet, "it was such a high for the guy who was remote. That was recognition. That was community."

Following the Nayars' example, the Sparks found ways of cultivating stakeholder relationships in the field. When they observed that teachers in the same community didn't communicate, they put them into WhatsApp groups, encouraging them to discuss challenges, exchange advice, and share examples of innovations they used in their classrooms. The Sparks were surprised at how quickly these groups evolved into marketplaces for ideas. For example, a Spark recalled one chat in Haryana where a teacher posted about his handmade Sampark-style Hindi teaching kit and, based on the response, began selling it for 650 rupees.

The Sparks also continued focusing on the relationship between officials and teachers. When Sampark expanded to new states, the Sparks observed that teachers were afraid to open Sampark's kits. "Historically," one official explained, "everything related to classroom materials was kept on record. If the government provided library books, [they] would check the number of books and their quality and status when they were monitoring the schools. So, the teachers used to keep the books hidden. To break that mentality was very difficult."

Changing teachers' mindsets would require embedding a more enabling (and less punitive) approach from the government. Constantly seeking ways to streamline the Sparks' work, Sampark's three-person technology team developed an offline mobile app where Sparks could input their monitoring data in under sixty seconds. The team created a similar app for government officials, where prompts became guardrails for behavior: they focused only on whether the materials and pedagogy were being *used*, with no mention of lost items or performance. If teachers were using the tools in innovative ways, officials were encouraged to celebrate them.

Over time, teachers became more open to voicing challenges, while officials became more encouraging of classroom innovation. Naveen Jain, the secretary of education in Rajasthan, described how he proactively "liked" and shared teachers' posts about their Sampark-inspired innovations on Facebook. He created a Star Teacher Award and a Teachers Innovation Club, an annual two-day workshop where 150 teachers developed new classroom tools with Jain and officials from multiple levels of the government. As one official who attended the workshop described:

> Everyone was able to collaborate and work together on developing new ideas. . . . There were no hierarchies, as everyone was speaking openly and collaborating at this workshop. . . . Usually any interaction between government officials and teachers was one directional, so this was different from our previous meetings with teachers.

To Vineet, these were positive signs. Officials and teachers were learning to cocreate together, allowing the education system to work differently going forward.

The Movement Accelerates

By the end of 2019, Sampark's team of 130 people had managed to reach 7 million students and 200,000 teachers in 90,000 public schools across six states.[10] Nine more states had approached Vineet, while nonprofits were contacting him every week for strategic advice. Even private schools wanted to buy materials from Sampark. "It was getting bigger than what we had imagined," Anupama noted.

An official in Uttarakhand (one of the first states in which Sampark launched) observed, "When I visit the school and see the ground-level work, I see a change in the vision of teachers [and] the capacity of students, their mastery. It is not imagination; it is reality." Through WhatsApp, social media, and local networks, teachers' new tools and methods were spreading. They were using basic materials from matchsticks to marbles in new ways to teach math. Teachers were systematically tracking student comprehension and reorganizing their activities based on what they learned.

Another official in Uttarakhand said that "students that are now in grades seven through ten look back and remember the impact of Didi." Vineet added:

> Didi brought the kind of emotion we needed—everybody was excited, everybody was singing and dancing. The teacher was credited with bringing the "magic box" into the classroom and there was love for her. For the first time, she was teaching English, and suddenly she was a respected participant in the community.

Across states, schools implemented a policy where the class that arrived first received Sampark's kit for the day. "From a situation where everybody used to come two hours late to school," Vineet explained, "everybody was coming one hour early." A principal in Uttarakhand noted that before, his students "were neither interested nor confident in English." Now, they could be heard gleefully singing Sampark Didi's English songs all their way home from school.

Teachers reported that students were eager to continue their learning from home. Many created their own learning materials out of recycled trash, garlands—whatever they could find. They flipped ahead in their Sampark workbooks at night and came to school *asking* the teacher for upcoming lessons. A teacher reflected on the change: "Learning has evolved from just memorizing and then forgetting into learning from the heart. . . . Sampark Didi motivates my students . . . they want to become her. She is a role model for them." Even parents had begun attending teacher conferences for the first time. As one principal described, "When parents come to the school, they say, 'My child is speaking English at home, saying, 'Hello, how are you?'"

Above all, students were learning. Academic scores were up by 32 percent according to Sampark's external reviewer.[11] Stories of Sampark's program spread quickly across communities. Parents were transferring their children from private schools back to government schools, which many principals and teachers attributed to the Sampark program. While the Sampark team hadn't expected it, parents were learning too. An official from Chhattisgarh, another early partner for Sampark, explained:

> In some places, mothers used to come to play with their children at the schools. They started peeping on the classes and seeing the audio box and [teaching materials], watching their kids performing in the school. Being illiterate, they also started to learn the tips and become more curious about how they could support the kids in their learning. As a result, we started "Mothers Orientation" in a big way across the state.

Seeing the impact firsthand, governments had woven Sampark into their capacity-building and accountability systems. "I had been in the department for twenty-five years," one official remarked, "and I had never seen any education program continuously reviewed by the chief minister."

Governments were updating their own pedagogies and materials following Sampark's model. Sampark had even begun to transfer ownership of printing workbooks and progress charts to governments.

From Vineet's perspective, all of this was evidence that Sampark's movement had taken off: "Everybody was talking about innovation in education. There would be experimentations far beyond what Sampark was doing, but now the yardstick was whether it could be full scale, if it was frugal, and if it was interesting. That muscle memory was here to stay."

The Tipping Point: Sampark TV

As the Covid-19 pandemic hit India in early 2020 and schools shut down across the country, over two hundred thousand teachers flocked to Sampark's Baithak app for support, crashing Sampark's servers.[12] "It has never happened in my life. I was so embarrassed," said Vineet. "It took us twenty days to fix it. We would build a server and then it would crash because usage was going up. We were adding ten to twelve thousand new teachers every day. . . . Teachers were frustrated. My employees were frustrated. It was very painful."

Once the app stabilized, it became a lifeline for daily users. Teachers were posting pictures of outdoor classrooms they had cocreated with their villages.[13] They were broadcasting Sampark Didi from loudspeakers of temples and churches. Sampark responded with a host of digital classroom innovations, like podcasts for teachers that could be facilitated over WhatsApp and Zoom. Vineet partnered with national TV broadcasters and arranged for Sampark's video content to be played on cable across the country.

In the middle of the pandemic, Vineet read articles describing Netflix's strategy for reaching millions of subscribers in India, tipping him off that something had "changed dramatically about consuming content in this country."[14] If Netflix could reach this scale, why not Sampark? He charged a team to explore what a Netflix model for education could look like. After eight months, the team had developed a small orange box with preloaded content called Sampark TV. Like Apple TV, this device could make any television "smart," but without requiring an internet connection. It was a one-stop shop of video lessons and activities covering all grade levels and subjects—designed, as always, to *complement* rather than replace teachers.

As schools began to reopen in 2021, the first Sampark TVs were piloted in five hundred schools. Students were ecstatic. Not only did it bring their favorite character, Didi, to life on a grand scale, but the cartoon star led a new type of assessment called *Didi Ke Sawaal* ("Didi's Questions"). Reminiscent of "Who Wants to Be a Millionaire?" Didi presented students with multiple-choice questions at the end of each lesson. If the students answered correctly, they would collectively earn points, which they could use to unlock hundreds of additional stories and videos. Students who used to be terrified by assessments were now eager to participate. Reflecting on Sampark's first analog tools, Anupama said, "We never in our wildest dreams thought that something like Sampark TV would appear."

From Vineet's perspective, the story of Sampark boiled down to two eras: before Sampark TV and after. The innovation spread the Sampark movement like wildfire. Teachers became more proactive than ever, collaborating with their communities to procure televisions. Parents were now moving their children from private to public schools in droves, and—for the first time in several districts' histories—government schools were oversubscribed. As one teacher in Gorakhpur noted:

> When the Sampark TV was introduced in this school, the parents were skeptical. They were initially concerned, asking, "Are my kids going to watch YouTube all day?" We called all the parents to the school to learn about the TV and how it works as an educational device. Now we hold regular meetings with them. The locality sees we have a Sampark TV, and now, they appreciate that. On holidays, they come to the school and want to learn more about its progress.

State officials were also invigorated. "Before [the] Sampark TV device came to our classrooms, we viewed 'smart classrooms' as 'fancy things,' unattainable until all other basic needs were met, like running water in the schools and sanitation," one government official from Varanasi remarked. "Our perception of how important it is for both students and teachers changed when it first arrived."

Best of all, the government was getting the credit—exactly what Sampark was hoping for. One teacher in Dehradun noted, "I'm thankful to the government for what they have done here—and I've called them and told them that directly. . . . We feel proud because we feel like we're teaching in a good institution." Governments, in turn, began investing in electrifying classrooms at scale. "For the first time in my life," described Vineet, "I have a situation where the demand is outstripping supply by ten to one. They want Sampark TV in every class. They want more and more subjects. They want more and more languages. It's a good problem to have."

Lessons Learned: Cultivating Regenerative Ecosystems

In early 2024, nearly a decade after that dismal day of school visits in Punjab, Vineet and Anupama were sitting in the back of a classroom in Maharashtra, one of their newest partner states. The room was overflowing with schoolchildren singing, dancing, and jumping out of their seats to answer questions their teacher was relaying in partnership with Sampark TV. Their local Spark had received an award for her relationship-building efforts with government officials, and when she arrived that day, the children rushed to her, calling her Sampark Didi. That, said the Spark, is when you know "you have accomplished what you set out to do." Government officials saw the impact of Sampark TV, with one noting:

> Children are now questioning things more often. There is a huge cultural shift occurring here—a historically protective society is now seeing certain ideals evolving, and parent perceptions are evolving as a result. . . . One example is how emotional parents are when they see how their children are learning via TVs. This is still a device that is lacking in most village homes, so this is very powerful to our rural families.

The Sampark story encapsulates what it means for catalysts to drive innovation at scale. Vineet and Anupama inspired and empowered the Sparks to become independent catalysts, who then activated the teachers and officials, who themselves learned to work in new ways together. Over time, this chain of catalysts pulled in skeptical colleagues, parents, and entire communities to cocreate on behalf of their children. If anything warrants being called a movement, Sampark is it.

The Nayars' story represents a key lesson in this book: scaling innovation is ultimately about inviting others to take ownership in shaping their own future. Catalysts find their "value zone" and use "contagion," as Vineet and Anupama put it early on, to activate others far beyond their immediate sphere of influence. They cultivate the movement by providing others with tools and systems to cocreate, building a regenerative ecosystem in the process.

Vineet and Anupama are confident Sampark will reach 20 million children by 2027—a deadline extended by two years owing to the pandemic. They are well on their way already, with 15 million children reached, 500,000 teachers trained, 250,000 teaching kits distributed, and 53,000 Sampark TVs in classrooms—all for $1 per child per year.[15]

As for the future of Sampark, the Nayars aren't concerned. From day one, the foundation was never an end in itself. It was a means to cultivate genius at scale. As catalysts, the Nayars know it is ultimately up to the teachers, governments, and communities to cocreate the future of education in India—to carry on the movement long after Sampark is gone.

The Way Forward

Cristina Ventura at White Star Capital

T his book is meant as a provocation: to show you the art of the possible and embolden you to cocreate the future you and your colleagues
imagine for your organization, your community, and beyond.[1] From
the beginning, we had one guiding question: How do great leaders drive
innovation at scale?

When we started our research for this book, we were not sure what we
would learn. The leaders we studied—and the stories we've shared—
reaffirmed the key lesson of *Collective Genius*. Leading innovation is not
about marshaling followers; it's about *architecting* an environment that
fosters cocreation—collaboration, experimentation, and learning. But our
new research showed us that the paradigm shift introduced there did not
go far enough. Democratizing innovation in-house is the foundation for
genius at scale. Great leaders of innovation today and tomorrow are also
bridgers and *catalysts* who forge partnerships and movements, spurring cocreation far beyond their organization's boundaries. Together, the ABCs
work in concert to amplify innovative ambitions and deliver on them—
beyond what a single organization can achieve alone.

Many leaders recognize the urgent need for this fundamental shift in
leadership. In our work we regularly meet senior executives who acknowledge the challenges posed by our dynamic, complex, and interconnected
global economy. At a town hall, you could hear a pin drop when the CEO
of a major industrial multinational said he had "no clear vision for their
future." He declared that "the company would have to find their future

together." An automotive CEO wrote a letter to the citizens of the European Union, imploring the general public and their stakeholders to see that no company, no matter how well run, can deliver an affordable electric vehicle alone; the private sector, government, and NGOs would have to "work horizontally" to build a prosperous, carbon-neutral future together.[2] But who will lead the way?

We think of the individuals in this book as *wayfinders*—exceptional business leaders who help orient us to where we are and where we want to go. Why wayfinders instead of pathfinders? A pathfinder has a destination in mind and blazes a trail for others to follow; a wayfinder discovers both the route and the goal on the way. Wayfinding epitomizes adaptability to ever-changing environments; we can never follow a wayfinder's footsteps exactly, but we can draw insight from them, finding our own way.

Wayfinding defies easy summaries with takeaway bullets. Our leaders navigated choppy waters on their innovation journeys, like ancient seafarers who used the sun, stars, ocean currents, cloud formations, or wildlife patterns to cross uncharted seas without sophisticated instruments. We've seen that wayfinding means slowing down in the short term to go faster and further in the long term. It requires taking the time to clarify the purpose that animates you and those working with you. It requires curiosity and diligence to gain an intimate understanding of the specific circumstances in which you're operating. Ultimately, it requires tenacity as you embrace the hard work of marrying bold ambition with grounded reality.

We leave you then with an invitation to turn inward: *How can you prepare yourself and others to lead innovation—with a realistic, yet optimistic, view of the demands ahead?* To support your reflections, we share some final vignettes of one more wayfinder, Cristina Ventura, a general partner at tech investment firm White Star Capital.[3] Ventura was the first leader we ever met whose formal job title is "chief catalyst officer."

Be Curious About Yourself and Others

"Cristina, what is your 'why'? And how would you like to leave a legacy?" asked Jennifer Woo, CEO and chair of Lane Crawford Joyce Group (LCJG). Ventura was stunned. It was 2013, and during her already accomplished career—at LVMH, Gucci, Prada, and most recently at Apple—no leader had ever asked her this question. Ventura had always devoted time to self-reflection. But Woo's simple yet profound gesture—her genuine curiosity about Ventura, at a human level—soon brought clarity. As she searched for her "honest answer within," Ventura realized that what ignited her passion throughout her career was "catalyzing evolution and personal growth" in others, so they could "make their own path to sustainable impact." After that interview, Ventura knew Woo was a leader with whom she could live out these values and continue to evolve herself.

Many people move through their careers, ascending corporate ranks to formal leadership positions without reflecting on the "why" that drives them. Perhaps no one has ever asked about your why, or you've never asked yourself. As we've illustrated throughout this book, leading innovation requires courage. It often feels like staring into a fog, and leaders need a sense of their why to guide them through messy terrain and have the confidence to act.

Woo's question was a gift that awakened the *catalyst* within Ventura and initiated conversations between them about their individual and shared values. A Spaniard who had been living in Hong Kong for a decade, Ventura shared that many Asian values—like family and community—deeply aligned with those she grew up with in Catalonia. As the head of her multigenerational family business, long regarded as Asia's premier luxury retail and brand management group, Woo emphasized her company's guiding principles: responsibility, sustainability, and leaving a meaningful legacy.

Woo's view of business resonated with Ventura, whose own parents were entrepreneurs. When the two discussed the future of LCJG, both agreed they were inspired by how the Asian customer was redefining the meaning of luxury consumption. Rather than seek flashy products in luxury, they sought personal meaning—"an experience, a lifestyle—something that makes you be the best version of yourself," said Ventura.

Out of their conversations emerged an entirely new position within LCJG, "chief catalyst officer." Woo asked Ventura to shape the role around her talents and passions. Ventura seized the opportunity by launching something new for the company: a corporate accelerator. The Cage, as they called it, would incubate new businesses at the intersection of technology and lifestyle—an intersection becoming ever more salient in the fashion industry. The Cage would provide entrepreneurs with the education, resources, and relationships needed to start a business. More than that, Ventura decided to formalize an onboarding process that would allow her to pass on the gift of clarity and orientation that Woo had given her.

Ventura developed a full-fledged curriculum, including self-discovery and meditation sessions, to help each young entrepreneur in the accelerator define their purpose and align it with their business strategy and ambitions. The process was unorthodox, encouraging self-awareness and self-management. Ventura asked questions to spark reflection and conversations that wandered into "existential explorations of the life experiences that had shaped them." As one young engineer put it, "I just wanted to start a business, do some technology. . . . But Cristina let me start to [clarify] how to align my purpose and values with my business. . . . This was life-changing thinking to me." For this entrepreneur, knowing her "why" and having a mentor who knew her deepest aspirations, not just her business model, proved invaluable as she weathered the inevitable ups and downs of leading a startup.[4]

Ventura understood that innovation starts with *meaningful* relationships. Instead of building large startup cohorts, she chose depth over scale, partnering only with "mission-driven entrepreneurs [committed to] making a tangible difference." By 2018, The Cage had graduated three cohorts, and upon graduation, every single one of its startups received funding, commercial agreements with LCJG or other companies, or some combination of both. As Ventura often says, "Values create value." We agree. Be curious—start a conversation about values with yourself and others. Ask the question: What is your "why"?

Dare to Try

From the beginning, The Cage was more than a startup accelerator for Ventura. It was a platform to amplify her impact. Ventura channeled all of her diverse experiences and relationships into building a vibrant ecosystem around The Cage's entrepreneurs. More than accelerating startups, The Cage became a generative community of academics, investors, and technologists, bound by a shared commitment to impact. The distinct value Ventura created stemmed from her willingness to push beyond her comfort zone and continually reinvent herself throughout what she called her "global, zigzag career."[5]

Ventura grew up in a small town outside of Barcelona. After university, she started her career in London at the UK headquarters of LVMH, a French multinational that manages over seventy-five luxury brands. Over seven years, she had five promotions at different brands within LVMH. Headhunters came calling as a result of her varied business development and operational roles. After accepting a position at Gucci with responsibilities in Europe and the Middle East, she was soon transferred to Asia—where, at age twenty-nine, she found herself managing thirteen hundred employees across fourteen countries. She then moved to regional retail director at the Prada Group, where she played a key role in launching its IPO in 2009.

Although moving to new continents where she knew no one and didn't speak the language was challenging, Ventura's curiosity—about what she might learn and who she might become—gave her the courage to accept these challenges. When she arrived in Hong Kong in 2005, she immersed herself in the culture and built relationships with whomever she could—from the man who sold flowers on her street, to local entrepreneurs, to senior executives of local firms and global conglomerates. Ventura did not discount any interaction as unimportant. The more time she spent with locals, the more aware she became that Asia was ahead of the West. In particular, the younger generations inspired her not just in their values-based approach to luxury, but in their willingness to push the frontiers of technological innovation.

Over the course of her various roles, Ventura developed a deep appreciation for the nuances of luxury brands, company cultures, and local consumer markets, while learning to continually adapt to new contexts. In 2011, she was recruited to open Apple's Asian market in Hong Kong and South China—what Ventura called a "game-changing" assignment.

In joining Apple, Ventura traded her designer wardrobe for T-shirts and jeans. Shifting from fashion to technology felt like a move to a new world. But her curiosity, openness, and willingness to learn allowed her to connect her past experiences to the opportunity before her. Apple, like the fashion brands she knew well, was about delivering a holistic luxury experience, but this time to the mass consumer. Ventura architected a team of mostly high-energy twenty-somethings, all of whom were consummate innovative problem-solvers. She found herself shuttling between Cupertino and Hong Kong where, she observed, "It helped that I was from neither the US nor Asia." Instead, her colleagues saw her as the perfect "bridge between East and West and luxury and technology." Working closely with her team and headquarters, she opened Apple's iconic flagship store in Hong Kong on September 18, 2011. During her two-year tenure at Apple, Ventura grew a high-performing team of fifteen hundred members to contribute to what became Apple's $8.8 billion market in China.[6]

At the intersection of her new tech expertise and her passion for innovation and sustainability, Ventura identified a new opportunity. She launched an entrepreneurial venture, LUXARITY (which combined the words "luxury" and "circularity"), a secondhand luxury goods pop-up store that donated all proceeds toward social initiatives and educational grants for design students.[7] This wasn't just any secondhand shopping experience; it was a call to join a sustainability and luxury movement. Ventura mobilized her Hong Kong network, connecting with her friends and many of the city's socialites and celebrities to donate luxury pieces from their wardrobes. She also partnered with blockchain experts to create a digital provenance for each item, so customers could digitally trace the story behind every piece—tapping into young consumers' desire for meaning and sustainability in luxury.

The relationships Ventura built through LUXARITY led to invitations to speak at several local design and tech schools. Ventura, a lifelong learner, had at several points in her career devoted her vacation time and salary bonuses to enrolling in executive education programs around the world.[8] In her words, the people she met through these courses, and the ideas and perspectives she was exposed to, "completely changed my life." Though she had never imagined herself at the front of a classroom, she gave teaching a try, bringing her own leadership style to the task. As a fellow instructor observed, Ventura's approach was less to teach and more to learn together with the students: "I personally haven't crossed [paths with] that many leaders who welcome and are humble enough to get down and dirty with students . . . to want to discuss their ideas and what they think. She genuinely gives anybody and everybody equal opportunity to have an opinion."

At multiple points in her career, Ventura stretched herself beyond what she thought possible. She approached every opportunity with grace, immersing herself in unfamiliar contexts, building authentic relationships, and learning from those around her. Her values gave her confidence to act in the scariest circumstances. Reinvention—periodically "resetting herself," as she put it—became energizing. The unexpected twists and turns of her career led to a unique combination of experiences that she now carried within her, generating new opportunities—new paths to impact—that she could never have foreseen. She channeled these all into each new phase of her work.

Ventura's journey offers a powerful reminder to seek out diverse experiences and embrace stretch assignments with courage and humility.[9] Dare to try; you never know where it will lead.

Connect the Dots: Scale Your Impact

In Hong Kong, Ventura was known for her superpower: the ability to forge value-adding connections across her expansive network, translating between East and West, luxury and technology, and corporates, startups, and academia. Whether it was an executive, entrepreneur, or professor, she described how once she "connected with someone on a human level" and aligned on core values, her instinct was to introduce them to others who could help them live their dreams.

Ventura approached introductions optimistically, hopeful that they could lead to value creation, but sharing her network without expecting anything in return. She invested significant time and resources in convening dinners and curating gatherings. She created a WhatsApp group, CatalystsXImpact, that soon grew to over six hundred catalysts across the globe who shared ideas, questions, and forged partnerships on the platform.

As much as she loved Hong Kong, during the pandemic, Ventura decided it was time to bring her chapter there to a close. Reinventing herself once more, she moved to Singapore. There, her philosophy of creating value through connections led to her next adventure.

Having seen the catalytic effect of capital on the lives of entrepreneurs and their stakeholders, Ventura imagined how she might scale her impact through investment. She became an adviser for LCJG and launched her own angel fund, VenturaXVentures.[10] Her fund became her new platform for driving "sustainable and responsible impact in business," as she put it, and empowering a new generation of entrepreneurs to do the same. As always, she invested only in founders with whom she shared values. And as with her previous roles, her contributions went beyond capital. She activated her global network of strategic investors, family offices, institutions, corporates, academia, and others, cultivating a broader ecosystem to support VenturaXVentures' mission: to *connect* global talent, *catalyze* growth, and *create* sustainable value for all stakeholders, including the planet.[11]

While launching her fund, Ventura continued broadening herself, working on ad hoc projects and joining advisory boards across government, fashion, philanthropy, and academia. She entertained attractive job offers, including CEO roles from major brands in Asia and Europe. But it was the tech investment firm founded by Eric Martineau-Fortin, cofounder and managing partner of White Star Capital and a longtime friend and thought partner, that she ultimately chose to join.[12] Martineau-Fortin was impressed by how Ventura had come to define her role as "an ecosystem generator" and made her an offer that no one else had: to become the chief catalyst officer of his venture firm and help transform its global network of partners into a generative, value-creating ecosystem.

Ventura accepted the offer. Through White Star Capital, she saw an opportunity to help even more entrepreneurs become leaders prepared to shape our collective future. But yet again, Ventura found herself out of her comfort zone. Not only was she suddenly the only woman in meetings, but most of her new colleagues were investment bankers, primarily making decisions through the lens of returns and efficiencies. Even in this new context, she found ways to live her philosophy of creating joint value through genuine connection.

In her first assignment, opening White Star's first Singapore office, Ventura's catalytic leadership was on full display. She hosted launch events to introduce White Star's team to local government officials, family offices, and startups, always stressing the importance of *quality* relationships to her new colleagues. One of her peers described her style as "old school," well-suited to the local culture. Ventura insisted that White Star had more to offer Singapore than just capital. She introduced her new team to Singapore's academic community, which soon sparked new collaborations: the launch of the White Star Capital STAR Impact Foundation, which aimed to democratize entrepreneurship by supporting individuals no matter their background or gender through scholarships, mentoring, and access to a global network of knowledge resources.

After facilitating a successful opening in Singapore, Ventura, now general partner, was charged with expanding White Star to the Middle East and North Africa. Ventura made frequent trips to the region in search of new partners and investment opportunities and soon found that Abu Dhabi in particular was innovating at the frontier of technology and sustainability. Ventura had come to believe that "if you start to recognize everyone in a room, it is time to be in a new room." So, in 2024, she decided to move from Singapore to Abu Dhabi, colocating her office with another venture fund—the founder of whom had been a key partner at The Cage—and start a new chapter in her catalytic leadership journey. When we asked her to describe what she hopes her legacy will be, Ventura remarked:

> Ultimately, my success will be measured by the growth, profitability, and societal impact of the companies we invest in, as well as the strength of the relationships we build with investors, partners, and the broader ecosystem. By ensuring a balance between financial returns and positive, measurable societal contributions, I want to create a legacy of sustainable, long-term value creation for all our stakeholders.

Like Ventura, you have unique experiences, talents, passions, and connections—your very own slice of genius. Generosity with your ideas and relationships enlarges you and your impact. Make the catalytic connections that unleash new possibilities for cocreation.

Let Your Values Be Your Guide

Like the leaders in this book, Ventura's wayfinding journey embraced continual experimentation and self-discovery. She grew and evolved as she traversed industries and geographies, but her values remained steady, as her source of orientation and guidance. Ventura's story illustrates the power of how a genuine gesture can have profound ripple effects. Woo's question—"What is your 'why'?"—invited Ventura to blossom. After that fateful meeting, Ventura embodied the role of the catalyst. At every turn, she passed on the gift of clarity and orientation to others through her genuine curiosity. She created access to opportunities that would help others fulfill their purpose in business and in life. These, to us, are hallmarks of great leadership.

Your leadership journey will be beset with conflicts, missteps, and failures. But as the leaders in this book demonstrate, let your values be your guide. The leaders whose stories we've shared endured much in their careers, yet they did not become cynical. They *chose* to be optimistic and believe in human potential and ingenuity. They saw *abundance* and possibility where others saw constraint. They were genuinely *curious* about others, especially those who were different from themselves. They were *generous* with their energy and attention and strove to ensure that all stakeholders met their priorities. And above all, they had *tenacity*—despite numerous obstacles, they were relentless in their pursuit of impact.

From Ajay Banga to Cristina Ventura, the leaders in this book live, scale, and sustain their values by creating space for others to try their own hand at the ABCs of leading innovation. The throughline of the ABCs is *development*—of oneself and others. Leading innovation "begins with self-awareness and inner alignment," Ventura tells us. Be inquisitive about who you are and why you are here. Identify your slice of genius and use these insights to pursue a purpose bold enough to deserve your dedication. With a spirit of abundance, curiosity, generosity, and tenacity, you can catalyze innovation at scale and create lasting impact for all.

Postscript

We hope we did justice to the leaders who shared their lives with us for this book. These are individuals who have figured out how to drive genius at scale. Portraits of leaders at the cutting edge in their professions often depict heroic solo figures, eager to maximize their fame and fortune. But the people in this book don't fit the stereotype. They are masters of cocreation in pursuit of ambitions greater than themselves. They scale their businesses by cultivating deep connections, including with the next generation of talent. These connections are the glue and grease that have allowed them to transform themselves, their organizations, and the world.

When the hard work of cocreation is proving too taxing (and we promise it will), perhaps you will find inspiration through a particular wayfinder in these chapters. Some found their "why" early in life; others clarified their values and expanded their ambitions only after a series of life experiments. Your future is only limited by your imagination and willingness to try. So, think big and get started—and don't try to go it alone.

Acknowledgments

The book in your hands is the culmination of a decade of collaboration, experimentation, and learning. It was an arduous and exhilarating journey, and it would not have been possible without the support and commitment of hundreds of partners.

First and foremost, we are indebted to the leaders and teams who allowed us to study the inner workings of their organizations up close and personal—most for years. We thank them for generously sharing their time and insights with us, and for their patience and encouragement throughout. Each of the chapters in this book was a production that involved exacting coordination behind the scenes. In addition to the many individuals who were willing to be interviewed and observed, we thank the assistants, communications teams, general counsels, and other stakeholders who made the research possible.

In preparing this book, we stand on the shoulders of scholars with expertise in leadership, innovation, organizational design, change management, technology evolution, social movements, and systems change, among other fields. In addition, each of us has benefited from opportunities to present our research to both academics and practicing leaders—from frontline staff to CEOs. We thank these individuals for their incisive questions and invaluable feedback that compelled us to collect additional data, revisit our analyses, and rewrite chapters to refine our argument.

We are deeply grateful to family, friends, and colleagues who read drafts of our work and helped us clarify our thinking and writing. In alphabetical order: Roger Breitbart, Lorraine Delhorne, Jan Dropmann, Gretchen Gavett, Joline Godfrey, Scott Halper, Elizabeth Heichler, Ann Le Cam, Ania Wieckowski Masinter, Sunand Menon, Prajna Murdaya, Taran Swan, Yvonne Tedards, Dana Teppert, Maurizio Travaglini, and Allison Wigen. Special thanks to two colleagues, Scott Anthony and Ryan Raffaelli, whose feedback propelled our manuscript forward at critical junctures.

We relied on editors at various stages in the process: Karl Weber, Rose Jacobs, Mark Rennella, June Lin, Lucy McCauley, and Jeremiah Hendren. We especially acknowledge Jeremiah, who elevated both the quality of our argument and the arc of our storytelling.

We also are indebted to research associate and graduate student Lydia Begag for her contributions to this book. She joined the team in 2022, collecting original data and coauthoring some of the case studies on which the chapters are based. She also contributed to drafting and editing chapters. As our project manager, she helped coordinate with our research sites, editors, and readers; finalized permissions; and compiled citations and references for the bibliography, the latter of which was completed by faculty support specialist Meggie Heffernan. Jen McNamara has also played a critical support role in all stages of the development of this book.

We would also like to thank our agent Carol Franco and our colleagues at Harvard Business Review Press. Jeff Kehoe, our editor, shared our passion for the book from day one and was committed to making sure we did our best work. We thank the anonymous reviewers he enlisted to read the manuscript, along with the team members who copyedited and prepared the manuscript for final publication and marketing.

Finally, we extend thanks to several divisions of Harvard Business School. HBS Online and the Multimedia Development Team helped us create multimedia material on our leaders and their companies, and our Baker Library colleagues helped us collect archival data. The Division of Research provided the significant resources required to complete this work.

A few words from Linda: From our first conversations, I knew that I had found not just an academic partner but a soulmate in Emily. I asked her very early in our relationship to coauthor what I was calling at that time *Collective Genius 2.0*. The vision for our book evolved as we worked together. The work was painstaking; Emily often led the way as we made sense of our voluminous data and developed the conceptual framework for our book. As anyone who has worked with Emily soon learns, she has much to offer our profession with her commitment to conducting rigorous and relevant research. In short, Emily has made me a better scholar.

I first met Jason when my coauthors and I were writing *Collective Genius: The Art and Practice of Leading Innovation* (2014). He was one of the young people we interviewed at IBM who was working on volunteer initiatives to develop profitable businesses that would meet the needs of the poor and vulnerable. Jason stayed in touch as he moved into senior roles at Salesforce and then Microsoft. He was always a voracious reader of the latest work on emerging technologies and kept me abreast of their transformative impact on business and leadership. When Emily and I were searching for an executive coauthor to keep us grounded, I immediately thought of Jason. Throughout our collaboration, he made sure we captured the pivotal role of purpose and empathy as enablers of innovation in practice.

I should mention again my research associate Lydia Begag, whose benefit to me went well beyond the tangible contributions listed above. Lydia joined me right out of college. With her prodigious intellect, she has been a conceptual sparring partner for so much of my work. Further, her generous spirit and dedication to doing exceptional work have served as an inspiration.

I have led numerous case discussions about the leaders in this book with executives in the General Management Program (GMP) over the last six years. I suspect I learned more from them than they did from me. GMPers have had an outsized influence on my thinking about scaling innovation.

Finally, I want to thank my family and friends who gave me the space and support required to write this book over almost a decade: the loves of my life, my husband, Roger Breitbart, and my son, Jonathan Hill Breitbart; my dear friends Joline Godfrey and Lorraine Delhorne, who reassured me during bouts of impostor syndrome; and my father, my role model, Clifford Hill Sr.

A few words from Emily: I am forever grateful to Linda and Jason for the opportunity to collaborate on the project of a lifetime. When I first met Linda, I was twenty-four. I had been applying for jobs for over a year with no success, and the future felt very uncertain. Linda took a chance on me, and with the utmost kindness and generosity, she opened doors to experiences and possibilities that I hadn't even known to dream of. When Jason joined our team, he brought a deep spirit of curiosity and collaboration. The mix of our backgrounds made for thought-provoking conversations every week—and at times spirited debates. I will cherish our partnership for not only expanding my thinking, but inspiring me to be a better person.

Spending the first chapter of my career on this book was both the greatest challenge and the greatest gift. To all the leaders and organizations, we studied: it is a privilege to know you. Your optimism, courage, humility, and commitment to impact energized me throughout this journey. Perhaps the greatest lesson I've gleaned from you is that one doesn't need to wait until reaching the top of a hierarchy to think big. You've taught me to see business—and the world—not only for what it is today, but for what it could be. To the many leaders out there not in this book, who are working every day to bring that future to fruition—thank you.

To my parents, Bill and Yvonne, thank you for always encouraging my creativity and for the countless late nights you spent teaching me to write when I was growing up. To my siblings—Jeremy, Stefanie, and Natalie—you constantly inspire me with your talents and your willingness to forge your own paths in life. To my friends, who graciously put up with me as I learned to balance work and life, thank you for your continuous encouragement. To my many professors and collaborators who have taught me so much—thank you for challenging and supporting me over the years.

And most of all, to my husband, Jan—thank you for your unwavering love, for being my sounding board, and for always keeping me grounded in what truly matters.

A few words from Jason: As the son of a Chicago blue-collar family, my dream when I was younger was just to find a decent job, maybe in something meaningful. I never could have imagined that I would lead projects in thirty-nine countries with organizations like Disney and NATO, let alone author a book that could potentially influence people's thinking and work. The journey has been both humbling and transformative.

My deepest gratitude goes to my wife, Xenia, who believed in this project even when I questioned my own contributions, and to my children, Jakob Wild, John Wild, Ethan Wild, and Noah Wild, who remind me daily why leadership is really needed for the next generation. I'm grateful to my mother, Diana Saltarelli, who instilled in me the values that guide my work, and my brother, Jamie Wild, who keeps me grounded with unconditional love. I grew up around people who were creative and believers, including my grandparents, Glen and Toby Johnson, who gave me the confidence to try to be my best.

Also, I'm so privileged to have incredible colleagues and friends who have shaped, supported, and believed in me: Harry Missirlian, Joel Koblentz, Eric Farley, Jade Nguyen-Strattner, Chris Press, and Valero Marin—thank you for your wisdom, challenge, and belief throughout my life. I'm grateful for having a first-row seat working for some of the greatest tech leaders of our generation: Lou Gerstner, Ginni Rometty, Marc Benioff, Satya Nadella, and others, learning their mindsets and behaviors by direct experience. Linda, I have learned so much from you that I am truly forever grateful. The passion for understanding what leadership truly means and your commitment to excellence in everything you do is inspiring. Emily, your gift for storytelling and bringing data to life is a real superpower. It's been a real honor to collaborate with and learn from both of you. All of you, in my view, embody the fact that leaders can be both super smart and kind.

. . .

It truly is an honor to tell the stories of the leaders chronicled in this book. We hope we have done justice to their legacies and to all who contributed to this project. For any shortcomings, we collectively accept responsibility.

Notes

We have posted online a full bibliography of over seven hundred books and articles that we relied on, available at https://hbr.org/book-resources.

Introduction

1. See Linda A. Hill, Greg Brandeau, Emily Truelove, and Kent Lineback, *Collective Genius: The Art and Practice of Leading Innovation* (Boston: Harvard Business Review Press, 2014). In *Collective Genius*, the authors make the central argument that innovation is the result of cocreation: collaboration, experimentation, and learning. For the research summary of why innovation requires collaboration, experimentation, and learning, see, in particular, chapters 1 and 2 of *Collective Genius*.

2. The research suggests there is no one best way to lead. For more work on leadership, see, for example, John Kotter, *Leading Change* (Boston: Harvard Business School Press, 1999); John P. Kotter, *John P. Kotter on What Leaders Really Do* (Boston: Harvard Business School Press, 1999); and John P. Kotter and Dan S. Cohen, *The Heart of Change: Real-Life Stories of How People Change Their Organizations* (Boston: Harvard Business School Press, 2002). Also see Warren Bennis and Burt Nanus, *Leaders: The Strategies for Taking Charge* (New York: HarperBusiness, 1997). Kotter and Bennis both make the distinction between leadership and management. Leadership is about coping with change: setting direction, aligning people, and motivating and inspiring. Management is about coping with complexity: planning and budgeting, organizing and staffing, controlling, and problem-solving. They both found that many companies lack agility and the capacity to adapt to new competitive environments because they are overmanaged and underled—a very important observation. Their work was focused on change, not innovation. Instead, these are related but different phenomena.

3. Our research took us deep inside the worlds of these leaders and the organizations they led. Our approach was ethnographic in nature; we wanted to see and experience the worlds of the individuals we studied through their eyes, as they experience it. Data collection involved interviews and observations of daily life in the leaders' organizations. During the pandemic, when we could not travel, we relied on videoconferencing to do our observations and interviews. In conducting interviews, we found the following useful: Robert Weiss, *Learning from Strangers: The Art and Method of Qualitative Interview Studies* (New York: Free Press, 1994) and Howard S. Becker, *Tricks of the Trade: How to Think About Your Research While You're Doing It* (Chicago: University of Chicago Press, 1998). For collecting observational data and writing ethnographic field notes, we drew on R. Emerson, R. Fretz, and L. Shaw, *Writing Ethnographic Fieldnotes* (Chicago: University of Chicago Press, 1995). Our analysis occurred in parallel with data collection. We found several scholars' work useful in guiding our analysis, including John Lofland, David A. Snow, Leon Anderson, and Lyn H. Lofland, *Analyzing Social Settings: A Guide to*

Qualitative Observation and Analysis (Boston: Cengage Learning, 2005); Kathy Charmaz, *Constructing Grounded Theory: A Practical Guide Through Qualitative Analysis* (Thousand Oaks, CA: Sage Publications, 2010); Ann Langley, "Strategies for Theorizing from Process Data," *Academy of Management Review* 24, no. 4 (1999): 691–710; and Amy C. Edmondson and Stacy E. McManus, "Methodological Fit in Management Field Research," *Academy of Management Review* 32, no. 4 (October 2007): 1246–64, https://doi.org/10.5465/amr.2007.26586086. When writing the stories of those we studied, we were inspired by J. Van Maanen, *Tales of the Field: On Writing Ethnography* (Chicago: University of Chicago Press, 2011); Karen Golden-Biddle and Karen Locke, "Appealing Work: An Investigation of How Ethnographic Texts Convince," *Organization Science* 4, no. 4 (1993): 595–616; Karen Locke and Karen Golden-Biddle, "Constructing Opportunities for Contribution: Structuring Intertextual Coherence and 'Problematizing' in Organizational Studies," *Academy of Management Journal* 40, no. 5 (1997): 1023–62; and D. Jean Clandinin and F. Michael Connelly, *Narrative Inquiry: Experience and Story in Qualitative Research* (San Francisco: Jossey-Bass Publishers, 2000). Throughout our research journey, data collection and analysis occurred in parallel. Our approach was inductive, even abductive; we asked not what "must" be but what "may" be. See Karen Locke, Karen Golden-Biddle, and Martha S. Feldman, "Making Doubt Generative: Rethinking the Role of Doubt in the Research Process," *Organization Science* 19, no. 6 (2008): 907–18. See also Lotte Bailyn, "Research as a Cognitive Process: Implications for Data Analysis," *Quality and Quantity* 11, no. 2 (1977): 97–117. Given our methodology, we cannot prove that leadership matters for innovation, but we believe that our findings are suggestive of its importance and offer promising avenues for future research.

4. Note that we studied additional leaders who showed great talent but, in the end, were unable to build teams or organizations that could innovate time and again. Therefore, they are not included in this book.

5. Here we build on the work of scholars like Greg Dees who studied entrepreneurial ecosystems of interconnected networks of individuals, organizations, and institutions within a specific sector or geography. These ecosystems consist of multiple stakeholders whose interactions foster an environment in which entrepreneurship can flourish. He includes financial capital providers, human capital, social capital, infrastructure, regulatory environment, cultural context, and market access. See, for example, Paul N. Bloom and J. Gregory Dees, "Cultivate Your Ecosystem," *Stanford Social Innovation Review* 6, no. 1 (2007): 47–53, https://doi.org/10.48558/QWAW-VP62. Our thinking was very influenced not only by the business research on ecosystems but also by the social enterprise research on ecosystems. To understand more on building movements—how people organize and work together to create systemic change—see Ron Adner, "Ecosystem as Structure: An Actionable Construct for Strategy," *Journal of Management* 43, no. 1 (January 2017): 39–58, https://doi.org/10.1177/0149206316678451; Ron Adner, *Winning the Right Game: How to Disrupt, Defend, and Deliver in a Changing World* (Cambridge, MA: MIT Press, 2021); Elizabeth J. Altman, Frank Nagle, and Michael L. Tushman, "The Translucent Hand of Managed Ecosystems: Engaging Communities for Value Creation and Capture," *Academy of Management Annals* 16, no. 1 (January 2022): 70–101, https://doi.org/10.5465/annals.2020.0244; Nathan Furr, Kate O'Keeffe, and Jeff Dyer, "Managing Multiparty Innovation," *Harvard Business Review*, November 2016; Nathan Furr and Kate O'Keeffe, "The Hybrid Start-Up," *Harvard Business Review*, March–April 2023; Douglas P. Hannah and Kathleen M. Eisenhardt, "How Firms Navigate Cooperation

and Competition in Nascent Ecosystems," *Strategic Management Journal* 39, no. 12 (December 2018): 3163–92, https://doi.org/10.1002/smj.2750; Brian Uzzi, "Social Structure and Competition in Interfirm Networks: The Paradox of Embeddedness," *Administrative Science Quarterly* 42, no. 1 (March 1997): 35, https://doi.org/10.2307 /2393808; Marco Iansiti and Roy Levien, *The Keystone Advantage: What the New Dynamics of Business Ecosystems Mean for Strategy, Innovation, and Sustainability* (Boston: Harvard Business School Press; London: McGraw-Hill, 2004); Marco Iansiti and Roy Levien, "Strategy as Ecology," *Harvard Business Review*, March 2004; and Peter Block, *Community: The Structure of Belonging* (San Francisco: Berrett-Koehler Publishers, 2008).

6. Great leaders of innovation at scale do not extract all the value for themselves; they help build and maintain a win-win ecosystem for all involved. See, for example, Iansiti and Levien, *The Keystone Advantage.* Our model of catalyst leadership and ecosystems is based on a biological metaphor, and like Iansiti and Levien, we emphasize that organizations must build interconnected ecosystems that can cocreate with all partners.

7. See, for example, chapter 2 of *Collective Genius,* which spells out the paradoxes inherent to leading innovation.

8. All quotations, unless otherwise noted, are based on our qualitative research. All dollar amounts are in US dollars.

Chapter 1

1. All information, including quotations, in this chapter is derived from cases authored or coauthored by Sunil Gupta and Linda A. Hill and published by Harvard Business Publishing about Mastercard, unless otherwise cited. We extend our deepest gratitude to Sunil Gupta for facilitating this research collaboration with Mastercard. For more information, see Sunil Gupta, Linda A. Hill, Julia Kelley, and Emily Tedards, "Mastercard: Creating a World Beyond Cash," Case 522-001 (Boston: Harvard Business School Publishing, April 2022); Linda A. Hill, Sunil Gupta, Emily Tedards, and Julia Kelley, "Mastercard Labs (A)," Case 422-080 (Boston: Harvard Business School Publishing, April 2022); and Linda A. Hill, Sunil Gupta, Emily Tedards, and Julia Kelley, "Mastercard Labs (B)," Case 422-081 (Boston: Harvard Business School Publishing, 2022).

2. Mastercard's market capitalization was approximately $13.29 billion at the end of 2006, following its IPO earlier that year. See "Mastercard Market Capitalization," CompaniesMarketCap, https://companiesmarketcap.com/mastercard/marketcap/.

3. Mastercard's market capitalization was approximately $334.97 billion at the end of 2020. See "Mastercard Market Capitalization," CompaniesMarketCap.

4. Mastercard, "Mastercard—A Global Technology Company in the Payments Industry," https://www.mastercard.us/.

5. Mastercard, "Brand History," https://www.mastercard.com/brandcenter/en-ca /brand-history.

6. For more on disruptive technologies and how incumbent firms respond to them, see Clayton M. Christensen, *The Innovator's Dilemma: When New Technologies Cause Great Firms to Fail,* Management of Innovation and Change Series (Boston: Harvard Business School Press, 1997); J. Eggers and K. F. Park, "Incumbent Adaptation to Technological Change: The Past, Present, and Future of Research on

Heterogeneous Incumbent Response," *Academy of Management Annals* 12, no. 1 (2018): 357–89; Marco Iansiti, "How the Incumbent Can Win: Managing Technological Transitions in the Semiconductor Industry," *Management Science* 46, no. 2 (2000): 169–85; Rosabeth Moss Kanter, *Evolve!: Succeeding in the Digital Culture of Tomorrow* (Boston: Harvard Business School Press, 2001); Charles A. O'Reilly and Michael L. Tushman, *Lead and Disrupt: How to Solve the Innovator's Dilemma* (Stanford, CA: Stanford University Press, 2016); Gary Pisano, *Creative Construction: The DNA of Sustained Innovation* (Boston: Harvard Business School Press, 1996); Ryan Raffaelli, "The Three Traps That Stymie Reinvention," *MIT Sloan Management Review*, Fall 2024, 46–52; and Michael L. Tushman, "Organizational Determinants of Technological Change: Toward a Sociology of Technological Evolution," *Research in Organizational Behavior* 14 (1992): 311–47.

7. See, for example, Linda A. Hill and Derek George, "The Board's New Innovation Imperative: Directors Need to Rethink Their Roles and Their Attitude to Risk," *Harvard Business Review*, November–December 2017, 102–09; and Linda A. Hill, Emily Tedards, and Taran Swan, "Drive Innovation with Better Decision-Making," *Harvard Business Review*, November–December 2021.

8. News18, "Maharashtra-Born Ajay Banga to Take Over as President of World Bank on June 2," News18, May 4, 2023, https://www.news18.com/amp/business /maharashtra-born-ajay-banga-to-take-over-as-president-of-world-bank-on-june-2 -7717375.html.

9. Mastercard's market capitalization was approximately $27.49 billion in July 2010, the same month that Ajay Banga became CEO. See "Mastercard Market Capitalization," CompaniesMarketCap.

10. For more reading on attention-based views to strategic change and leadership, see William Ocasio, Tomi Laamanen, and Eero Vaara, "Communication and Attention Dynamics: An Attention-Based View of Strategic Change," *Strategic Management Journal* 39, no. 1 (2018): 155–67, https://doi.org/10.1002/smj.2702.

11. See, for example, John P. Kotter, *A Sense of Urgency* (Boston: Harvard Business Press, 2008) and John P. Kotter, *Leading Change* (Boston: Harvard Business School Press, 1996).

12. As the key underlying technology for all digital wallets and tap-to-pay solutions, tokenization is like a virtual credit card number in that it links sensitive data, like a credit card number, with nonsensitive characters called a "token."

13. APIs (Application Programming Interfaces) are digital tools that enable different software applications and systems to interact with each other. An API "plug and play" approach enhances this seamless data exchange, enabling businesses to connect quickly to various data sources and enhancing efficiency and speed along the way. For more information on APIs, please see Michael Goodwin, "What Is an API?," *IBM Think*, April 9, 2024, https://www.ibm.com /think/topics/api.

14. These figures are found in an HBS case study Sunil Gupta wrote about Mastercard driving financial inclusion. For more information, see Sunil Gupta, Rajiv Lal, and Natalie Kindred, "MasterCard: Driving Financial Inclusion," Case 515-035 (Boston: Harvard Business School Publishing, October 2014).

15. Gupta, Lal, and Kindred, "MasterCard: Driving Financial Inclusion."

16. Gupta, Lal, and Kindred, "MasterCard: Driving Financial Inclusion." For more information, see National Identity Management Commission (NIMC), "Formal

Launch of E-ID Card in Nigeria," NIMC, August 28, 2014, https://nimc.gov.ng/formal-launch-of-e-id-card-in-nigeria/.

17. Mastercard Center for Inclusive Growth, https://www.mastercardcenter.org/.

18. World Bank, "World Bank Group and Coalition Partners Make Commitments to Accelerate Universal Financial Access," press release, April 17, 2015, https://www.worldbank.org/en/news/press-release/2015/04/17/world-bank-group-coalition-partners-make-commitments-accelerate-universal-financial-access.

19. Hayden Harrison, "Banking for Humanity: Making the Digital Economy Work for All," Mastercard Newsroom, n.d., https://www.mastercard.com/news/perspectives/featured-topics/start-with-people-and-start-something-priceless/banking-for-humanity/.

20. For more information on the choice of Michael Miebach as CEO of Mastercard, see Richard Haythornthwaite and Ajay Banga, "The Former and Current Chairs of Mastercard on Executing a Strategic CEO Succession," *Harvard Business Review*, March–April 2021.

21. World Bank, "Ajay Banga Becomes World Bank Group President," World Bank Timeline, June 2, 2023, https://timeline.worldbank.org/en/timeline/eventdetail/05430d92-cc46-4fc6-8579-da1da0356f85.

Chapter 2

1. All information, including quotations, in this chapter is derived from a four-part case series published by Harvard Business Publishing, "Michael Ku and Global Clinical Supply at Pfizer Inc.: Bringing Hope to Patients," unless otherwise cited. On four occasions over the course of nine years of longitudinal data collection, Pfizer covered partial travel expenses. After collecting data on Pfizer GCS, Linda's consulting firm was hired by GCS and other groups at divisions at the company to deliver workshops on leadership and innovation.

2. For more information, see Albert Bourla, *Moonshot: Inside Pfizer's Nine-Month Race to Make the Impossible Possible* (New York: Harper Business, 2022) and Albert Bourla, "The CEO of Pfizer on Developing a Vaccine in Record Time," *Harvard Business Review*, May 2021. See also Danforth Dialogues, "Leaders Reflect on Leadership During the Pandemic," Morehouse School of Medicine, January 3, 2024, https://www.msm.edu/RSSFeedArticles/2024/January/DanforthDialogues.php#.

3. "Which Covid-19 Vaccine Saved the Most Lives in 2021?," *Economist*, July 13, 2022, https://www.economist.com/graphic-detail/2022/07/13/which-covid-19-vaccine-saved-the-most-lives-in-2021.

4. "Fact Check: COVID-19 Vaccines Did Have Clinical Trials," Reuters, February 2, 2021, https://www.reuters.com/article/world/fact-check-covid-19-vaccines-did-have-clinical-trials-idUSKBN2A22CD/ and "Pfizer and BioNTech Announce Vaccine Candidate Against COVID-19," Pfizer, November 9, 2020, https://www.pfizer.com/news/press-release/press-release-detail/pfizer-and-biontech-announce-vaccine-candidate-against.

5. Pfizer, "Delivering Hope: Pfizer-BioNTech COVID-19 Vaccine Clinical Supply Chain Journey," YouTube video, August 6, 2021, https://www.youtube.com/watch?v=gU4efmo0Ag8.

6. Pfizer, "Delivering Hope."

7. Pfizer, "Delivering Hope."

8. Chapters 1, 2, and 6 of *Collective Genius: The Art and Practice of Leading Innovation* summarize the research that supports the conclusion that most innovative problem-solving is the result of the collaboration of individuals with different perspectives and expertise who are able to leverage that diversity by working through the inevitable conflicts that arise. The authors make the argument for why "creative abrasion," or the ability to generate a marketplace of ideas through debate and discourse is, therefore, a critical capability for innovation. See Linda A. Hill, Greg Brandeau, Emily Truelove, and Kent Lineback, *Collective Genius: The Art and Practice of Leading Innovation* (Boston: Harvard Business Review Press, 2014), chapters 1, 2, and 6. The term "creative abrasion" was first used by Jerry Hirshberg; see Jerry Hirshberg, *The Creative Priority: Driving Innovative Business in the Real World* (New York: Harper Business, 1998). Dorothy Leonard's work on creative abrasion has shaped our thinking as well. See, for example, Dorothy Leonard and Walter Swap, *When Sparks Fly: Igniting Creativity in Groups* (Boston: Harvard Business School Press, 1999). We also drew on the following works: Keith Sawyer, *Group Genius: The Creative Power of Collaboration* (New York: Basic Books, 2007); Frank Lewis Dyer and Thomas Commerford Martin, *Edison: His Life and Inventions* (New York: Harper & Brothers, 1929), chapter 24; Jane Magruder Watkins and Bernard J. Mohr, *Appreciative Inquiry: Change at the Speed of Imagination* (San Francisco: Jossey-Bass/Pfeiffer, 2001); John Child, "Commentary on Constructive Conflict," in *Mary Parker Follett: Prophet of Management: A Celebration of Writings from the 1920s*, ed. Pauline Graham (Washington, DC: Beard Books, 2003), 89; and Kathleen M. Eisenhardt, Jean L. Kahwajy, and L. J. Bourgeois III, "How Management Teams Can Have a Good Fight," *Harvard Business Review*, July–August 1997. Finally, our point of view has been strongly influenced by a body of research on leveraging diversity. See Robin J. Ely and David A. Thomas, "Cultural Diversity at Work: The Moderating Effects of Work Group Perspectives on Diversity," *Administrative Science Quarterly* 46 (June 2001): 229–73; Doris Kearns Goodwin, *Team of Rivals: The Political Genius of Abraham Lincoln* (New York: Simon & Schuster, 2005); Boris Groysberg et al., "Too Many Cooks Spoil the Broth: How High-Status Individuals Decrease Group Effectiveness," *Organization Science* 21, no. 3 (2010): 1–16; Karen A. Jehn, "A Multimethod Examination of the Benefits and Detriments of Intragroup Conflict," *Administrative Science Quarterly* 40, no. 2 (June 1995): 256–82; Frans Johansson, *The Medici Effect: Breakthrough Insights at the Intersection of Ideas, Concepts, and Cultures* (Boston: Harvard Business School Press, 2004); Scott E. Page, *The Difference: How the Power of Diversity Creates Better Groups, Firms, Schools, and Societies* (Princeton, NJ: Princeton University Press, 2008); and finally, J. Richard Hackman, *Collaborative Intelligence: Using Teams to Solve Hard Problems* (San Francisco: Berrett-Koehler, 2011).

9. Chapter 4 of *Collective Genius: The Art and Practice of Leading Innovation* summarizes why a sense of shared purpose is foundational to building an innovative culture, a culture in which people are willing to do the hard emotional and intellectual work of collaboration, experimentation, and learning with diverse others. Shared purpose helps people feel part of a community engaged in something meaningful, larger than any individual could accomplish alone, as all feel responsible for contributing to that shared purpose. See Hill, Brandeau, Truelove, and Lineback, *Collective Genius*, chapter 4. For more work on the importance of purpose, see, for example, Michael Beer et al., *Higher Ambition: How Great Leaders Create Economic and Social Value* (Boston:

Harvard Business Review Press, 2011); Sumantra Ghoshal and Christopher A. Bartlett, *The Individualized Corporation: A Fundamentally New Approach to Management* (New York: Harper Business, 1997), chapters 8–9; Ranjay Gulati, *Deep Purpose: The Heart and Soul of High-Performance Companies* (New York: Harper Business, 2022); Doug A. Ready and Emily Truelove, "The Power of Collective Ambition," *Harvard Business Review*, December 2011; Joel Podolny, Rakesh Khurana, and Marya Hill-Popper, "Revisiting the Meaning of Leadership," *Research in Organizational Behavior* 26, no. 1 (2005): 1–36; and John Henry Clippinger, *A Crowd of One: The Future of Individual Identity* (New York: PublicAffairs, 2007). For more on community building and social capital, see Robert Putnam, "Bowling Alone: America's Declining Social Capital," *Journal of Democracy* 6, no. 1 (1995): 65–78; Henry Mintzberg, "Rebuilding Companies as Communities," *Harvard Business Review*, July 2009; and Gerben S. van der Vegt and J. Stuart Bunderson, "Learning and Performance in Multidisciplinary Teams: The Importance of Collective Team Identification," *Academy of Management Journal* 48, no. 3 (2005): 532–47.

10. For examples of how to build customer-centric organizations, see Ranjay Gulati, *Reorganize for Resiliency: Putting Customers at the Center of Your Business* (Boston: Harvard Business Press, 2010); Alec Rawson et al., "The Truth About Customer Experience," *Harvard Business Review*, September 2013; James L. Heskett et al., *The Ownership Quotient: Putting the Service Profit Chain to Work for Unbeatable Competitive Advantage* (Boston: Harvard Business Press, 2008); and James Kalbach, *The Jobs to Be Done Playbook: Align Your Markets, Organizations, and Strategy Around Customer Needs* (New York: Two Waves Books, 2020).

11. Building a customer-centric organization requires breaking down silos and building a more cross-functional way of working to deliver for customers. See, for example, Gulati, *Reorganize for Resiliency*. For an example of what it takes to build an organization able to deliver a differentiated end-to-end customer experience, see B. Joseph Pine II and James H. Gilmore, *The Experience Economy: Competing for Customer Time, Attention, and Money* (Boston: Harvard Business Review Press, 2020).

12. Einstein's quote about "combinational chemistry" is referenced in *Collective Genius*, while his reminder to look at "old problems from a new angle" is derived from his book that he coauthored with Leopold Infeld, *The Evolution of Physics*.

13. Most of the innovative solutions GCS was pursuing were process innovations. For more on process innovation, see, for example, the work of Marco Iansiti, *Technology Integration: Making Critical Choices in a Dynamic World* (Boston: Harvard Business School Press, 1998); Marco Iansiti and Karim R. Lakhani, "Rearchitecting the Firm," in *Competing in the Age of AI: Strategy and Leadership When Algorithms and Networks Run the World* (Boston: Harvard Business Review Press, 2020); Gary P. Pisano, *The Development Factory: Unlocking the Potential of Process Innovation* (Boston: Harvard Business School Press, 1996); and Gary P. Pisano and Willy C. Shih, *Producing Prosperity: Why America Needs a Manufacturing Renaissance* (Boston: Harvard Business Review Press, 2012).

14. For examples of why balancing advocacy versus inquiry by leaders is critical to innovative problem-solving, see Hal Gregersen, *Questions Are the Answer: A Breakthrough Approach to Your Most Vexing Problems at Work and in Life* (New York: Harper Business, 2018) and Peter M. Senge, *The Fifth Discipline: The Art and*

Practice of the Learning Organization, rev. and updated ed. (New York: Currency, 2006), chapter 10.

15. For examples of why contextual intelligence of different geographic markets is critical to business success, see Pankaj Ghemawat, *Redefining Global Strategy: Crossing Borders in a World Where Differences Still Matter* (Boston: Harvard Business School Press, 2007) and Tarun Khanna, "Contextual Intelligence," *Harvard Business Review*, September 2014.

16. Integrative decision-making often leads to more innovative solutions. See, for example, Mary Parker Follett, *Creative Experience* (Bristol, UK: Thoemmes Press, 2001). Follett discusses the importance of not settling for choice A or B but rather creating an innovative third way that combines elements of and improves on both A and B. An integrative solution is an approach that solves a conflict by accommodating the real demands of all the parties involved. The result is often represented more aptly as a mosaic rather than a melting pot of the varied talents and perspectives of those involved. Also see Roger Martin, *The Opposable Mind: How Successful Leaders Win Through Integrative Thinking* (Boston: Harvard Business School Press, 2007) and Roger Martin, "How Successful Leaders Think," *Harvard Business Review*, June 2007.

17. See, for example, John J. Gabarro, *The Dynamics of Taking Charge* (Boston: Harvard Business School Press, 1987); Daniel Goleman, *Emotional Intelligence: Why It Can Matter More Than IQ* (New York: Bantam, 2005); Daniel Goleman, *Social Intelligence: The New Science of Human Relationships* (New York: Bantam, 2007); and Linda A. Hill and Kent Lineback, *Being the Boss: The Three Imperatives of Becoming a Great Leader* (Boston: Harvard Business Review Press, 2011).

18. For research on the importance of psychological safety, see Amy C. Edmondson, "Psychological Safety and Learning Behavior in Work Teams," *Administrative Science Quarterly* 44, no. 2 (1999): 350–83 and Amy C. Edmondson, *Teaming: How Organizations Learn, Innovate, and Compete in the Knowledge Economy* (San Francisco: Jossey-Bass, 2021).

19. A growing body of research indicates that a leader's rhetoric and storytelling capabilities do have impact on their capacity to influence others and lead change. For example, see John P. Kotter, *The Heart of Change* (Boston: Harvard Business School Press, 2002); Belle Halpern and Kathy Lubar, *Leadership Presence: Dramatic Techniques to Reach Out, Motivate, and Inspire* (New York: Avery, 2004); Stephen Denning, *The Leader's Guide to Storytelling: Mastering the Art and Discipline of Business Narrative*, rev. and updated ed. (San Francisco: Jossey-Bass, 2011); and David Marquet, *Leadership Is Language: The Hidden Power of What You Say—and What You Don't* (New York: Portfolio, 2020).

20. For more information on what it takes to get employees to adopt digital tools and use data effectively when making decisions, see Linda A. Hill et al., "Where Can Digital Transformation Take You? Insights from 1,700 Leaders," Harvard Business School Working Knowledge, January 31, 2022, https://www.library.hbs .edu/working-knowledge/leading-in-the-digital-era-where-can-digital -transformation-take-you; Linda A. Hill et al., "Digital Transformation: A New Roadmap for Success," Harvard Business School Working Knowledge, February 7, 2022, https://www.library.hbs.edu/working-knowledge/leading-in-the-digital-era-a -new-roadmap-for-success; and Linda A. Hill et al., "Curiosity, Not Coding: 6 Skills Leaders Need in the Digital Age," Harvard Business School Working

Knowledge, February 14, 2022, https://www.library.hbs.edu/working-knowledge/six
-unexpected-traits-leaders-need-in-the-digital-era. We have continued to collect
data from executives across the globe, and having surveyed over 8,300 executives as
of September 2025, we have observed that the results are in line with our initial
findings. Also see Marco Iansiti and Satya Nadella, "Democratizing Transformation," *Harvard Business Review*, May–June 2022.

21. The terminology "data-informed" and "data-driven" is something we studied in
a research stream about what it takes to lead during a digital era. See Hill et al., "Where
Can Digital Transformation Take You?"; Hill et al., "Digital Transformation: A New
Roadmap for Success"; and Hill et al., "Curiosity, Not Coding: 6 Skills Leaders Need
in the Digital Age."

22. Michael Ku said that he adopted the phrase after reading *Collective Genius*. See
Hill et al., *Collective Genius*.

23. See "FDA Authorizes Use of Pfizer's COVID Vaccine for 5- to
11-Year-Olds," NPR, October 29, 2021, https://www.npr.org/sections/health-shots
/2021/10/29/1049704374/fda-authorizes-use-of-pfizers-covid-vaccine-for-5-to-11
-year-olds; Pfizer, "Pfizer and BioNTech Granted FDA Emergency Use Authorization of Omicron BA.4/BA.5-Adapted Bivalent COVID-19 Vaccine Booster for
Ages 12 Years and Older," press release, August 31, 2022, https://www.pfizer.com
/news/press-release/press-release-detail/pfizer-and-biontech-granted-fda
-emergency-use-authorization#; Pfizer, "Pfizer and BioNTech Receive U.S. FDA
Emergency Use Authorization for Omicron BA.4/BA.5-Adapted Bivalent
COVID-19 Vaccine Booster in Children 5 Through 11 Years of Age," press release,
October 12, 2022, https://www.pfizer.com/news/press-release/press-release-detail
/pfizer-and-biontech-receive-us-fda-emergency-use-1; and Pfizer, "Pfizer Re-
ceives U.S. FDA Emergency Use Authorization for Novel COVID-19 Oral
Antiviral Candidate," press release, December 22, 2021, https://www.pfizer.com
/news/press-release/press-release-detail/pfizer-receives-us-fda-emergency-use
-authorization-novel.

24. John Kotter found that many leaders in incumbent organizations are unable to
cope with both complexity and change; too often these organizations end up being what
he describes as overmanaged and underled. Michael Ku, in contrast, did not fall into
this trap despite the complexity of GCS's work. See John P. Kotter, *Leading Change*
(Boston: Harvard Business School Press, 1996).

Chapter 3

1. All information, including quotations, in this chapter is derived from a case
study on Procter & Gamble, unless otherwise cited. See Emily Truelove, Linda A.
Hill, and Emily Tedards, "Kathy Fish at Procter & Gamble: Navigating Industry
Disruption by Disrupting from Within," Case 421-012 (Boston: Harvard Business
School, July 2020).

2. Statista, "Market Share of the Leading Liquid Laundry Detergent Brands in
the United States in 2022," https://www.statista.com/statistics/188716/top-liquid
-laundry-detergent-brands-in-the-united-states/.

3. Mason Swimming, "Kathy Fish—Feature About AMO50," January 16,
2020, https://www.masonswimming.org/page/news/333637/kathy-fish---feature
-about-amo50.

4. Many books have discussed Procter & Gamble's strategy and tactics to drive product innovation. For example, see Scott D. Anthony and David S. Duncan, *Building a Growth Factory: Four Components That Make Innovation Repeatable* (Boston: Harvard Business Review Press, 2012) and Alan G. Lafley and Roger L. Martin, *Playing to Win: How Strategy Really Works* (Boston: Harvard Business Review Press, 2013).

5. Beauty Packaging, "Big Executive Changes at Procter & Gamble," November 14, 2013, https://www.beautypackaging.com/contents/view_breaking-news/2013 -11-14/big-executive-changes-at-procter-and-gamble/.

6. There has been extensive research on the pros and cons of different change strategies. Because the objective is to transform culture, the choice of a more bottom-up approach is consistent with the research. For example, see Rosabeth Moss Kanter, *The Change Masters: Innovations for Productivity in the American Corporation* (New York: Simon & Schuster, 1983); Michael Beer et al., *Higher Ambition: How Great Leaders Create Economic and Social Value* (Boston: Harvard Business Review Press, 2011); and Ryan Raffaelli, "Leading and Managing Change," Industry and Background Note 415-040 (Boston: Harvard Business School Publishing, 2014).

7. World Economic Forum, "Procter & Gamble," https://www.weforum.org /organizations/procter-gamble/.

8. Linda A. Hill, Emily Tedards, and Taran Swan, "Drive Innovation with Better Decision-Making," *Harvard Business Review*, November–December 2021.

9. Developed by Eric Ries. See *The Lean Startup: How Today's Entrepreneurs Use Continuous Innovation to Create Radically Successful Businesses* (New York: Crown Business, 2011).

10. In *Collective Genius*, the coauthors provide a comprehensive summary of why recursive experimentation (i.e., more discovery-driven learning) is critical to innovation and the challenges companies run into when trying to adopt it. See Linda A. Hill et al., *Collective Genius: The Art and Practice of Leading Innovation* (Boston: Harvard Business Review Press, 2014), chapter 7. To learn more about discovery-driven learning methodologies, see Tim Brown, *Change by Design: How Design Thinking Creates New Alternatives for Business and Society* (New York: HarperCollins Publishers, 2009); Rita Gunther McGrath and Ian C. MacMillan, *Discovery-Driven Growth: A Breakthrough Process to Reduce Risk and Seize Opportunity* (Boston: Harvard Business School Press, 2009); Stefan Thomke and Eric von Hippel, "Customers as Innovators: A New Way to Create Value," *Harvard Business Review*, April 2002; Stefan Thomke and Jim Manzi, "The Discipline of Business Experimentation: Increase Your Chances of Success with Innovation Test-Drives," *Harvard Business Review*, December 2014; and Tom Kelley and Jonathan Littman, *The Art of Innovation: Lessons in Creativity from IDEO, America's Leading Design Firm* (New York: Currency, 2001).

11. This idea of shifting from an orchestra to a jazz ensemble is from one of the leaders we studied in *Collective Genius*. See Hill et al., "Why Collective Genius Needs Leadership: The Paradoxes of Innovation," in *Collective Genius*, 44–62.

12. Edison's quote appears in *Collective Genius*. See Hill et al., *Collective Genius*, chapter 1.

13. To understand the cultural barriers to adopting a more discovery-driven learning approach to innovation, see *Collective Genius*. See Hill et al., *Collective Genius*,

chapter 7; Scott Kirsner, "The Barriers Big Companies Face When They Try to Act Like Lean Startups," hbr.org, August 16, 2016, https://hbr.org/2016/08/the-barriers -big-companies-face-when-they-try-to-act-like-lean-startups; and Stefan H. Thomke, *Experimentation Works: The Surprising Power of Business Experiments* (Boston: Harvard Business Review Press, 2020).

14. For more information, see Ries, *The Lean Startup* and Steve Blank, *The Four Steps to the Epiphany: Successful Strategies for Products That Win* (Pescadero, CA: K&S Ranch Publishing, 2005).

15. Serial entrepreneurs (including the former CEO of Bionic, David S. Kidder) wrote a playbook on the interventions they introduced to Procter & Gamble to build their capabilities to innovate. See David S. Kidder and Christina Wallace, *New to Big: How Companies Can Create Like Entrepreneurs, Invest Like VCs, and Install a Permanent Operating System for Growth* (New York: Crown Currency, 2019).

16. In *Being the Boss*, the coauthors make the distinction between "value creators" and "game changers." Value creators focus on delivering what they "should" be delivering, while game changers focus on what they "could" be doing. When Linda presented the distinction between value creators and game changers to Kathy Fish and her colleagues, they concluded the company was rewarding people for being value creators and not game changers. The new career track was designed to encourage more game-changing behavior. For more information, see Linda A. Hill and Kent Lineback, *Being the Boss: The Three Imperatives for Becoming a Great Leader* (Boston: Harvard Business Review Press, 2011).

17. Psychological safety in organizations fosters an environment where individuals feel secure to take risks, voice concerns, and learn from failures. For more reading on the different types of failures, see Amy C. Edmondson, *The Right Kind of Wrong: The Science of Failing Well* (New York: Simon Element, 2023).

18. To learn more about changes Procter & Gamble has made to improve its capacity to launch new products, see Peter Koen et al., "Scaling Up Transformational Innovations," *Harvard Business Review*, November–December 2024.

19. Procter & Gamble, "Superiority: A Higher Standard of Excellence," 2021 Annual Report, https://us.pg.com/annualreport2021/superiority-a-higher-standard-of -excellence/.

20. Mason Swimming, "Kathy Fish—Feature About AMO50."

Chapter 4

1. A quote provided by Dr. Rakesh Suri for the purposes of foregrounding the importance of learning in this chapter.

2. All information, including quotations and statistics, in this chapter is derived from a case series published by Harvard Business Publishing unless otherwise cited. See Linda A. Hill and Emily Tedards, "Cleveland Clinic Abu Dhabi," Case 422-058 (Boston: Harvard Business School, 2022); Linda A. Hill and Emily Tedards, "Cleveland Clinic Abu Dhabi (Abridged)," Case 422-056 (Boston: Harvard Business School, 2022); Linda A. Hill and Emily Tedards, "Cleveland Clinic Abu Dhabi: Leading Through the Fog of the COVID-19 Pandemic," Case 422-057 (Boston: Harvard Business School, 2022); and Linda A. Hill and Lydia Begag, "Dr. Tom Mihaljevic and Cleveland Clinic," Case 424-031 (Boston: Harvard Business School, 2024). We extend our deepest gratitude to Frances X. Frei, Amy Edmondson, and their coauthors for

their contributions to the research on Cleveland Clinic. See Frances X. Frei, Amy C. Edmondson, Eliot Sherman, and Christine Harris-Van Keuren, "Cleveland Clinic," Case 607-143 (Boston: Harvard Business School, 2007) and Amy C. Edmondson and Michaela J. Kerrissey, "Enabling Teamwork at the Cleveland Clinic," Case 621-040 (Boston: Harvard Business School, 2020).

3. Emirates News Agency (WAM), "Agreement Between Health Authority Abu Dhabi and Cleveland Clinic to Manage Sheikh Khalifa Medical City," June 5, 2007, https://www.wam.ae/en/article/hsyin34d-agreement-between-health-authority-cleveland.

4. Value-based care (as opposed to fee-for-service care) refers to health-care delivery models based on patient health outcomes as opposed to the quantity of services provided. These models are focused on improving the quality of the patient experience and delivering better health outcomes, while also reducing the overall cost of care. For more value-based care models, see, for example, Michael E. Porter and Elizabeth Olmsted Teisberg, *Redefining Health Care: Creating Value-Based Competition on Results* (Boston: Harvard Business School Press, 2006).

5. The notion of a "learning organization" first appeared in the early 1990s, when so many incumbents were stumbling in what was becoming an ever more volatile and complex global economy. To be agile in today's competitive environment in which ability and speed are key, continuous learning has become an imperative. Unfortunately, there are many barriers to building learning organizations. Two leading scholars on learning organizations are Donald A. Schön and Peter M. Senge. Other research includes, for example, Francesca Gino and Gary P. Pisano, "Why Leaders Don't Learn from Success," *Harvard Business Review*, April 2011 and Jean-François Harvey, Henrik Bresman, Amy C. Edmondson, and Gary P. Pisano, "A Strategic View of Team Learning in Organizations," *Academy of Management Annals* 16, no. 2 (July 2022): 476–507, https://doi.org/10.5465/annals.2020.0352.

6. Donald A. Schön, *The Reflective Practitioner: How Professionals Think in Action* (New York: Basic Books, 1983).

7. Michael Ku struggled with the same challenge of getting people in his organization to feel psychologically safe enough to share their thoughts, in large measure because they wanted to avoid conflict. Therefore, his team struggled with creative abrasion. Here, we see the importance of creating an environment of psychological safety to create the conditions for organizational learning. See, for example, Amy Edmondson's research on the impact of psychological safety on learning: Amy Edmondson, "Psychological Safety and Learning Behavior in Work Teams," *Administrative Science Quarterly* 44, no. 2 (1999): 350–83; Amy Edmondson, "The Competitive Imperative of Learning," *Harvard Business Review*, July–August 2008; Amy C. Edmondson, "Strategies for Learning from Failure," *Harvard Business Review*, April 2011; and Amy Edmondson, *Teaming: How Organizations Learn, Innovate, and Compete in the Knowledge Economy* (San Francisco: Jossey-Bass, 2012).

8. We found that in innovative teams and organizations, the culture created was one in which individuals felt both a sense of autonomy and a sense of responsibility to deliver on the collective purpose. Hence, individuals felt like they belonged to a community in which there was a foundation of mutual influence and mutual trust that made them feel psychologically safe enough to take risks and innovate. See Linda A. Hill, Greg Brandeau, Emily Truelove, and Kent Lineback, *Collective Genius: The Art and Practice of Leading Innovation* (Boston: Harvard Business Review Press, 2014), chapter 2.

9. Cleveland Clinic, "Mission, Vision & Values," https://my.clevelandclinic.org /about/overview/who-we-are/mission-vision-values.

10. Organizations have found that despite making major investments in digital tools and data, individuals do not necessarily embrace and use them to deliver on organizational objectives. There is a growing body of research that describes how to overcome barriers to adoption and to get people to develop what we refer to as digital dexterity—the willingness and ability to embrace emerging technologies. For more information, see Linda A. Hill et al., "Where Can Digital Transformation Take You? Insights from 1,700 Leaders," Harvard Business School Working Knowledge, January 31, 2022, https://www.library.hbs.edu/working-knowledge/leading-in-the-digital -era-where-can-digital-transformation-take-you; Linda A. Hill et al., "Digital Transformation: A New Roadmap for Success," Harvard Business School Working Knowledge, February 7, 2022, https://www.library.hbs.edu/working-knowledge /leading-in-the-digital-era-a-new-roadmap-for-success; and Linda A. Hill et al., "Curiosity, Not Coding: 6 Skills Leaders Need in the Digital Age," Harvard Business School Working Knowledge, February 14, 2022, https://www.library.hbs.edu/working -knowledge/six-unexpected-traits-leaders-need-in-the-digital-era. We have continued to collect data from executives across the globe, and having surveyed over 8,300 executives as of March 2025, we have observed that the results are in line with our initial findings. For other research, see, for example, Marco Iansiti and Satya Nadella, "Democratizing Transformation," *Harvard Business Review*, May–June 2022; and Tsedal Neeley and Paul Leonardi, "Developing a Digital Mindset," *Harvard Business Review*, May–June 2022.

11. A/B testing is a method to compare two versions of a prototype to figure out which works more effectively. For more information on A/B testing and experimentation, please see Eric T. Peterson, "A Refresher on A/B Testing," *Harvard Business Review*, June 22, 2017 and Stefan H. Thomke, *Experimentation Works: The Surprising Power of Business Experiments* (Boston: Harvard Business Review Press, 2020).

12. One Cleveland Clinic is a governance framework that Cleveland Clinic enterprise uses. The organization is an operating company in which the executive team assumes responsibility for a global portfolio of activities. For more information, please see Hill and Begag, "Dr. Tom Mihaljevic and Cleveland Clinic," Case 424-031.

13. These are statistics that Cleveland Clinic Abu Dhabi provided to the authors of this book at the time of the case development process in 2020.

14. Peter M. Senge, *The Fifth Discipline: The Art and Practice of the Learning Organization* (New York: Doubleday, 1990).

Part II

1. Too often when developing strategic alliances up front, leaders devote most of their time and attention to governance and legal matters. But to achieve desired performance outcomes, more attention should be paid to the role that inter*personal* trust plays in building the inter*organizational* trust required to achieve desired performance outcomes. In fact, working through elaborate contractual arrangements too early can risk damaging the development of trust. There is some evidence that the more effective way to start these relationships is to begin with a simple MOU to guide the first months of interaction. See, for example, J. P. Eggers and K. Francis Park, "Incumbent Adaptation

to Technological Change: The Past, Present, and Future of Research on Heterogeneous Incumbent Response," *Academy of Management Annals* 12, no. 1 (2018): 357–89, https://doi.org/10.5465/annals.2016.0051; Andrew Shipilov, Nathan Furr, and Tobias Studer Andersson, "Looking to Boost Innovation? Partner with a Startup," hbr.org, May 27, 2020, https://hbr.org/2020/05/looking-to-boost-innovation-partner-with-a-startup; Nathan Furr, Kate O'Keeffe, and Jeff Dyer, "Managing Multiparty Innovation," *Harvard Business Review*, November 2016; Yves L. Doz and Gary Hamel, *Alliance Advantage: The Art of Creating Value Through Partnering* (Boston: Harvard Business School Press, 1998); and Sascha Albers, Franz Wohlgezogen, and Edward J. Zajac, "Strategic Alliance Structures: An Organization Design Perspective," *Journal of Management* 42, no. 3 (March 2016): 582–614, https://doi.org/10.1177/0149206313488209.

2. Effective working relationships are characterized by three conditions: mutual commitment, mutual trust, and mutual influence. See, for example, John J. Gabarro, *The Dynamics of Taking Charge* (Boston: Harvard Business School Press, 1987) and Linda A. Hill and Kent Lineback, *Being the Boss: The 3 Imperatives for Becoming a Great Leader* (Boston: Harvard Business Review Press, 2011). There is a considerable body of research—although much of it is more macro in orientation (interorganizational trust versus interpersonal trust) that looks at the conditions and processes that need to be in place for strategic alliances to generate and/or scale innovative solutions. See, for example, Sascha Albers, Franz Wohlgezogen, and Edward J. Zajac, "Strategic Alliance Structures: An Organization Design Perspective," *Journal of Management* 42, no. 3 (March 2016): 582–614, https://doi.org/10.1177/0149206313488209; Yves L. Doz and Gary Hamel, *Alliance Advantage: The Art of Creating Value Through Partnering* (Boston: Harvard Business School Press, 1998); Vincenzo Perrone, Akbar Zaheer, and Bill McEvily, "Free to Be Trusted? Organizational Constraints on Trust in Boundary Spanners," *Organization Science* 14, no. 4 (August 2003): 422–39, https://doi.org/10.1287/orsc.14.4.422.17487; Akbar Zaheer, Bill McEvily, and Vincenzo Perrone, "Does Trust Matter? Exploring the Effects of Interorganizational and Interpersonal Trust on Performance," *Organization Science* 9, no. 2 (April 1998): 141–59, https://doi.org/10.1287/orsc.9.2.141; Herminia Ibarra and Morten T. Hansen, "Are You a Collaborative Leader?," *Harvard Business Review*, July–August 2011; Henry Adobor, "The Role of Personal Relationships in Inter-Firm Alliances: Benefits, Dysfunctions, and Some Suggestions," *Business Horizons* 49, no. 6 (November 2006): 473–86, https://doi.org/10.1016/j.bushor.2006.03.003; Howard E. Aldrich and C. Marlene Fiol, "Fools Rush In? The Institutional Context of Industry Creation," *Academy of Management Review* 19, no. 4 (October 1994): 645–70, https://doi.org/10.5465/amr.1994.9412190214; T. K. Das and Bing-Sheng Teng, "Between Trust and Control: Developing Confidence in Partner Cooperation in Alliances," *Academy of Management Review* 23, no. 3 (July 1998): 491–512, https://doi.org/10.2307/259291; Jeffrey H. Dyer, Prashant Kale, and Harbir Singh, "How to Make Strategic Alliances Work," *MIT Sloan Management Review*, July 15, 2001, https://sloanreview.mit.edu/article/how-to-make-strategic-alliances-work/; Ranjay Gulati, "Alliances and Networks," *Strategic Management Journal* 19, no. 4 (April 1998): 293–317; Ranjay Gulati, Franz Wohlgezogen, and Pavel Zhelyazkov, "The Two Facets of Collaboration: Cooperation and Coordination in Strategic Alliances," *Academy of Management Annals* 6, no. 1 (May 2012): 531–83, https://doi.org/10.1080/19416520.2012.691646; and Denise M. Rousseau, Sim B. Sitkin, Ronald S. Burt, and Colin Camerer, "Not So Different After All: A Cross-Discipline View of Trust,"

Academy of Management Review 23, no. 3 (July 1998): 393–404, https://doi.org/10.5465
/amr.1998.926617.

3. There is a body of research on the importance and challenges of boundary-spanning roles. See, for example, Howard Aldrich and Diane Herker, "Boundary Spanning Roles and Organization Structure," *Academy of Management Review* 2, no. 2 (April 1977): 217–30, https://doi.org/10.2307/257905; Kate Williams, "Hybrid Knowledge Production and Evaluation at the World Bank," *Policy and Society* 41, no. 4 (November 10, 2022): 513–27, https://doi.org/10.1093/polsoc/puac009; Ronald Burt, *Structural Holes: The Social Structure of Competition* (Boston: Harvard Business School Press, 1992); Richard Leifer and George P. Huber, "Relations Among Perceived Environmental Uncertainty, Organization Structure, and Boundary-Spanning Behavior," *Administrative Science Quarterly* 22, no. 2 (June 1977): 235–47, https://doi .org/10.2307/2391958; Morten Hansen, "Introducing T-Shaped Managers: Knowledge Management's Next Generation," *Harvard Business Review*, March 2001; and Rob Cross, *Beyond Collaboration Overload: How to Work Smarter, Get Ahead, and Restore Your Well-Being* (Boston: Harvard Business Review Press, 2021). Most of this work looks at bilateral relationships and less at what it takes for individuals to negotiate relationships across multiple parties at the same time—the challenge many of our bridgers faced. Some exceptions to this, include, for example, Michael L. Tushman, Wendy K. Smith, and Andy Binns, "The Ambidextrous CEO," *Harvard Business Review*, June 2011; M. L. Tushman and T. J. Scanlan, "Boundary Spanning Individuals: Their Role in Information Transfer and Their Antecedents," *Academy of Management Journal* 24, no. 2 (June 1, 1981): 289–305, https://doi.org/10.2307/255842; Linda A. Hill, *Becoming a Manager: How New Managers Master the Challenges of Leadership*, 2nd ed. (Boston: Harvard Business School Press, 2003); Linda A. Hill and Kent Lineback, "Are You a Good Boss—or a Great One?," *Harvard Business Review*, January–February 2011; and Hill and Lineback, *Being the Boss*, particularly the chapters on managing your network. There is more discussion on negotiating multilateral relationships in part III of this book.

4. In a classic article, James March describes the inherent tension in designing an organization better suited for innovation as opposed to execution. His work has evolved into the extensive literature on ambidextrous organizations. See James G. March, "Exploration and Exploitation in Organizational Learning," *Organization Science* 2, no. 1 (February 1991): 71–87, https://doi.org/10.1287/orsc.2.1.71. Incumbents are creating centers of excellence (dedicated units organized to foster cocreation separate from the core business) in order to innovate with more speed at scale. See, for example, Andrew Shipilov, Nathan Furr, and Tobias Studer Andersson, "Looking to Boost Innovation? Partner with a Startup," hbr.org, May 27, 2020, https://hbr.org/2020/05 /looking-to-boost-innovation-partner-with-a-startup; Scott D. Anthony, Clark G. Gilbert, and Mark W. Johnson, *Dual Transformation: How to Reposition Today's Business While Creating the Future* (Boston: Harvard Business Review Press, 2017); Andrew Binns, Charles A. O'Reilly, and Michael Tushman, *Corporate Explorer: How Corporations Beat Startups at the Innovation Game* (Hoboken, NJ: Wiley, 2022); Kim B. Clark and Rebecca Henderson, "Architectural Innovation: The Reconfiguration of Existing Product Technologies and the Failure of Established Firms," *Administrative Science Quarterly* 35, no. 1 (1990): 9–30; Kathleen M. Eisenhardt and Shona L. Brown, *Competing on the Edge: Strategy as Structured Chaos* (Boston: Harvard Business School Press, 1998); Charles A. O'Reilly III and Michael L. Tushman, "The Ambidextrous

Organization," *Harvard Business Review*, April 2004; Michael Tushman and Charles A. O'Reilly III, "Ambidextrous Organizations: Managing Evolutionary and Revolutionary Change," *California Management Review* 38, no. 4 (1996): 8–30; Charles A. O'Reilly III and Michael L. Tushman, *Lead and Disrupt: How to Solve the Innovator's Dilemma* (Stanford, CA: Stanford Business Books, 2016); and Michael Tushman and Charles A. O'Reilly, *Winning Through Innovation: A Practical Guide to Leading Organizational Change and Renewal* (Boston: Harvard Business School Press, 1997).

5. Generating innovative solutions is challenging, but launching and scaling them is even more difficult. The research on ambidextrous organizations emphasizes the challenges encountered when moving an idea from the center of excellence to the core business to scale it. See, for example, Peter Koen et al., "Scaling Up Transformational Innovations," *Harvard Business Review*, November–December 2024.

6. One of us, Linda Hill, has been working with Ann Le Cam, Sunand Menon, Karina Grazina, and Lydia Begag, a team of executives and academic researchers, to conduct a series of global surveys and roundtables to better understand the challenges of leadership and innovation in the digital era. Since 2022, we have continued to collect data from executives across the globe, and have surveyed over 8,300 executives from over 100 countries across 6 continents as of September 2025. In our data set over the years, we have found that companies are continuing to leverage innovation labs and corporate accelerators. Forty-five percent of survey participants for the 2025 survey noted that their companies have an innovation lab or corporate accelerator. Twenty-eight percent reported that innovation labs or corporate accelerators have a *moderate* impact on their organization, 38 percent reported that innovation labs or corporate accelerators have a *significant* impact on their organization, and 19 percent reported that innovation labs or corporate accelerators have an *extreme* impact on their organizations.

Chapter 5

1. This quote is from an excerpt of Ed Bastian's keynote address at the 2020 Consumer Electronics Show. See Delta Air Lines, "Video: Delta CEO Ed Bastian CES 2020 Opening Keynote (Full Length)," press release, January 7, 2020, https://news .delta.com/video-delta-ceo-ed-bastian-ces-2020-opening-keynote-full-length.

2. All information, including quotations, in this chapter is derived from the case study published by Harvard Business Publishing unless otherwise cited. See Linda A. Hill and Emily Tedards, "Nicole M. Jones and The Hangar: Delta Air Lines' Global Innovation Center," Case 422-042 (Boston: Harvard Business School, 2021; revised 2022) and Linda A. Hill and Lydia Begag, "OneTen at Delta Air Lines: Catalyzing Family-Sustaining Careers for Black Talent (A)," Case 423-072 (Boston: Harvard Business Publishing, 2023; revised May 2023).

3. Hill and Tedards, "Nicole M. Jones and The Hangar" and Hill and Begag, "OneTen at Delta Air Lines."

4. Hill and Tedards, "Nicole M. Jones and The Hangar" and Hill and Begag, "OneTen at Delta Air Lines."

5. Delta Air Lines, "Video: Delta CEO Ed Bastian CES 2020 Opening Keynote (Full Length)."

6. In designing her team and selecting team members, Nicole Jones made choices consistent with those of the three architect leaders we profiled in part I of the book. She worked to develop a team that was willing and able to cocreate with others, meaning they were able to collaborate, experiment, and learn with others.

7. As we saw in chapter 3 about Kathy Fish at P&G, Nicole Jones and her team introduced a discovery-driven learning methodology to Delta. Instead of lean innovation, they relied on a design-thinking methodology. To learn more about discovery-driven learning methodologies, see Tim Brown, *Change by Design: How Design Thinking Creates New Alternatives for Business and Society* (New York: HarperCollins Publishers, 2009); Rita Gunther McGrath and Ian C. MacMillan, *Discovery-Driven Growth: A Breakthrough Process to Reduce Risk and Seize Opportunity* (Boston: Harvard Business School Press, 2009); Stefan Thomke and Eric von Hippel, "Customers as Innovators: A New Way to Create Value," *Harvard Business Review*, April 2002; Stefan Thomke and Jim Manzi, "The Discipline of Business Experimentation: Increase Your Chances of Success with Innovation Test-Drives," *Harvard Business Review*, December 2014; and Tom Kelley and Jonathan Littman, *The Art of Innovation: Lessons in Creativity from IDEO, America's Leading Design Firm* (New York: Currency, 2001).

8. Clear, "CLEAR—Travel Faster Through Airport Security," https://www.clearme.com/ and Shivani Vora, "How Clear Can Speed Up the Airport Screening Process," *New York Times*, November 17, 2017, https://www.nytimes.com/2017/11/17/travel/clear-airport-screening.html.

9. There is considerable research to suggest that The Hangar's approach to decision-making is more likely to lead to making decisions that meet the needs of the customer. See, for example, Linda A. Hill, Emily Tedards, and Taran Swan, "Drive Innovation with Better Decision-Making," *Harvard Business Review*, November–December 2021. For examples of how to build customer-centric organizations, see Ranjay Gulati, *Reorganize for Resiliency: Putting Customers at the Center of Your Business* (Boston: Harvard Business Review Press, 2010); Alec Rawson et al., "The Truth About Customer Experience," *Harvard Business Review*, September 2013; James L. Heskett et al., *The Ownership Quotient: Putting the Service Profit Chain to Work for Unbeatable Competitive Advantage* (Boston: Harvard Business Press, 2008); and James Kalbach, *The Jobs to Be Done Playbook: Align Your Markets, Organizations, and Strategy Around Customer Needs* (New York: Two Waves Books, 2020). Building a customer-centric organization requires breaking down silos and building a more cross-functional way of working to deliver for customers. See, for example, Ranjay Gulati, *Reorganize for Resiliency: Putting Customers at the Center of Your Business* (Boston: Harvard Business Press, 2010). For an example of what it takes to build an organization able to deliver a differentiated end-to-end customer experience, see B. Joseph Pine II and James H. Gilmore, *The Experience Economy: Competing for Customer Time, Attention, and Money* (Boston: Harvard Business Review Press, 2020). The customer-centric approach is also more likely to lead to buy-in from others, increasing the likelihood that the decision will actually be implemented. See, for example, John P. Kotter, *Leading Change* (Boston: Harvard Business School Press, 1996); Ryan Raffaelli, "Leading and Managing Change," Industry and Background Note 415-040 (Boston: Harvard Business School Publishing, 2014); Michael Beer, *High Commitment, High Performance* (San Francisco: Jossey-Bass, 2009); Robert B. Cialdini, *Influence, New and Expanded: The Psychology of Persuasion* (New York: Harper Business, 2021); and Richard Tanner Pascale and Jerry Sternin, "Your Company's Secret Change Agents," *Harvard Business Review*, May 2005.

10. As in the case of Ajay Banga at Mastercard (chapter 1), APIs act as a kind of messenger that allows one software system to communicate and connect with another.

11. See part II, note 5. As we wrote there, generating innovative solutions is challenging, but launching and scaling them through the core business is even more

difficult. For more information, see Peter Koen et al., "Scaling Up Transformational Innovations," *Harvard Business Review*, November–December 2024.

12. "O'Hare Loses Its Status as the World's Busiest," *Chicago Tribune*, August 20, 2021, https://www.chicagotribune.com/2000/01/04/ohare-loses-its-status-as-the-worlds-busiest/.

13. We saw this same challenge in chapter 3 at P&G. Design thinking and lean innovation are both methodologies that help individuals stay focused on and learn more about customer pain points and desires.

14. In this book, we define trust and credibility as it was defined in Linda A. Hill and Kent Lineback, *Being the Boss*. We define interpersonal *trust* as whether or not someone is perceived as competent (knowing the right thing to do) and a person of character (wanting to do the right thing). We define *credibility* as whether or not someone is perceived as being trustworthy and having enough influence to get the right thing done. Both trust and credibility are based on reputation, but even more on individuals' firsthand experiences with each other. Over time, The Hangar team was perceived as trustworthy and credible. For more information, see Linda A. Hill and Kent Lineback, *Being the Boss: The 3 Imperatives for Becoming a Great Leader* (Boston: Harvard Business Review Press, 2011).

Chapter 6

1. Words of His Highness Sheikh Mohammed Bin Rashid Al Maktoum, as inscribed on the Museum of the Future, Dubai, UAE.

2. All information, including quotations, in this chapter is derived from a case series published by Harvard Business Publishing unless otherwise cited. See Linda A. Hill, Emily Tedards, and Lydia Begag, "Accelerating the Accelerator: Raja Al Mazrouei at DIFC Fintech Hive," Case 423-064 (Boston: Harvard Business School Publishing, 2023; revised May 2023) and Linda A. Hill and Lydia Begag, "Astyanax Kanakakis at norbloc: A Founder's Experience with the DIFC Fintech Hive," Case 423-066 (Boston: Harvard Business School Publishing, 2023).

3. Daniel Shepherd, "DIFC FinTech Hive Makes Global Finance's World Best Innovation Labs 2021 List," TahawulTech.com, June 24, 2021, https://www.tahawultech.com/news/difc-fintech-hive-makes-global-finances-world-best-innovation-labs-2021-list/.

4. Parag Deulgaonkar, "12% of Dubai GDP from DIFC," *Emirates 24/7*, February 4, 2014, https://www.emirates247.com/business/economy-finance/12-of-dubai-gdp-from-difc-2014-02-04-1.537222.

5. Emirates News Agency, "DIFC Posts Strong Growth in First Half of 2016," August 31, 2016, https://www.wam.ae/en/details/1395299412842.

6. Jackson Mueller and Michael S. Piwowar, "FinTech in the Middle East: An Analysis of the Industry and the Regulatory Landscape," Milken Institute, December 2019, https://milkeninstitute.org/sites/default/files/reports-pdf/FinTech%20in%20the%20Middle%20East-FINAL-121119.pdf and Nada Al Rifai, "Middle East Fintech Investments Make Up Just 1% of Global Total–Bahrain Fintech Bay CEO," *Zawya*, March 4, 2019, https://www.zawya.com/en/business/middle-east-fintech-investments-make-up-just-1-of-global-total-bahrain-fintech-bay-ceo-t3wi5vqo.

7. On average, 14 percent of the Middle East's adult population had bank accounts in 2014. World Economic Forum, "The World's Unbanked in 6 Charts," September 2017, https://www.weforum.org/stories/2017/09/the-worlds-unbanked-in-6-charts.

8. GSMA Intelligence, *The Mobile Economy: Middle East and North Africa 2016*, GSMA, 2016, https://data.gsmaintelligence.com/api-web/v2/research-file-download?id =18809379&file=the-mobile-economy-middle-east-and-north-africa-2016 -1482139999344.pdf.

9. For more research on growing economies and building competitive nations, see Michael E. Porter, *The Competitive Advantage of Nations* (New York: Free Press, 1998); Richard L. Florida, *Cities and the Creative Class* (London: Routledge, 2005); Richard H. K. Vietor, *How Countries Compete: Strategy, Structure, and Government in the Global Economy* (Boston: Harvard Business School Press, 2007); and Tarun Khanna, Krishna G. Palepu, and Jayant Sinha, "Strategies That Fit Emerging Markets," *Harvard Business Review*, June 2005.

10. The research on strategic alliances identifies factors to consider in selecting which organizations to partner with. These factors go beyond the capabilities that the partner will bring (factors that will make it harder to build collaborative relationships like vast differences in culture, physical proximity, or operating model). See, for example, J. P. Eggers and K. Francis Park, "Incumbent Adaptation to Technological Change: The Past, Present, and Future of Research on Heterogeneous Incumbent Response," *Academy of Management Annals* 12, no. 1 (2018): 357–89, https://doi.org/10 .5465/annals.2016.0051; Andrew Shipilov, Nathan Furr, and Tobias Studer Andersson, "Looking to Boost Innovation? Partner with a Startup," hbr.org, May 27, 2020, https://hbr.org/2020/05/looking-to-boost-innovation-partner-with-a-startup; Nathan Furr, Kate O'Keeffe, and Jeff Dyer, "Managing Multiparty Innovation," *Harvard Business Review*, November 2016; Yves L. Doz and Gary Hamel, *Alliance Advantage: The Art of Creating Value Through Partnering* (Boston: Harvard Business School Press, 1998); Sascha Albers, Franz Wohlgezogen, and Edward J. Zajac, "Strategic Alliance Structures: An Organization Design Perspective," *Journal of Management* 42, no. 3 (March 2016): 582–614, https://doi.org/10.1177/0149206313488209; Lee Fleming, Santiago Mingo, and David Chen, "Collaborative Brokerage, Generative Creativity, and Creative Success," *Administrative Science Quarterly* 52, no. 3 (2007): 443–75; and David Obstfeld, "Social Networks, the Tertius Iungens Orientation, and Involvement in Innovation," *Administrative Science Quarterly* 50, no. 1 (March 2005): 100–30, https://doi.org/10.2189/asqu.2005.50.1.100.

11. For research on the importance of contextual intelligence, see Tarun Khanna, "Contextual Intelligence," *Harvard Business Review*, September 2004 and Anthony J. Mayo and Nitin Nohria, "Zeitgeist Leadership," *Harvard Business Review*, October 2005.

12. Bridgers have to be able to help others communicate across their differences if parties are to understand each other's perspectives and develop a common language. See, for example, the following research on managing differences: Linda A. Hill, Greg Brandeau, Emily Truelove, and Kent Lineback, *Collective Genius: The Art and Practice of Leading Innovation* (Boston: Harvard Business Review Press, 2014), chapters 1, 2, and 6; John Child, "Commentary on Constructive Conflict," in *Mary Parker Follett: Prophet of Management: A Celebration of Writings from the 1920s*, ed. Pauline Graham (Washington, DC: Beard Books, 2003), 89; Kathleen M. Eisenhardt, Jean L. Kahwajy, and L. J. Bourgeois III, "How Management Teams Can Have a Good Fight," *Harvard Business Review*, July–August 1997; Robin J. Ely and David A. Thomas, "Cultural Diversity at Work: The Moderating Effects of Work Group Perspectives on Diversity," *Administrative Science Quarterly* 46 (June 2001): 229–73; Doris Kearns Goodwin, *Team of Rivals: The Political Genius of Abraham Lincoln* (New York: Simon & Schuster, 2005); Boris

Groysberg et al., "Too Many Cooks Spoil the Broth: How High-Status Individuals Decrease Group Effectiveness," *Organization Science* 21, no. 3 (2010): 1–16; Karen A. Jehn, "A Multimethod Examination of the Benefits and Detriments of Intragroup Conflict," *Administrative Science Quarterly* 40, no. 2 (June 1995): 256–82; Frans Johansson, *The Medici Effect: Breakthrough Insights at the Intersection of Ideas, Concepts, and Cultures* (Boston: Harvard Business School Press, 2004); Scott E. Page, *The Difference: How the Power of Diversity Creates Better Groups, Firms, Schools, and Societies* (Princeton, NJ: Princeton University Press, 2008); J. Richard Hackman, *Collaborative Intelligence: Using Teams to Solve Hard Problems* (San Francisco: Berrett-Koehler, 2011); and E. Jeffrey Conklin, *Dialogue Mapping: Building Shared Understanding of Wicked Problems* (Hoboken, NJ: Wiley, 2006). In helping others understand and work thorough the inevitable conflicts that arise when doing translation work, bridgers have to be skilled at conflict management. For some of the research on managing conflict, see Kerry Patterson, Joseph Grenny, Ron McMillan, and Al Switzler, *Crucial Conversations: Tools for Talking When Stakes Are High* (New York: McGraw-Hill, 2021); Douglas Stone, Bruce Patton, and Sheila Heen, *Difficult Conversations: How to Discuss What Matters Most* (New York: Penguin Books, 2022); Deborah Borisoff and David A. Victor, *Conflict Management: A Communication Skills Approach* (Englewood Cliffs, NJ: Prentice-Hall, Inc., 1989); Carsten K. W. De Dreu and Michelle J. Gelfand, "Conflict in the Workplace: Sources, Functions, and Dynamics Across Multiple Levels of Analysis," in *The Psychology of Conflict Management in Organizations*, ed. Carsten K. W. De Dreu and Michelle J. Gelfand (New York: Lawrence Erlbaum Associates, 2007), 3–54; Goodwin, *Team of Rivals*; Linda A. Hill and Allison J. Wigen, "Tom Kalil: Leading Technology & Innovation at the White House," Case 417-021 (Boston: Harvard Business School Publishing, 2016; revised March 2019); Morten Hansen, "Introducing T-Shaped Managers: Knowledge Management's Next Generation," *Harvard Business Review*, March 2001; and Diya Kapur Misra, Linda A. Hill, Gaurav Laroia, and Christiane Hamacher, "A Better Way to Unlock Innovation and Drive Change," *MIT Sloan Management Review*, Fall 2024, https://sloanreview.mit.edu /article/a-better-way-to-unlock-innovation-and-drive-change/.

13. For more research on how integrative decision-making often leads to more innovative solutions, see, for example, Mary Parker Follett, *Creative Experience* (Bristol, UK: Thoemmes Press, 2001). Follett discusses the importance of not settling for choice A or B, but, rather, creating an innovative third way that combines elements of and improves on both A and B. An integrative solution is an approach that solves a conflict by accommodating the real demands of all the parties involved. The result is often represented more aptly as a mosaic rather than a melting pot of the varied talents and perspectives of those involved. Also, see Roger Martin, *The Opposable Mind: How Successful Leaders Win Through Integrative Thinking* (Boston: Harvard Business Press, 2007) and Roger Martin, "How Successful Leaders Think," *Harvard Business Review*, June 2007.

14. For research on the importance of "both/and" thinking, see Wendy K. Smith and Marianne W. Lewis, *Both/And Thinking: Embracing Creative Tensions to Solve Your Toughest Problems* (Boston: Harvard Business Review Press, 2022) and Hill, Brandeau, Truelove, and Lineback, *Collective Genius*, chapter 2.

15. See Ranjay Gulati, Franz Wohlgezogen, and Pavel Zhelyazkov, "The Two Facets of Collaboration: Cooperation and Coordination in Strategic Alliances," *Academy of Management Annals* 6, no. 1 (May 2012): 531–83, https://doi.org/10.1080

/19416520.2012.691646, for how to make integration choices that will facilitate coordination of work and collaboration with others outside organizational boundaries. See also Adam Kahane, *Collaborating with the Enemy: How to Work with People You Don't Agree with or Like or Trust* (Oakland, CA: Berrett-Koehler Publishers, Inc., 2017) and Rosabeth Moss Kanter, *Thinking Outside the Building: How Advanced Leaders Can Change the World One Smart Innovation at a Time* (New York: PublicAffairs, 2020).

Chapter 7

1. All information, including quotations, in this chapter is derived from a number of cases published by Harvard Business Publishing about Mastercard, unless otherwise cited. We extend our deepest gratitude to Sunil Gupta, for facilitating this research collaboration with Mastercard. For more information, please see Sunil Gupta, Linda A. Hill, Julia Kelley, and Emily Tedards, "Mastercard: Creating a World Beyond Cash," Case 522-001 (Boston: Harvard Business School Publishing, April 2022); Linda A. Hill, Sunil Gupta, Emily Tedards, and Julia Kelley, "Mastercard Labs (A)," Case 422-080 (Boston: Harvard Business School Publishing, April 2022); and Linda A. Hill, Sunil Gupta, Emily Tedards, and Julia Kelley, "Mastercard Labs (B)," Case 422-081 (Boston: Harvard Business School Publishing, 2022).

2. Mastercard, "A World Beyond Cash: Priceless. Mastercard Annual Report," 2011, https://www.annualreports.com/HostedData/AnnualReportArchive/m/NYSE _MA_2011.pdf.

3. See Mastercard Labs company document in exhibit 5 of the Mastercard Labs (A) case study. Hill, Gupta, Tedards, and Kelley, "Mastercard Labs (A)."

4. Research on ambidextrous organizations explores why you must set up a separate unit for innovation. Explicit and implicit in these arguments about ambidexterity is the idea that innovation will not happen in the core. As a result, there is a body of research on what it takes to prime the core. See, for example, Andrew Shipilov, Nathan Furr, and Tobias Studer Andersson, "Looking to Boost Innovation? Partner with a Startup," hbr.org, May 27, 2020, https://hbr.org/2020/05/looking-to-boost -innovation-partner-with-a-startup; Scott D. Anthony, Clark G. Gilbert, and Mark W. Johnson, *Dual Transformation: How to Reposition Today's Business While Creating the Future* (Boston: Harvard Business Review Press, 2017); Andrew Binns, Charles A. O'Reilly, and Michael Tushman, *Corporate Explorer: How Corporations Beat Startups at the Innovation Game* (Hoboken, NJ: Wiley, 2022); Kim B. Clark and Rebecca Henderson, "Architectural Innovation: The Reconfiguration of Existing Product Technologies and the Failure of Established Firms," *Administrative Science Quarterly* 35, no. 1 (1990): 9–30; Kathleen M. Eisenhardt and Shona L. Brown, *Competing on the Edge: Strategy as Structured Chaos* (Boston: Harvard Business School Press, 1998); Charles A. O'Reilly III and Michael L. Tushman, "The Ambidextrous Organization," *Harvard Business Review*, April 2004; Michael Tushman and Charles A. O'Reilly III, "Ambidextrous Organizations: Managing Evolutionary and Revolutionary Change," *California Management Review* 38, no. 4 (1996): 8–30; Charles A. O'Reilly III and Michael L. Tushman, *Lead and Disrupt: How to Solve the Innovator's Dilemma* (Stanford, CA: Stanford Business Books, 2016); and Michael Tushman and Charles A. O'Reilly III, *Winning through Innovation: A Practical Guide to Leading Organizational Change and Renewal* (Boston: Harvard Business School Press, 1997).

5. For more information on innovation metrics, see Scott D. Anthony, Steven Fransblow, and Steve Wunker, "Measuring the Black Box: How to Design and Implement Innovation Metrics," *Chief Executive*, December 2007; Eric Ries, *The Lean Startup: How Today's Entrepreneurs Use Continuous Innovation to Create Radically Successful Businesses* (New York: Currency, 2011); and Evans Baiya and Ron Price, *The Innovator's Advantage: Revealing the Hidden Connection Between People and Process* (Meridian, ID: Aloha Publishing, 2017).

6. Mastercard, "A World Beyond Cash: Priceless. Mastercard Annual Report," 2011.

7. Mastercard, "MasterCard Announces Acquisition of VocaLink," press release, July 21, 2016, https://investor.mastercard.com/investor-news/investor-news-details /2016/MasterCard-Announces-Acquisition-of-VocaLink/default.aspx.

8. "Mastercard Study Shows Consumers Globally Make the Move to Contactless Payments for Everyday Purchases, Seeking Touch-Free Payment Experiences," Business Wire, April 29, 2020, https://www.businesswire.com/news/home/20200429005592/en /Mastercard-Study-Shows-Consumers-Globally-Make-the-Move-to-Contactless -Payments-for-Everyday-Purchases-Seeking-Touch-Free-Payment-Experiences.

9. Richard Haythornthwaite and Ajay Banga, "The Former and Current Chairs of Mastercard on Executing a Strategic CEO Succession," *Harvard Business Review*, March–April 2021.

10. Hill, Gupta, Tedards, and Kelley, "Mastercard Labs (B)."

Part III

1. Our thinking on the catalyst role was shaped by the work on social movements, institutional emergence, systems change, and open innovation, as well as the work on strategic alliances, interorganizational networks, and ecosystems in business. We find that the body of research on social movements has focused more on the evolution of movements over time than the body of research on strategic alliances and ecosystems in business and open innovation. The latter two research streams have focused more on the initial conditions of these ecosystems or open innovation efforts and their impact on achieving desired outcomes. See, for example, Paul N. Bloom and J. Gregory Dees, "Cultivate Your Ecosystem," *Stanford Social Innovation Review* 6, no. 1 (2007): 47–53, https://doi.org/10.48558/QWAW-VP62; Peter Block, *Community: The Structure of Belonging* (San Francisco: Berrett-Koehler Publishers, 2008); J. Gregory Dees, Jed Emerson, and Peter Economy, *Enterprising Nonprofits: A Toolkit for Social Entrepreneurs* (New York: Wiley, 2001); J. Gregory Dees, Jed Emerson, and Peter Economy, *Strategic Tools for Social Entrepreneurs: Enhancing the Performance of Your Enterprising Nonprofit* (New York: John Wiley & Sons, Inc., 2002); Sarah A. Soule, Brayden G. King, Ed Walker, and Mary-Hunter McDonnell, *Contention and Corporate Social Responsibility* (Cambridge, UK: Cambridge University Press, 2016); David A. Snow and Sarah A. Soule, *A Primer on Social Movements* (New York: W. W. Norton & Company, 2009); David A. Snow, Sarah A. Soule, and Hanspeter Kriesi, *The Blackwell Companion to Social Movements* (Malden, MA: Blackwell Publishing, 2004); Gerald F. Davis, Doug McAdam, W. Richard Scott, and Mayer N. Zald, eds., *Social Movements and Organization Theory* (Cambridge, UK: Cambridge University Press, 2005); Julie Battilana, "Agency and Institutions: The Enabling Role of Individuals' Social Position," *Organization* 13, no. 5 (2006): 653–76, https://doi.org/10.1177/1350508406067008;

Julie Battilana, Bernard Leca, and Eva Boxenbaum, "How Actors Change Institutions: Towards a Theory of Institutional Entrepreneurship," *Academy of Management Annals* 3, no. 1 (January 2009): 65–107, https://doi.org/10.5465/19416520903053598; Paul J. DiMaggio, "Interest and Agency in Institutional Theory," in *Institutional Patterns and Organizations: Culture and Environment* (Cambridge, MA: Ballinger Publishing, 1988); Amy C. Edmondson and Jean-François Harvey, *Extreme Teaming: Lessons in Complex, Cross-Sector Leadership* (Bingley, UK: Emerald Publishing, 2017); Amy C. Edmondson and Susan Salter Reynolds, *Building the Future: Big Teaming for Audacious Innovation* (Oakland, CA: Berrett-Koehler Publishers, 2016); John Elkington and Pamela Hartigan, *The Power of Unreasonable People: How Social Entrepreneurs Create Markets That Change the World* (Boston: Harvard Business Press, 2008); Kate Odziemkowska and Yiying Zhu, "How Social Movements Catalyze Firm Innovation," *Organization Science*, January 17, 2025, https://doi.org/10.1287/orsc.2023.17497; John F. Padgett and Walter W. Powell, *The Emergence of Organizations and Markets* (Princeton, NJ: Princeton University Press, 2012); Peter Senge, Hal Hamilton, and John Kania, "Co-Creating the Future: The Dawn of System Leadership," *Rotman Management Magazine*, 2015; Beverly Schwartz, *Rippling: How Social Entrepreneurs Spread Innovation Throughout the World* (San Francisco: Jossey-Bass, 2012); and Doug McAdam and David Snow, *Social Movements: Readings on Their Emergence, Mobilization and Dynamics* (Los Angeles: Roxbury Publishing, 1997). For some of the work on strategic alliances, networks, and ecosystems in business, see endnote 1 and 2 in the part II introduction of this book and endnote 10 in chapter 6. Notable works from this body of research that we have relied on include Henry Adobor, "The Role of Personal Relationships in Inter-Firm Alliances: Benefits, Dysfunctions, and Some Suggestions," *Business Horizons* 49, no. 6 (November 2006): 473–86, https://doi.org/10.1016/j.bushor.2006.03 .003; T. K. Das and Bing-Sheng Teng, "Between Trust and Control: Developing Confidence in Partner Cooperation in Alliances," *Academy of Management Review* 23, no. 3 (July 1998): 491–512, https://doi.org/10.2307/259291; Rosabeth Moss Kanter, *Thinking Outside the Building: How Advanced Leaders Can Change the World One Smart Innovation at a Time* (New York: Public Affairs, 2020); David Obstfeld, "Social Networks, the Tertius Iungens Orientation, and Involvement in Innovation," *Administrative Science Quarterly* 50, no. 1 (March 2005): 100–30, https://doi.org/10.2189/asqu .2005.50.1.100; Charles Dhanaraj and Arvind Parkhe, "Orchestrating Innovation Networks," *Academy of Management Review* 31, no. 3 (July 2006): 659–69, https://doi .org/10.5465/amr.2006.21318923; Ranjay Gulati, Paul R. Lawrence, and Phanish Puranam, "Adaptation in Vertical Relationships: Beyond Incentive Conflict," *Strategic Management Journal* 26, no. 5 (May 2005): 415–40, https://doi.org/10.1002/smj.458; Ranjay Gulati, Franz Wohlgezogen, and Pavel Zhelyazkov, "The Two Facets of Collaboration: Cooperation and Coordination in Strategic Alliances," *Academy of Management Annals* 6, no. 1 (May 2012): 531–83, https://doi.org/10.1080/19416520 .2012.691646; Kathleen M. Eisenhardt and Jeffrey A. Martin, "Dynamic Capabilities: What Are They?," *Strategic Management Journal* 21, no. 10–11 (October 2000): 1105–21; and Michael Docherty, *Collective Disruption: How Corporations & Startups Can Co-Create Transformative New Businesses* (New York: Polarity Press, 2015). For the work on open innovation, see, for example, Carliss Y. Baldwin and Eric Von Hippel, "Modeling a Paradigm Shift: From Producer Innovation to User and Open Collaborative Innovation," *Organization Science* 22, no. 6 (2011): 1399–1417; Yochai Benkler, *The Wealth of Networks: How Social Production Transforms Markets and Freedom* (New Haven,

CT: Yale University Press, 2006); Kevin J. Boudreau and Karim R. Lakhani, "Using the Crowd as an Innovation Partner," *Harvard Business Review*, April 2013; Andrew King and Karim R. Lakhani, "Using Open Innovation to Identify the Best Ideas," *MIT Sloan Management Review*, September 11, 2013, https://sloanreview.mit.edu/article /using-open-innovation-to-identify-the-best-ideas/; Henry William Chesbrough, *Open Innovation: The New Imperative for Creating and Profiting from Technology* (Boston: Harvard Business School Press, 2003); Eric von Hippel, *Democratizing Innovation* (Cambridge, MA; London: MIT Press, 2005); Karim R. Lakhani, Hila Lifshitz-Assaf, and Michael Tushman, "Open Innovation and Organization Boundaries: Task Decomposition, Knowledge Distribution and the Locus of Innovation," in *Handbook of Economic Organization: Integrating Economic and Organization Theory*, ed. Anna Grandori (Northampton, UK: Edward Elgar Publishing, 2013), 355–82; James Surowiecki, *The Wisdom of Crowds* (New York: Anchor Books, 2005); Walter W. Powell, "Neither Market Nor Hierarchy: Network Forms of Organization," *Research in Organizational Behavior* 12 (1990): 295–336; Douglas Thomas and John Seely Brown, *A New Culture of Learning: Cultivating the Imagination for a World of Constant Change* (CreateSpace Independent Publishing, 2011); Clay Shirky, *Here Comes Everybody: The Power of Organizing Without Organizations* (New York: Penguin Press, 2008); and Kathleen M. Eisenhardt and Donald N. Sull, "Strategy as Simple Rules," *Harvard Business Review*, January 2001.

2. Our catalyst leaders saw themselves more as "orchestors" than "brokers," to adopt the language of Shipilov, Furr, and Andersson. They define orchestors as companies that connected multiple parties and encouraged them to work directly with each other (what we refer to as multiparty coalitions), whereas brokers kept multiple parties separate and required those parties to work through them. See Nathan Furr and Andrew Shipilov, "Building the Right Ecosystem for Innovation," *MIT Sloan Management Review*, Summer 2018, 59–64, https://sloanreview.mit.edu/article /building-the-right-ecosystem-for-innovation/. In addition, the successful catalyst leaders we studied adopted a win-win mindset when building their ecosystems. They shared the value created and worked to understand each stakeholder's unique priorities and interests and create the conditions necessary for them to fulfill them. See, for example, Ron Adner, "Sharing Value for Ecosystem Success," *MIT Sloan Management Review*, November 1, 2021, https://sloanreview.mit.edu/article/sharing -value-for-ecosystem-success/. Adner describes the need to let go of an "ego-system" mindset on p. 85. On p. 86, he writes, "It almost always makes sense for companies to strive for leadership within their industries—winning that position brings great profit and pride. But ecosystems present a different hierarchy. In a successful ecosystem, there are no losers—only partners that win in different ways." For more reading on this topic, see Ron Adner, *Winning the Right Game: How to Disrupt, Defend, and Deliver in a Changing World* (Cambridge, MA: MIT Press, 2021); Elizabeth J. Altman, Frank Nagle, and Michael L. Tushman, "The Translucent Hand of Managed Ecosystems: Engaging Communities for Value Creation and Capture," *Academy of Management Annals* 16, no. 1 (January 2022): 70–101, https://doi.org/10.5465 /annals.2020.0244; Marco Iansiti and Roy Levien, *The Keystone Advantage: What the New Dynamics of Business Ecosystems Mean for Strategy, Innovation, and Sustainability* (Boston: Harvard Business School Press, 2004); and Nathan Furr, Kate O'Keeffe, and Jeff Dyer, "Managing Multiparty Innovation," *Harvard Business Review*, November 2016.

3. The catalysts we profile are also exceptional architects and bridgers and devote considerable time and attention to developing the architecting, bridging, and catalyzing skills of their colleagues.

Chapter 8

1. This quote has been edited slightly to include and embrace both Akira's and Kevin's voices. They often complete each other's sentences.

2. All information, including quotations, in this chapter is derived from a case study published by Harvard Business Publishing about avatarin, unless otherwise cited. See Linda A. Hill and Emily Tedards, "Akira Fukabori and Kevin Kajitani at avatarin (A)," Case 421-089 (Boston: Harvard Business School Publishing, 2021). We extend our deepest gratitude to Jeremy Dann and Daniel Paredes for their contributions to the research on Akira Fukabori and ANA. See Jeremy Dann and Daniel Paredes, "All Nippon Airways' 'Blue Wing': Elevating Social Impact," Case Study SCG-548 (Los Angeles: USC-Marshall/Lloyd Greif Center for Entrepreneurial Studies, revised February 2020).

3. This statistic, estimating that 6 percent of the world's population flies in a single year, is based on an analysis by one air safety specialist. Christine Negroni, "How Much of the World's Population Has Flown in an Airplane?," *Smithsonian Magazine*, January 6, 2016, https://www.smithsonianmag.com/air-space-magazine/how-much-worlds -population-has-flown-airplane-180957719/.

4. avatarin, "Vision: About avatarin," https://about.avatarin.com/en/concept/.

5. S. Nakahara and M. Ichikawa, "Mortality in the 2011 Tsunami in Japan," *Journal of Epidemiology* 23, no. 1 (2013): 70–73, https://doi.org/10.2188/jea.je20120114.

6. At this point, avatarin is what is referred to as a "hybrid" startup because it is still fully located within the incumbent organization. Hybrid startups enjoy the benefits of being part of a large entity, including access to financial and other tangible resources as well as the legitimacy that most startups hold when they approach outside stakeholders. However, as the literature on ambidexterity (see the endnotes in part II's introduction) indicated, hybrid startups have to navigate the challenge associated with being so closely tethered to the core business when trying to pursue breakthrough innovation.

7. The research on partnerships is clear that if a potential partner is not committed from initial interactions with them (i.e., not having the right "confident building steps," as Doz calls them), chances are it will be difficult to get this alliance off the ground. Some of the research has also specified that "early signals" like the interest of senior executives as well as resources (time, finances, etc.) need to be invested in a partnership early on for it to really take off. For more on this topic, see Yves L. Doz, "The Evolution of Cooperation in Strategic Alliances: Initial Conditions or Learning Processes?," *Strategic Management Journal* 17, no. S1 (Summer 1996): 55–83, https://doi .org/10.1002/smj.4250171006; Nathan Furr, Kate O'Keeffe, and Jeff Dyer, "Managing Multiparty Innovation," *Harvard Business Review*, November 2016; and Sascha Albers, Franz Wohlgezogen, and Edward J. Zajac, "Strategic Alliance Structures: An Organization Design Perspective," *Journal of Management* 42, no. 3 (March 2016): 582–614, https://doi.org/10.1177/0149206313488209.

8. When building multiparty coalitions, catalysts must contend with the paradoxes outlined in the introduction of this book and elaborated on in chapter 2 of *Collective Genius*—especially in the paradox between meeting the unique needs of the individual

parties and of the collective. As we saw in chapter 6 with Raja Al Mazrouei, when conflict was escalating, she was willing and able to be more directive in her approach, providing both parties with feedback on the impact of their behaviors on each other and reminding them of their shared intention. Catalysts must be even more skilled at working across differences than bridgers, reconciling a complex web of differences as they build an ecosystem of diverse parties often from different industries and sectors.

9. Eventually avatarin does become a separate company but remains closely connected to ANA. ANA recognized that avatarin needed to become independent, because ANA did not have the resources (including financial resources) required to scale avatarin.

10. Japan Aerospace Exploration Agency (JAXA), "avatarin and JAXA Kick-Off Co-Creation Project to Advance 'Space Avatar' Technology with Cooperation from the University of Tokyo," press release, July 16, 2021, https://global.jaxa.jp/press/2021/07/20210716-1_e.html.

11. Norbert Gehrke, "Six Companies Invest a Total of JPY 3.7bn in avatarin," *Medium*, July 17, 2024, https://medium.com/tokyo-fintech/six-companies-invest-a-total-of-jpy-3-7bn-in-avatarin-a87ee3cb483d.

12. XPRIZE Foundation, "Nimbro Announced as Winner of the $10m ANA Avatar XPRIZE," XPRIZE, November 6, 2022, https://www.xprize.org/prizes/avatar/articles/ana-avatar-xprize-winners.

13. Kaitlyn Tiffany, "Digital Smell Technology Could Let Us Transmit Odors in Online Chats," NBC News, November 27, 2018, https://www.nbcnews.com/mach/science/digital-smell-technology-could-let-us-transmit-odors-online-chats-ncna940121.

Chapter 9

1. This chapter is primarily based on ethnographic research (interviews and field-based observations) on Ndidi Nwuneli and her several organizations between 2019 and 2025, with supplemental information included from public sources and cited accordingly. We are grateful to Ndidi Nwuneli and her colleagues for their support regarding this chapter.

2. This anecdote is the opening of Ndidi's 2021 book. See Ndidi Okonkwo Nwuneli, *Food Entrepreneurs in Africa: Scaling Resilient Agriculture Businesses* (London; New York: Routledge, Taylor & Francis Group, 2021).

3. United Nations, "World Population Prospects—Population Division," https://population.un.org/wpp/.

4. Mapping is a critical function in building ecosystems. It is a learning-by-doing process, because you can't know in advance what you don't know. The problem and the solutions are still uncertain or being sorted out. It is often hard to predict who the stakeholders will be, the capabilities and resources that will be required, and the obstacles that will have to be overcome. In Furr and Shipilov's discussion of "adaptive" as opposed to "centralized" ecosystems, they use Mastercard as an example of a company good at building adaptive ecosystems. See Nathan Furr and Andrew Shipilov, "Building the Right Ecosystem for Innovation," *MIT Sloan Management Review*, Summer 2018, 59–64, https://sloanreview.mit.edu/article/building-the-right-ecosystem-for-innovation/. See p. 61 in which they remark, "You need to start by defining the 'battlefield'—or the area to explore. From there, you can begin to assemble an ecosystem to explore the challenge and refine it as your understanding about the opportunity evolves."

5. World Economic Forum, "2 Truths about Africa's Agriculture," January 22, 2016, https://www.weforum.org/stories/2016/01/how-africa-can-feed-the-world/.

6. MarketForces Africa, "Stanbic IBTC Appoints Ndidi Nwuneli Board Member," March 24, 2023, https://dmarketforces.com/stanbic-ibtc-appoints-ndidi-nwuneli-board-member/.

7. L. D. S. Tapsoba, S. M. A. Kiemde, B. F. Lamond, and J. Lépine, "On the Potential of Packaging for Reducing Fruit and Vegetable Losses in Sub-Saharan Africa," *Foods* 11, no. 7 (2022): 952, https://doi.org/10.3390/foods11070952.

8. Ecofin Agency, "West Africa's Ban on Imported Whole Milk Powder Could Hurt Local Processors, Expert Warns," November 8, 2024, https://www.ecofinagency .com/homepage/0811-46115-west-africas-ban-on-imported-whole-milk-powder-could -hurt-local-processors-expert-warns.

9. Aimée Knight, "What Is a Smallholder Farmer?," Heifer International, April 14, 2022. https://www.heifer.org/blog/what-is-a-smallholder-farmer.html.

10. Sahel Consulting: Agriculture & Nutrition Ltd., https://sahelconsult.com/.

11. "AACE Foods sources its products from over 10,000 smallholder farmers in rural communities across Nigeria and West Africa in value chains that include Maize, Ginger, Chili, Turmeric, Onions, Soy Beans, Cowpea, Peanut etc." For more information, please see Inclusive Business Action Network, "AACE Foods: Local Agroprocessing in Nigeria," https://www.inclusivebusiness.net/page/project-profile-aace-foods -local-agroprocessing-in-nigeria.

12. The term "hidden middle" Nwuneli drew from the following report emphasizing the importance of SMEs in the development of the African Economy: Alliance for a Green Revolution in Africa (AGRA), *Africa Agriculture Status Report: The Hidden Middle: A Quiet Revolution in the Private Sector Driving Agricultural Transformation* 7 (Nairobi, Kenya: AGRA, 2019).

13. Ndidi wrote a book about these findings. See Nwuneli, *Food Entrepreneurs in Africa*.

14. Ndidi Okonkwo Nwuneli, "Nourishing Africa's 2.4 Billion: Leapfrogging Through Innovation and Technology," seminar transcript (Cambridge, MA: Mossavar-Rahmani Center for Business and Government, Harvard Kennedy School, October 16, 2019), https://www.hks.harvard.edu/sites/default/files/centers/mrcbg/files /Nourishing%20Africa%20Leapfrogging%20Through%20Innovation%20and%20 Technology.pdf.

15. See Ndidi Okonkwo Nwuneli, *Social Innovation in Africa: A Practical Guide for Scaling Impact* (London; New York: Routledge, Taylor & Francis Group, 2016). Ndidi would go on to write another book on agribusiness and innovation in Africa, published in 2021. See Nwuneli, *Food Entrepreneurs in Africa*.

16. Gareth Hodder, Brenda Migwalla, and Stephen Pickup, "Africa's Agricultural Revolution: From Self-Sufficiency to Global Food Powerhouse," White & Case, July 12, 2023, https://www.whitecase.com/insight-our-thinking/africa-focus-summer -2023-africas-agricultural-revolution.

17. Seko Baga Bio Maro Bio Sia et al., "The Economic Impact of COVID-19 on Africa and the Countermeasures," *Open Journal of Business and Management* 11, no. 2 (2023): 1–15.

18. Mastercard Foundation, "Program to Train 20,000 Young Agripreneurs and Provide Grants to Nigerian MSMEs," March 15, 2021, https://mastercardfdn.org/en /news/program-to-train-20000-young-agripreneurs-and-provide-grants-to-nigerian -msmes/.

19. Again, we see that mapping is a continual learning-by-doing process and, as a consequence, the mix of stakeholders can grow and shift over time. Ndidi Nwuneli and her team had left out a key constituency that they could have been leveraging. Not surprisingly, the SMEs often trusted organizations in their local communities with whom they had experience, rather than the global organizations with whom they had no experience. As Ajay Banga from Mastercard observed in chapter 1, multinationals had to earn credibility with local communities.

20. Mastercard Foundation, "Program to Train 20,000 Young Agripreneurs and Provide Grants to Nigerian MSMEs," March 15, 2021, https://mastercardfdn.org/en /news/program-to-train-20000-young-agripreneurs-and-provide-grants-to-nigerian -msmes.

21. African Food Changemakers, "About Us," https://afchub.org/about.

22. We found that digital tools were essential to building and maintaining the social fabric of most of the ecosystems we studied; however, the bridgers and catalysts in this book all agreed there was no substitute for face-to-face interactions. As we saw, for instance, with Raja Al Mazrouei or Akira Fukabori and Kevin Kajitani, building partnerships and movements required our leaders to devote significant time, attention, and energy.

23. For more information on the types of narrative changers that Ndidi Nwuneli and her team work on, please see African Food Changemakers Hub, https://afchub.org/.

24. Based on 2023 numbers from an AFC company document.

25. Based on 2023 numbers from an AFC company document.

26. "ONE Campaign Announces Ndidi Okonkwo Nwuneli as New CEO," ONE .org, February 20, 2024, https://www.one.org/us/press/one-campaign-announces-ndidi -okonkwo-nwuneli-as-new-ceo/.

Chapter 10

1. The World's 50 Best Restaurants, "Osteria Francescana," https://www .theworlds50best.com/awards/best-of-the-best/osteria-francescana.html.

2. This chapter was developed with the research support of research associate and graduate student Lydia Begag, who played a central role in collecting, drafting, and refining the data and chapter material. This chapter is primarily based on ethnographic research (interviews and field-based observations) on the Francescana Family businesses between 2022 and 2025. This research was conducted for the purposes of developing a multimedia case study on Massimo, Lara, and their teams in Modena and around the world. For more information, see Linda A. Hill, Allison J. Wigen, David Habeeb, and Lydia Begag, "Francescana Family: Leading a Global Food Movement," Multimedia Case (Boston: Harvard Business School Publishing, forthcoming). Supplemental information included from public sources is cited accordingly. All quotes from Bernardo Paladini and Mattia Agazzi are from a recording of a public panel event they participated in, in Miami, Florida, in July 2024. The topic of the panel was mentorship in the culinary world. We would also like to acknowledge the contributions of Francesca Gino to research on rebel talent, including Massimo Bottura. See Francesca Gino, *Rebel Talent: Why It Pays to Break the Rules at Work and in Life* (New York: Dey Street Books, 2018).

3. Scaling usually refers to growing a business to an ever-larger size. An assump- tion in business is usually that bigger means better. Massimo Bottura and Lara Gilmore have, in fact, grown their business over time; they have numerous restaurants and

refettorios in multiple markets across the globe. But in this chapter, we are referring primarily to scaling their values—best summarized in this chapter by their slow food, fast cars philosophy. See, for example, Nathan Furr, Susannah Harmon Furr, and John Kay, "It's Time to Reimagine Scale," hbr.org, November 22, 2024, https://hbr.org/2024/11/its-time-to-reimagine-scale. In Furr, Furr, and Kay's article, they describe another top restaurant committed to scaling or spreading their idea to "rearchitect the food industry to support life and nutrition in the long run" and their objective being to support small farms because not only are they ecologically sound, but they can help create healthy communities.

4. Massimo Bottura and Lara Gilmore, "This Is Not Tuscany," in *Slow Food, Fast Cars: Casa Maria Luigia—Stories and Recipes* (New York: Phaidon, 2023), 6.

5. Bottura and Gilmore, "Slow Food," in *Slow Food, Fast Cars*, 151.

6. For more information on the Slow Food movement, please see the Slow Food website: "Slow Food," https://www.slowfood.com/ as well as scholarly work on the Slow Food movement. See, for example, Charlene Zietsma, Peter Groenewegen, Danielle M. Logue, and C. R. (Bob) Hinings, "Field or Fields? Building the Scaffolding for Cumulation of Research on Institutional Fields," *Academy of Management Annals* 11, no. 1 (2017): 391–450, https://doi.org/10.5465/annals.2014.0052; Stephen Schneider, "Good, Clean, Fair: The Rhetoric of the Slow Food Movement," *College English* 70, no. 4 (2008): 384–402, http://www.jstor.org/stable/25472277; and Érica Maria Calíope Sobreira, Danielle Mantovani, and Áurio Leocádio, "Slow Food as an Alternative Food Consumption: Approaches, Principles and Product Attributes," *Research, Society and Development* 11, no. 3 (2022), http://dx.doi.org/10.33448/rsd-v11i3.26771.

7. Spencer Bailey, "Massimo Bottura on Ethics, Aesthetics, and Slow Food," *Time Sensitive* (podcast), December 11, 2025, https://timesensitive.fm/episode/massimo-bottura-on-ethics-aesthetics-and-slow-food/. This podcast episode was recorded in front of a live audience at Refettorio Harlem, inside the Emanuel AME Church in Harlem, on December 11, 2023, which one of the *Genius at Scale* coauthors (Linda, and research associate and graduate student Lydia Begag) attended in person.

8. Jeff Gordinier, "Massimo Bottura, the Chef Behind the World's Best Restaurant," *New York Times*, October 17, 2016, https://www.nytimes.com/2016/10/17/t-magazine/massimo-bottura-chef-osteria-francescana.html.

9. Fine Dining Lovers, "World's 50 Best Restaurants 2012: Osteria Francescana, Number 5 on the List," May 1, 2012, https://www.finedininglovers.com/explore/videos/worlds-50-best-restaurants-2012-osteria-francescana-number-5-list.

10. There is a common myth across disciplines that stars are born, not made. The research suggests otherwise. What we know how to do is based largely on what we get to do (i.e., the opportunities we are afforded). Stars are great at learning from experience; they seek out and are offered stretch assignments that let them develop key attributes and talents. They establish developmental relationships that get them access to challenging learning opportunities with considerable autonomy and visibility. If they make missteps, their mentors do not punish them but rather help them reflect and learn from failures. See, for example, Linda A. Hill, *Becoming a Manager: How New Managers Master the Challenges of Leadership*, 2nd ed. (Boston: Harvard Business School Press, 2003); Douglas A. Ready, Jay A. Conger, and Linda A. Hill, "Are You a High Potential?," *Harvard Business Review*, June 2010; Morgan W. McCall Jr., *High Flyers: Developing the Next Generation of Leaders* (Boston: Harvard Business School Press, 1998); Morgan W. McCall Jr. and Michael M. Lombardo, *The Lessons of Experience*

(Lanham, MD: Lexington Books, 1988); Boris Groysberg, *Chasing Stars: The Myth of Talent and the Portability of Performance* (Princeton, NJ: Princeton University Press, 2010); Adam Grant, *Originals: How Non-Conformists Move the World* (New York: Penguin Books, 2017); Donald Schön, *The Reflective Practitioner* (New York: Basic Books, 1984); Malcolm Gladwell, *Outliers: The Story of Success* (New York: Little, Brown, 2008); and Linda A. Hill, Nancy A. Kamprath, and Leticia Garcia, "Beyond the Myth of the Perfect Mentor: Take Charge and Build Your Personal Board of Directors," Background Note 491-096 (Boston: Harvard Business School, March 1991, rev. October 2022).

11. Jeff Gordinier, "Massimo Bottura, the Chef Behind the World's Best Restaurant," *New York Times*, October 17, 2016, https://www.nytimes.com/2016/10/17/t -magazine/massimo-bottura-chef-osteria-francescana.html.

12. Larry Olmsted, "The Biggest Italian Dinner in History, Thanks to Social Media," *Forbes*, October 17, 2012, https://www.forbes.com/sites/larryolmsted/2012/10 /17/the-biggest-italian-dinner-in-history-thanks-to-social-media/.

13. World Food Programme, "5 Facts about Food Waste and Hunger," June 25, 2024, https://www.wfp.org/stories/5-facts-about-food-waste-and-hunger and Hannah Ritchie, Pablo Rosado, and Max Roser, "Hunger and Undernourishment," Our World in Data, 2023, https://ourworldindata.org/hunger-and-undernourishment.

14. The word "refettorio" comes from the Latin *reficere*, meaning "to re-make," but also "to restore." Food for Soul's refettorios are redesigned community spaces meant for social connection over the breaking of bread together.

15. Bailey, "Massimo Bottura on Ethics, Aesthetics, and Slow Food."

16. More and more businesspeople are striving to give voice to their prosocial values by addressing social challenges as they build profitable businesses. There is a growing body of research on the advantages and challenges of trying to achieve both, especially given short-term market pressures. See, for example, Clayton M. Christensen, Heiner Bauman, Rudy Ruggles, and Thomas M. Sadtler, "Disruptive Innovation for Social Change," *Harvard Business Review*, December 2006; Marc R. Benioff and Monica Langley, *Trailblazer: The Power of Business as the Greatest Platform for Change* (New York: Currency, 2019); Mihaly Csikszentmihalyi, *Good Work: When Excellence and Ethics Meet* (New York: Basic Books, 2001); Robert G. Eccles, "Moving Beyond ESG," *Harvard Business Review*, September–October 2024; John Elkington and Pamela Hartigan, *The Power of Unreasonable People: How Social Entrepreneurs Create Markets That Change the World* (Boston: Harvard Business Press, 2008); Vijay Govindarajan and Chris Trimble, *Reverse Innovation: Create Far from Home, Win Everywhere* (Boston: Harvard Business Review Press, 2012); Geoffrey Jones, *Deeply Responsible Business: A Global History of Values-Driven Leadership* (Cambridge, MA: Harvard University Press, 2023); Rosabeth Moss Kanter, *Thinking Outside the Building: How Advanced Leaders Can Change the World One Smart Innovation at a Time* (New York: PublicAffairs, 2020); Peter M. Senge, *The Necessary Revolution: How Individuals and Organizations Are Working Together to Create a Sustainable World* (New York: Crown Publishing Group, 2008); John Mackey and Rajendra Sisodia, *Conscious Capitalism: Liberating the Heroic Spirit of Business* (Boston: Harvard Business Review Press, 2014); Jacqueline Novogratz, *The Blue Sweater: Bridging the Gap Between Rich and Poor in an Interconnected World* (New York: Rodale, 2009); Jacqueline Novogratz, *Manifesto for a Moral Revolution: Practices to Build a Better World* (New York: Henry Holt and Company, 2020); Satya Nadella, Greg Shaw, and Jill Tracie Nichols, *Hit Refresh: The Quest to Rediscover Microsoft's Soul and*

Imagine a Better Future for Everyone (New York: Harper Business, 2017); C. K. Prahalad, *The Fortune at the Bottom of the Pyramid: Eradicating Poverty Through Profits*, rev. and updated 5th anniversary ed. (Upper Saddle River, NJ: Wharton School Publishing, 2010); Lynn Sharp Paine, *Value Shift: Why Companies Must Merge Social and Financial Imperatives to Achieve Superior Performance* (New York; Toronto: McGraw-Hill, 2003); Rebecca Henderson, "Innovation in the 21st Century: Architectural Change, Purpose, and the Challenges of Our Time," *Management Science* 67, no. 9 (September 2021): 5479–88, https://doi.org/10.1287/mnsc.2020.3746; Rebecca Henderson, *Reimagining Capitalism in a World on Fire* (New York: PublicAffairs, 2020); and Paul Polman and Andrew Winston, *Net Positive: How Courageous Companies Thrive by Giving More Than They Take* (Boston: Harvard Business Review Press, 2021).

17. "Refettorio Harlem," https://www.refettorioharlem.org/.

18. "Refettorio Harlem," https://www.refettorioharlem.org/.

19. Bottura and Gilmore, "This House Is a Hotel," in *Slow Food, Fast Cars*, 44.

20. Lela London, "Massimo Bottura on Slow Food, Fast Cars and All Those Michelin Stars," *Forbes*, December 5, 2023, https://www.forbes.com/sites/lelalondon/2023/12/05/massimo-bottura-on-slow-food-fast-cars-and-all-those-michelin-stars/.

21. Rachael Hogg, "How Caroline Caporossi and Jessica Rosval Are Helping Migrant Women Put Down Roots and Flourish in Modena, Italy," The World's 50 Best Restaurants, November 7, 2024, https://www.theworlds50best.com/stories/News/champions-of-change-2024-jessica-rosval-caroline-caporossi-roots-modena-italy.html.

22. "Al Gatto Verde," *Michelin Guide*, https://guide.michelin.com/us/en/emilia-romagna/modena/restaurant/al-gatto-verde.

23. "Casa Maria Luigia—Modena—a Michelin Guide Hotel," *Michelin Guide*, https://guide.michelin.com/us/en/hotels-stays/Modena/casa-maria-luigia-13611?arr=2024-10-22&dep=2024-10-23.

24. Mariarosaria Bruno, "Mattia Agazzi on Cooking for Gucci Osteria Massimo Bottura in Beverly Hills," *Fine Dining Lovers*, October 11, 2021, https://www.finedininglovers.com/article/mattia-agazzi-gucci-osteria-massimo-bottura-beverly-hills.

25. Stefania Virone Vitor, "A Conversation with Chef Jessica Rosval of Casa Maria Luigia," *La Cucina Italiana*, September 19, 2021, https://www.lacucinaitaliana.com/trends/restaurants-and-chefs/chef-jessica-rosval-bottura-casa-maria-luigia-modena.

26. "Food for Soul," https://www.foodforsoul.it/.

Chapter 11

1. All information about Sampark Foundation, including quotations and statistics, in this chapter is derived from a case study published by Harvard Business Publishing about Sampark Foundation, or is derived from a number of interviews with Sampark staff, Indian government officials, and primary school teachers, conducted on the ground in India in January 2024. All quotes from the January 2024 interviews that are included in this chapter have been read and approved by everyone interviewed for publication in this chapter. For the case study, see Linda A. Hill and Emily Tedards, "Vineet Nayar and Sampark Foundation: Frugal Innovation at Scale (A)," Case 421-015, rev. 2021 (Boston: Harvard Business School, 2020). We extend our deepest gratitude to V. Kasturi Rangan for his contributions to the research on Sampark Foundation. See V. Kasturi Rangan and Shweta Bagai, "Sampark Foundation: Transforming Primary Education in India," Case 518-006 (Boston: Harvard Business School, July 2017).

In 2021, Linda was invited to join the board of Sampark Foundation.

2. We refer to Vineet and Anupama by their first names in this chapter since they share a surname.

3. *The Right of Children to Free and Compulsory Education Act*, No. 35 of 2009, Acts of Parliament (India), 2009, https://www.education.gov.in/rte.

4. These are statistics Sampark Foundation provided to the authors of this book at the time of the case development process in 2019.

5. These are statistics HCL Technologies provided to the case study authors at the time of the case development process. For more information on Vineet Nayar's time at HCL Technologies and the impact made from "Employees First, Customers Second," see HCL Technologies, *Employees First Mini-Book*, https://www.hcltech.com/sites/default/files/documents/resources/brochure/files/emplyeesfirstminibook.pdf.

6. The story of Vineet Nayar's cultural transformation of HCL Technologies is told in chapter 3 of *Collective Genius: The Art and Practice of Leading Innovation*, titled "Recasting the Role of the Leader: Vineet Nayar at HCL Technologies." This chapter is based on qualitative data collected on Vineet Nayar and HCL Technologies and published in two HBS case studies. For a more enriched description of Vineet Nayar's tenure at HCL, please consult Linda A. Hill, Tarun Khanna, and Emily A. Stecker, "HCL Technologies (A)," Case 408-004 (Boston: Harvard Business School Publishing, August 2007); and Linda A. Hill and Tarun Khanna, "HCL Technologies (B)," Case 408-006 (Boston: Harvard Business School Publishing, August 2007). For more information on HCL and Indian management practices, please see Peter Cappelli et al., *The India Way: How India's Top Business Leaders Are Revolutionizing Management* (Boston: Harvard Business Press, 2010).

7. Laura Garnett, "How a People-First Culture Is Transforming Education in India," *Forbes*, May 8, 2018, https://www.forbes.com/sites/lauragarnett/2018/05/08/how-a-people-first-culture-is-transforming-education-in-india/.

8. The Sparks were on the front line when it came to building and maintaining relationships with and between the teachers and government officials. There is limited grounded research on how to be an effective boundary-spanner in strategic alliances or ecosystems as they evolve. For more information, see Sascha Albers, Franz Wohlgezogen, and Edward J. Zajac, "Strategic Alliance Structures: An Organization Design Perspective," *Journal of Management* 42, no. 3 (March 2016): 582–614, https://doi.org/10.1177/0149206313488209. As Albers et al. point out, much of the available research on boundary-spanning is often conceptualized as a single interpersonal tie at the interface between organizations working together, when in fact there is likely a complex network of interpersonal ties among alliances or ecosystem partners (recall in chapter 5 all the relationships Nicole Jones and her team had to manage at Delta Air Lines). Albers et al. call for more research on just how dense, broad, and active relationships among boundary-spanners should be. They propose that a broad, dense, and active interface should facilitate "exploitation-focused learning, that is, the refinement and improvement of existing processes and capabilities" (p. 594) as well as more explorative forms of learning, such as innovation. In addition, Albers et al. offer an insightful discussion of the benefits of building in more structure (standard practices and policies; clarification of roles and responsibilities) to facilitate and guide the establishment of healthy social connections. Structure can lead to better coordination of work and trust across stakeholders, that is, if it still allows for improvisation and agility. The Sparks had much to learn about how to build robust relationships with teachers and government employees and encourage productive relationships between these two stakehold-

ers. For research on what it takes to build connections with stakeholders from different sectors, see, for example, Nick Lovegrove and Matthew Thomas, "Triple-Strength Leadership," *Harvard Business Review*, September 2013.

9. For research on the role of digital tools to support bottom-up innovation by making knowledge-sharing and collective learning easier and processes more transparent, see, for example, Michael Schrage, *Shared Minds: The New Technologies of Collaboration* (New York: Random House, 1990); Clay Shirky, *Here Comes Everybody: The Power of Organizing without Organizations* (New York: Penguin Press, 2008); Andrew McAfee, *Enterprise 2.0: New Collaborative Tools for Your Organization's Toughest Challenges* (Boston: Harvard Business Press, 2009); and Andrew McAfee and Erik Brynjolfsson, *Machine, Platform, Crowd: Harnessing Our Digital Future* (New York: W. W. Norton & Company, 2017).

10. These are statistics Sampark Foundation provided to the authors of this book at the time of the case development process in 2019. For more information, see a company document in exhibit 3 of Hill and Tedards, "Vineet Nayar and Sampark Foundation: Frugal Innovation at Scale (A)."

11. Sampark Foundation, "Frugal Innovation in Education: Achieving Big Impact with Small Changes," *Sampark Foundation blog*, January 24, 2025, https://www .samparkfoundation.org/blog/frugal-innovation-in-education-achieving-big-impact -with-small-changes.

12. See Anil Swarup, "Sampark Foundation," *Millennium Post*, September 9, 2020, https://www.millenniumpost.in/opinion/sampark-foundation-417801 and Sudhir Chowdhary, "Baithak Aims to Reform the Learning Curve of Students in Rural India," *Financial Express*, April 20, 2020, https://www.financialexpress.com/business/industry -baithak-aims-to-reform-the-learning-curve-of-students-in-rural-india-1933384/.

13. Sampark facilitated the creation of communities of practice or networks of teachers who shared their tacit knowledge and learnings with each other. For more on creating communities of practice and associated learning and development on the job, see Etienne Wenger, Richard McDermott, and William M. Snyder, *Cultivating Communities of Practice: A Guide to Managing Knowledge* (Boston: Harvard Business School Press, 2002) and Donald Schön, *The Reflective Practitioner* (New York: Basic Books, 1984). As the teachers interacted with each other, they began to create and share their own innovative solutions. For research on how to access certain knowledge and tools (such as online communities and maker spaces) to facilitate customer innovation (or in this instance, teacher innovation), see Eric von Hippel, *Democratizing Innovation* (Cambridge, MA: MIT Press, 2005).

14. Krishna Gopalan and Abhik Sen, "Netflix: Popular OTT Platform in India," *Business Today*, https://www.businesstoday.in/interactive/immersive/netflix-india -popular-ott-platform-in-india/ and Prerna Lidhoo, Abhik Sen, and Sourav Majumdar, "Netflix and Its Battle for India," *Fortune India*, February 24, 2021, https://www .fortuneindia.com/enterprise/netflix-and-its-battle-for-india/105217.

15. These statistics are as of March 2025. See Sampark Foundation, https://www .samparkfoundation.org.

Epilogue

1. This chapter was developed with the research support of research associate and graduate student Lydia Begag, who played a central role in collecting, drafting, and refining the data and chapter material.

2. One of the coauthors of this book (Linda) was in attendance when the leader in the first example, the CEO of a major industrial company, made the remarks above. His employees were stunned. The second example refers to a letter written by Luca de Meo, former CEO of Renault Group in March 2024, ahead of the EU elections. It is entitled "Letter to Europe: Advocacy for a Sustainable, Inclusive and Competitive Auto Industry."

3. All mentions of Cristina Ventura's story in this chapter are based on three cases about Cristina Ventura and her time at Lane Crawford Joyce Group and White Star Capital and supplemented with ethnographic research (interviews and field-based observations) between 2020 and 2025, including research collected on the ground in Singapore, Dubai, and Abu Dhabi. See Linda A. Hill and Allison J. Wigen, "Cristina Ventura: Leading Innovation in the Luxury Industry," Multimedia/Video Case 420-711 (Boston: Harvard Business School, 2019); Linda A. Hill and Allison J. Wigen, "Cristina Ventura: Leading Innovation in the Luxury Industry," Case Supplement N419-083 (Boston: Harvard Business School, 2019); Linda A. Hill, Allison J. Wigen, and Ruth Page, "Cristina Ventura: The Career of a Catalyst," Multimedia Case 425-708 (Boston: Harvard Business School, August 2024); and Linda A. Hill, Allison J. Wigen, Dave Habeeb, and Ruth Page, "Cristina Ventura at White Star Capital," Multimedia Case 425-710 (Boston: Harvard Business School, 2025). We extend our deepest gratitude to Marta Elvira and her collaborators for their contributions to the research on Cristina Ventura. See Marta Elvira and Marta Villamor, "A Catalyst Journey During Corona Times (A)," Case DPO-733-E (Barcelona: IESE Publishing, 2021); Marta Elvira and Marta Villamor, "A Catalyst Journey During Corona Times (B)," Case DPO-734-E (Barcelona: IESE Publishing, 2021); and Marta Elvira and Catalina Mesa Sclarrotta, "A Catalyst Journey During Corona Times (C)," Case DPO-744-E (Barcelona: IESE Publishing, 2021).

4. Research shows us that knowing your personal "why" and values can serve as an internal compass to help you make complex decisions (especially those involving trade-offs), be resilient in the face of challenges and stress, be more authentic in your relationships, and in the long run, help you find a deeper sense of happiness and sense of fulfillment. See, for example, Bill George with Peter Sims, *True North: Discover Your Authentic Leadership* (San Francisco: Jossey-Bass, 2007); Simon Sinek, *Start with Why: How Great Leaders Inspire Everyone to Take Action* (New York: Portfolio, 2011); Herminia Ibarra, "The Authenticity Paradox," *Harvard Business Review*, January–February 2015; and Linda A. Hill, "Exercising Moral Courage: A Developmental Agenda," in *Moral Leadership: The Theory and Practice of Power, Judgement, and Policy*, ed. Deborah L. Rhode (San Francisco: Jossey-Bass, 2006), 267–90.

5. In today's world, leaders are expected to be able to collaborate across functions and/or geographies. Consequently, having an enterprise-wide mindset is fast becoming a leadership imperative. The most effective way to develop this mindset is to have experience working in different functions and geographies. See, for example, Morten T. Hansen and Bolko von Oetinger, "Introducing T-Shaped Managers: Knowledge Management's Next Generation," *Harvard Business Review*, March 2001 and Douglas A. Ready and M. Ellen Peebles, "Developing the Next Generation of Enterprise Leaders," *MIT Sloan Management Review*, Fall 2015, https://sloanreview.mit.edu/article/developing-the-next-generation-of-enterprise-leaders/.

6. Eric Jackson, "The 8 Most Important Things Not Being Covered About Apple's Quarter," *Forbes*, July 20, 2011, https://www.forbes.com/sites/ericjackson/2011/07/20/the-8-most-important-things-not-being-covered-about-apples-quarter/.

7. LCJG eventually acquired LUXARITY. It is now a nonprofit social venture.

8. Cristina is an alumnus of Harvard, Stanford, INSEAD, and MIT, and a Kauffman Fellow.

9. Stretch assignments are key to an individual's leadership development, as are developmental relationships. See, for example, Linda A. Hill, *Becoming a Manager: How New Managers Master the Challenges of Leadership*, 2nd ed. (Boston: Harvard Business School Press, 2003); Morgan W. McCall Jr., *High Flyers: Developing the Next Generation of Leaders* (Boston: Harvard Business School Press, 1998); Douglas A. Ready, Jay A. Conger, and Linda A. Hill, "Are You a High Potential?," *Harvard Business Review*, June 2010; and Linda A. Hill, Nancy A. Kamprath, and Leticia Garcia, "Beyond the Myth of the Perfect Mentor: Take Charge and Build Your Personal Board of Directors," Background Note 491-096 (Boston: Harvard Business School, March 1991, rev. October 2022).

10. VenturaXVentures, "VenturaXVentures," https://www.venturaxventures.com/.

11. Cristina is a systems thinker. To better understand the systems thinking she engages in, see, for example, Donella H. Meadows, *Thinking in Systems: A Primer* (White River Junction, VT: Chelsea Green Publishing, 2008).

12. Eric Martineau-Fortin cofounded White Star Capital in 2007 with Jean-Francois Marcoux. Since its inception, White Star Capital has grown into an international, multistage technology investment platform with a presence in twelve cities across North America, Europe, and Asia.

Index

Endnotes have not been indexed. Our research builds on a foundation of multidisciplinary research; see citations in our online bibliography, available at hbr.org/book-resources.

About the Authors

LINDA A. HILL is the Wallace Brett Donham Professor of Business Administration at Harvard Business School, faculty chair of the Leadership Initiative, and one of the world's top experts on leadership and innovation. Recognized twice by Thinkers50 as a top ten management thinker globally (2013, 2021), she received the Thinkers50 Innovation Award in 2015 and was named an Innovation Luminary by Front End of Innovation in 2025.

Hill has authored or coauthored many influential and award-winning books, articles, and multimedia programs, including the acclaimed *Collective Genius: The Art and Practice of Leading Innovation*, named by *Business Insider* as one of the "20 Best Business Books" and selected for the inaugural Thinkers50 Booklist of management classics. Her TED Talk on managing for collective creativity has over 3.1 million views. She also coauthored *Being the Boss: The 3 Imperatives for Becoming a Great Leader*, which the *Wall Street Journal* named one of the "Five Best Business Books to Read for Your Career."

Hill cofounded Paradox Strategies and InnovationForce—a SaaS company that uses AI to accelerate innovation and was named by *Fast Company* as an "Innovative Company to Watch" in 2023 and 2024. She serves on the boards of Relay Therapeutics, the Kresge Foundation, ArtCenter College of Design, and Team8 Fintech. She is on the advisory boards of Eight Inc., the Morgan Stanley Institute for Sustainable Investment, the United Nations Institute for Training and Research, the Aspen Institute's Leadership and Business & Society programs, and Mass General Brigham.

Her consulting and executive education work spans leadership development, innovation, digital transformation, and implementation of global strategies with organizations including Amazon, Egon Zehnder, Google, Microsoft, Mitsubishi, NASA, Novartis, Salesforce.com, the Federal Reserve Bank, and the Abu Dhabi Investment Authority.

Hill earned her PhD in Behavioral Sciences from the University of Chicago and her BA, summa cum laude, in psychology from Bryn Mawr College.

EMILY TEDARDS is a doctoral student in Organizational Behavior at Harvard Business School and a Doctoral Fellow for the Reimagining the Economy initiative at Harvard Kennedy School. Her research focuses on cross-sector collaboration, organization design, and innovation, with particular attention to how business, government, and civil society actors work together to address complex challenges—from regional development and climate change to the transformation of industries and nations.

Before beginning her PhD, Tedards conducted qualitative research on multinational companies, startups, and nonprofits across the globe. She has published more than twenty case studies and articles on leadership, innovation ecosystems, digital transformation, and corporate accelerators and innovation labs. She has also served as a research consultant for the United Nations, Harvard Business School's Institute for Strategy and Competitiveness, and several nonprofits and think tanks. She studied global liberal studies and philosophy at New York University and earned her master's degree from the London School of Economics and Political Science.

JASON WILD is cofounder and CEO of Wild Innovation & Strategy Excellence, providing exclusive advisory services to CEOs and CXOs on growth, innovation, and transformation. For over a decade at IBM, he led global innovation initiatives and launched several multibillion-dollar growth businesses, including an engineering services organization that exceeded $1 billion in revenue within three years and the launches of Smarter Cities and WatsonX.

At Salesforce, Wild built and scaled the award-winning innovation program Ignite from twenty people to hundreds over seven years, recognized by Gartner as the gold standard in strategic innovation. He later served as Global Vice President at Microsoft, responsible for CEO Co-Innovation and Customer Engagement, including the launch of Generative AI.

Wild has advised senior leadership at Disney, Under Armour, Bank of America, NATO, the city of Paris, and the government of Singapore. He has led transformative projects in thirty-nine countries, including preparing the city of Rio de Janeiro for the Olympics and serving the unbanked in developing markets. His thought leadership has been featured in *Harvard Business Review*, *Fortune*, and the *Journal of Marketing*.

Wild earned his MBA from Emory University and BA, magna cum laude, from Loyola University Chicago.